Trailing Daniel Boone

Other titles by Randell Jones

Before They Were Heroes at King's Mountain
2011, Daniel Boone Footsteps, publisher
Willie Parker Peace History Book Award, 2011
North Carolina Society of Historians

A Guide to the Overmountain Victory National Historic Trail
2011, Daniel Boone Footsteps, publisher
Willie Parker Peace History Book Award, 2011

In the Footsteps of Daniel Boone, 2005, John F. Blair, Publisher
Willie Parker Peace History Book Award, 2006

On the Trail of Daniel Boone, companion DVD,
2005, Daniel Boone Footsteps, publisher
Paul Green Multimedia Award, 2006

In the Footsteps of Davy Crockett, 2006, John F. Blair, Publisher

Scoundrels, Rogues, and Heroes of the Old North State
by Dr. H.G. Jones, co-editors: Randell Jones and Caitlin Jones
2004, The History Press

All titles available through Daniel Boone Footsteps
www.danielboonefootsteps.com
1959 N. Peace Haven Rd., #105
Winston-Salem, NC 27106
DBooneFootsteps@gmail.com

www.danielboonefootsteps.com

TRAILING DANIEL BOONE

Trailing
Daniel Boone

by Randell Jones

Daniel Boone Footsteps
Winston-Salem, North Carolina

2012 Kentucky History Award,
Kentucky Historical Society

2012 Willie Parker Peace
History Book Award,
North Carolina Society of Historians

Daniel Boone Footsteps
www.danielboonefootsteps.com
DBooneFootsteps@gmail.com

TRAILING DANIEL BOONE

For my daughters
and all their revolutions

TRAILING DANIEL BOONE

It seems strange that the Wilderness Road,
naturally one of the most beautiful in the world,
and historically one of the most interesting,
should have been so long 'unhonored and unsung.'

- Mrs. Lindsay Patterson,
North Carolina Society,
Daughters of the American Revolution,
state conference,
Charlotte, 1913

TRAILING DANIEL BOONE

Preface

If you like a good story, you have chosen your topic well in selecting this book to read. What follows is the surprising account of a remarkable effort undertaken a century ago by a group of dedicated women who were committed to commemorating a significant part of America's frontier history. The story that appears here is not the story that I imagined I would find when I began my research. It is a much richer tale and one I have thoroughly enjoyed reconstructing and putting together for you. I use the word "reconstructing" advisedly, as I have learned that too little of this record is remembered today, even by those with an organizational connection. But that has made the project that much more rewarding for me, and I am delighted and honored to present it now so that due recognition can be given to the stalwart actors in this story during the centennial observance of the events described here.

Countless times in my research I discovered and uncovered connections among people, places, and times that surprised and delighted me. I hope you share in those delights as well. Most of all, I want you to share the experience of these intrepid women, by putting yourself in their shoes or imagining that your great-grandmother or your great-great grandmother had joined in the effort. One hundred years ago, America was a much different place than today, one that few of us can readily imagine. Through our reading, many of us, perhaps, may know more about the pioneer era than we do about the early years of the 20th century. As the centennial of this three-year, trail-marking effort unfolds during 2012-2015, I hope this book helps readers connect with America's broader story during the first two decades of the 20th century and inspires many to read more. Every era of America's history has its heroes and troublemakers. But every facet of America's real, underlying history is driven along by the actions and efforts of ordinary, everyday people wanting to do the right thing for the right reasons and working with pride and perseverance to make the country and the world a better place for everyone. The Daughters of the American Revolution in this account are some of those everyday people, but I trust that you will find them, as I did, to be the real heroes of the day.

Names, Titles, and Abbreviations

In writing about Daughters of the American Revolution in the 21st century, it is appropriate to use the member's name and not her husband's. Such was not the case a century ago. The historic record of the early 20th century is filled with references given in the preferred style of the day, referring to members with their husband's name. In many cases, the accounts provided the member's name offset with parentheses and sometimes with the husband's name offset with parentheses. The Progressive Era was a time of transition, when women were striving for a new status and for Equal Suffrage. The practice of referring to women, in general, and to DAR members, in particular, was in flux. To keep the account true to the era, I have continued the practice as used in the historic accounts, but with the addition of fully indentifying information usually on the first mention of a person. So be prepared. Most of the accounts refer to "Mrs. (husband's name)," and by using that, I intend to honor the women making their way in the world they inhabited, not to diminish them or to hide who they were.

Quoted materials retain the capitalization (or not) of DAR titles as reported, as well as use periods to identify DAR as an abbreviation, (i.e., D.A.R.) as it was done at the time. Some accounts referred to "D.A.Rs" without a closing period after the "Rs."

Daniel Boone's Trail

The name used for the 1912-1915 trail-marking project varied over the years and among the different participants and observers. In speeches, reports, and in newspaper accounts, it was variously called "the Daniel Boone Trail," "the Boone Trail," and "Daniel Boone's Trail." The last was used on the tablets placed by North Carolina, Tennessee, and Kentucky. Virginia dropped the possessive form, using "Daniel Boone Trail" on its tablets. When not quoting, I have tried to use consistently "Daniel Boone's Trail," intending by that usage to recognize the name given by the Daughters to the project and thus differentiating that commemorative route from any other route that can be suggested and perhaps argued adequately for recognition as a historic track over which Daniel Boone trod from time to time and for whatever reason. "Daniel Boone's Trail" is the route defined by the Daughters of the American Revolution during that 1912-1915 project regardless of the historical accuracy of their markers' placements relative to what later scholarship may have shown about where Daniel Boone walked. Because I know this is an issue with some, I wish to declare my views up front: where the Daughters placed the markers in 1913, 1914, and 1915 is where they belong. I believe those markers are now part of our collective history and this book celebrates that historic trail-marking project. The Daughters were commemorating Daniel Boone; I did the same with my 2005 book, *In the Footsteps of Daniel Boone*. This current book, *Trailing Daniel Boone*, has a different focus. It is a story about the Daughters of the American Revolution in the early 20th century and it celebrates the trail they created.

The Full Story

As I have discovered with all the books I have written, someone somewhere knows something I did not find in my research. I welcome input from readers on additional aspects of the story that may not have been included. My goal is help gather the whole story to one place so that others will not have to piece it together again in the future. Please write to me or email me with additional information which you believe adds to the telling. I will especially welcome old photographs of markers and dedication ceremonies and images of DAR members who participated in the project. As much information as you can provide regarding dates and places will be a help to us all.

I trust this book serves as an obvious expression of my deep regard for the Daughters of the American Revolution, especially those from 1912-1915 who put Daniel Boone's Trail on the ground. I offer them and their fellow Daughters who have followed them through a century my heartiest congratulations on a job well done and I offer my sincerest gratitude for their service to America. As the National Society, Daughters of the American Revolution, celebrates its 125th anniversary in 2015, I hope the coincident observance of the centennial of marking Daniel Boone's Trail provides ample opportunity for patriotic Americans all across the country to express their own appreciation of the Daughters of the American Revolution for their service to the United States of America.

RJ
Winston-Salem
2012

Contents

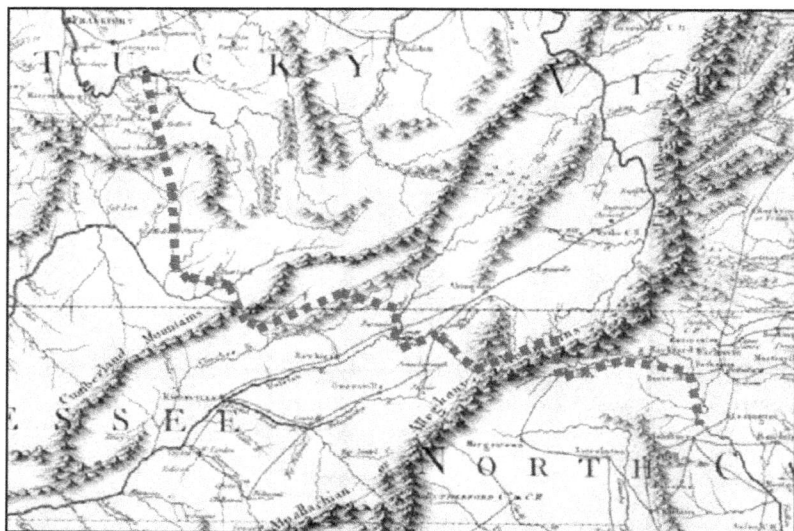

Daniel Boone's Trail

Daughters of the American Revolution
1912-1915

This Rugged Way

"Ihave been asked by those who grope in darkness, if we are doing things of importance, or if we are organized for social pleasure? Daughters of the American Revolution, you need no tongue to proclaim your deeds; does not the winding trail of Daniel Boone across our glorious mountains tell its own story? Each gleaming tablet speaks with a thousand tongues. The way is so plain that 'wayfaring men tho' fools shall not err therein.' The state owes a debt of gratitude to the noble woman who has led us step by step up this rugged way. Some day we will climb higher still and on the pinnacle we will carve the name of Mrs. Lindsay Patterson."[1]

Mrs. Mary S. Mercer[2], Committee on Patriotic Education
North Carolina Society, DAR State Conference, Durham, N.C., Nov. 3 and 4, 1914

The unbridled appreciation of Mary Mercer for Mrs. Lindsay Patterson represented how the Daughters of the American Revolution, at least those in four states, felt about the woman who had organized the marking of Daniel Boone's Trail during the second decade of the 20th century. Mrs. Patterson was roundly praised—and deservedly so by any objective measure. But she was appropriately modest, recognizing the efforts of so many others even before the work was finished. "The Chairman begs to thank," she had declared

This Rugged Way

from the lectern in 1913, "all of the Daughters whose sympathy and help have made possible marking Daniel Boone's Trail through North Carolina."[3] She would tender additional praise and appreciation of many others throughout the project during the three years it took to complete.

Mrs. Lindsay Patterson served as chairman of the Daniel Boone Trail Committee, not only for North Carolina but for the interstate effort. She was the first to think of the idea of marking the trail and she successfully promoted it within the organization to Daughters of the American Revolution in North Carolina, Tennessee, Virginia, and Kentucky. From 1912 to 1915, she marshaled the energy and the enthusiasm of all those Daughters who wanted to make the trail a reality and she enlisted the help of outside volunteers and advisors. It is safe to say that without the effort of Mrs. Lindsay Patterson, there would have been no Daniel Boone's Trail a century ago and probably none today as all such efforts since have relied so prominently on the record these Daughters left behind.

A Centennial Celebration

This is the story of how Daniel Boone's Trail came to be marked one hundred years ago across the landscape of four states, represented by 45 bronze and cast iron markers. They were placed at historically meaningful spots and erected across a challenging terrain at a time before good roads and bridges would have made the task decidedly less taxing. This is a story of love of country, of deep respect for history and heritage, and of a constant abiding commitment to carry forward to future generations enduring stories of America's creation, struggles, and resilience. Such stories never grow old and never go out of style, for each new generation must revisit the paths of its predecessors and learn anew what it meant and means to be American then and now. Each must then carry that spirit forward, facing the challenges of its own time, of course, but always striving in concert with the trust and faith in principles of its ancestral generations so that this country can continue to be a blessing to all people who look to the United States of America for strength, encouragement, and direction.

This is a story about women of another era—the Progressive Era, about women not yet accorded the right to vote and relegated to a supporting role in a man's world, but working diligently for the betterment and improvement of society, including their own status. This is the story of particular women—strong women, intelligent women, savvy women, women who moved America forward—women of the early 20th century who served with pride and distinction as Daughters of the American Revolution.

Memorial Continental Hall,
National Society, Daughters of the American Revolution,
Washington, D.C., 2011 (left) and 1911

This Rugged Way

TRAILING DANIEL BOONE

4

This Great and Good Work

Daniel Boone, America's pioneer hero, has had his champions over the years, Mrs. Lindsay Patterson among them. She and others have shown their admiration in remarkable ways. So it was, in 1912, that one of Boone's relatives by marriage, a great nephew of Daniel Boone's wife, Rebecca Bryan, the man claimed, undertook the building of a monument singlehandedly, although he never would have thought it would come to that.

Esquire

William Lewis Bryan was one of the real characters of Boone, North Carolina, in the early years of the new century. He was a native of Watauga County, born in Meat Camp in November 1837, a mere 17 years after Daniel Boone had died in Missouri a few weeks shy of his 86th birthday. Bryan was in his mid-70s in 1912, some ten years beyond the usual life expectancy of the day. Some of the people who knew him best might have said that longevity was because he was just too ornery to pass on.

Bryan had been the first mayor of Boone when the town was chartered in 1872, but he had been there long before, arriving in 1857. When he was only 20, he worked as a store clerk for Jacob Rintils. He watched the town grow slowly from its simple, rural beginnings as a community surrounding (Jordan) Councill's Store, the name first used for the settlement and for the post office. He was there when the town became the county seat as Watauga County was formed by the North Carolina General Assembly in 1849 and the name Boone was bestowed on the settlement. When Councill's Store post office became the Boone post office, the town of Boone boasted a commercial center with a few stores, three sawmills, a brick courthouse, and a brick jail with an iron cage inside. At an elevation of over 3,330 feet above sea level, it was then the highest county seat in the country east of the Rocky Mountains.[1] [2] [3]

Watauga County continued to grow some, but not so rapidly. In 1880, the population was about 8,200 and 30 years later was only 5,000 more. The county was a part of the state in the mountain region known as the "Lost Provinces." Watauga County and Boone sat on the Blue Ridge plateau isolated and engaged in only limited commerce with the piedmont communities to the east, hampered, as it was, by a lack of adequate communication, meaning good roads and railways. In fact, Boone would, for a time, establish more reliable commercial connections to communities in Tennessee to its west than with fellow North Carolina towns. In the middle of the 19th century trade had been conducted by wagon. Produce in the form of hides and tallow, beeswax, butter, and cranberries had been carried out on wagons pulled by teams of horses. Drovers had pushed down the mountain herds of cattle, hogs, horses, and mules. They went to Richmond to the north and to Charleston to the south. And, without railroads and adequate roadways into the mountains, the means of trade had scarcely improved in the last 50 years. Early in the second decade of the promising 20th century, the town of Boone was ready for change.[4]

William Bryan had seen a thing or two in his time in Watauga County and he had his strong opinions about the way things ought to be. After all, he had been there longer than most everyone else in town. He was not so pleased that all these newcomers did not have the same regard for the history of the area that he had, and he wanted to do something to remind them of the town's worthy heritage. Bryan was well known and probably genuinely respected by those who had known him over the years. But to the newer members of the town of Boone in 1912, he may have been regarded simply as the town's loveable old curmudgeon. As an honorific befitting a man of his longevity and standing in the community, the editor of the *Watauga Democrat* often applied "Esquire" when writing about Bryan. It was a nice touch equivalent to using "mister." Three years later, author John Preston Arthur applied another apparent honorific to Bryan, calling him "colonel." (No biography of W.L. Bryan mentions any military service.) Arthur was also accorded the same honorific by the community about the same time.

The Great Pioneer

In the spring of 1912, Bryan had an idea to honor the ancestral relative he claimed as a hero of America's pioneer days and a favorite son of North Carolina. He wrote out his idea carefully and entrusted his letter to his friend, R.C. Rivers, the editor and proprietor of the *Watauga Democrat*.

April 25, 1912

"The Daniel Boone Monument

Mr. Editor: Will you kindly allow me space in your columns to say that I have been for some little time trying to gather up a little fund to be used in the erection of a monument to the honor and memory of the great pioneer, Daniel Boone, who had a camp or cabin near our court house in what is now known as East Boone, and near where the young men's dormitory now stands. We want to erect the monument where the Boone cabin stood, if we can arrange to do so, if not, as near that spot as possible.

"I think it would be well to call a meeting of the citizens relative to this matter, and I would like every township to be represented for I am of the opinion that the feet of Daniel Boone have trodden the earth, perhaps, in every township in the county. I should like for all the people to become interested in this matter and look upon it as a county enterprise. It is no trouble to still see his old paths or trails in various places, more especially on the east side of the Blue Ridge, where he was approaching near the top of the mountain. I can show them to anyone who wishes to see them, at different crossings of the Blue Ridge.

"I will gladly receive donations from anyone wishing to help in this great and good work, and will publish each month the names of those giving or sending us funds for this work, and the amounts given by each one, and it need not be confined to Watauga county. We will be glad to have help from any one in or out of the State, so far as that goes. We want to make the nicest thing we can and that will all depend upon the amount of money we can raise for the purpose. I want to hear from some of the citizens as to the calling of the meeting, time, etc.
W.L. Bryan"[5]

As it happened, Watauga County was also exploring at the time the notion of holding its first county fair. The organizers were looking for support and contributions from the civic-minded citizenry, especially those who could contribute substantially. Among those they hoped to hear from was a Winston-Salem attorney, Lindsay Patterson, who owned large tracts of land in Watauga and Ashe counties.

In the second decade of the 20th century, the Town of Boone was a rural village nestled within the rolling hillsides on the Blue Ridge Plateau. from the collection of Sarah Spencer at the *Watauga County Public Library*

From time to time, Patterson advertised the prize livestock he offered from his farms. One such ad ran in the spring of 1912:

"Fine Stock For Sale

Shetland ponies, Shropshire Sheep, Jersey Milk Cows, Short Horn Cattle

All young stock suitable for breeding purposes. Grandsons and grand-daughters of the two most famous short horn sires, *Choice Good*, and *Whiteball Sultan*.

If interested, write the undersigned at Winston-Salem, N.C. or Harrison Baker, Sands, Watauga Co., N.C.

Lindsay Patterson"[6]

Patterson did, in fact, visit Boone that May and contributed $25 toward funding the county fair planned for September.

A month after putting forth his idea for a monument to Daniel Boone, Bryan gave a report in another letter to the editor. He was not excited by the responses he had received and stated simply that nothing would begin until adequate contributions were received.

May 30, 1912

"The Daniel Boone Monument

Following are the names and amounts contributed or subscribed to the fund to be used in erecting a monument to the memory and honor of Daniel Boone the great pioneer of this county:" [Bryan's list gave 22 names including prominent men of the community. Among them was Blanford B. Dougherty, co-founder and president of Appalachian Training School. Contributions were $5 (3), $1 (7), 50 cents (8), and 25 cents (4), all together totaling $27.][7]

"We desire to get this monument completed within the next month and hope the people will send in their contributions to this honorable undertaking without being begged for it. Every man, woman and child in the county ought to be glad to help a little in this work. We really can't do anything else to perpetuate his great name only to erect something in his memory. We suggest the people to send in what they feel willing to give to myself or R.C. Rivers, one of us can be found at home at almost any time or if it is more convenient they can leave it with any of the merchants of the town, and take a receipt for it if you want to. Please think about it.

Very truly yours,

W.L. Bryan"[8]

Another few weeks passed, and little more apparently happened regarding contributions. Bryan took ill for a while, and as the summer solstice approached and the sun was reaching its zenith, the good promoter's irritability was also on a sharp rise.

The editor of the *Watauga Democrat* noted in his listing of items of local interest that Bryan had not been feeling well recently. "Glad to see Esq. W.L. Bryan out again after an illness of more than two weeks," the editor wrote. "He is still very weak, but is improving very nicely." Apparently, Bryan had stopped by the newspaper office to drop off his latest missive, one that closed his indiscriminate and stern warning to all citizens with the incongruous "very truly."

June 20, 1912
"General Notice
I hereby notify all persons, whomsoever, old, young, big, little, black or white, not to secure any cherries from the trees in my fields or along the fences; By climbing, pulling down the limbs or breaking them off, or knocking them off with sticks, poles, or rocks. Last year we did not get a cherry, but this year I propose to protect them, as we need them ourselves. If we have a surplus we are willing to divide, if asked for them. Our lands are posted and we expect protection of our stuff inside our fields. If this notice is violated we will try to enforce the town and State laws made and provided in such cases. Very truly,
W.L. Bryan
Boone, N.C., June 19"[9]

By mid-summer, William Bryan, Esq. had probably become more than a little disappointed at the meager response to his overtures for financial support to build a monument to Daniel Boone. It was important to him and, as happens so often with creative visionaries, he just could not fathom how others could not possibly be enthralled by what he saw so clearly as a worthy project. Soon enough, he began to wear the mantle of crusty ol' codger. Once again he called upon the good graces of his colleague in community efforts, R.C. Rivers, to run a letter on page one of the *Watauga Democrat*.

Bryan's letter revealed his admiration for Daniel Boone, his frustration with elected officials, and read almost as a harangue of the citizenry. His passions must have gotten the better of him, for his run-on sentences suggest that he dashed off this piece without likely giving it a second reading. Of course, the letter appeared as it was typeset, and some of the grammatical errors could have been those of the newspaper, but Rivers probably gave it extra attention, knowing all too well that he would likely get an earful from Bryan if he did not reproduce the letter exactly as the good gentleman presented it.

July 25, 1912
"Please Read This
It seems that I have heretofore failed to interest you in what I have tried to say to you through the paper in regard to the little monument I have been trying to raise means to erect in memory of the great pioneer Daniel Boone. I can't understand why the people would not be interested in the enterprise. the [*sic*] people don't seem to know that he with his comrades located and placed nearly all the most valuable farm lands in this county, in the hands of the early settlers, without charge in this way, [*sic*] He located the lands on all the rivers and creeks while he hunted the country for game to live on he was shaping things for the settlers as well. He in doing this work had to face the Indian as well as the dangerous wild beasts of the forest, and as soon as soon as [*sic*] matters were planned and arranged for the settlers this most wonderful man would move on farther westardly [*sic*] and the settlers of the new country followed him thus the great man spent his days, and lots of the citizens of Watauga county today live on trails that Daniel

helped to make by the tread of his feet in the long gone by days [*sic*] yet the old trails many of them are still visible in many places in Watauga and adjoining counties These statements are facts. Then why not erect a monument in memory of this great name that will live after we are all gone. It will only cost about $150.00. It will not hurt the people to make this little contribution, and every man, woman and child should be glad to put in a small amount in this worthy enterprise.

"I tried to get the county commissioners to give us $50.00, but they were so saving that they would not give us so much as one cent. I see that Carter county, Teen. [*sic*], is building one, and the county gave $500.00 to aid in its erection. It seems to me that our county could have helped in this enterprise to the amount of $50.00 without hurting the tax payers of the county.

"I insist upon the good citizens of the county helping us in this little enterprise at once. We are desirous of beginning the work within the next few days. It will take about 4,000 pounds of cement, besides sand and other material, to do this work. So please kindly give the matter a little thought and don't forget to send in the cash to help to erect it, and oblige,
Very truly yours,
W.L. Bryan
Boone, N.C."[10]

R.C. Rivers offered his own remarks regarding the matter on page 3 under Local News:
"On the first page of this paper is an article by W.L. Bryan, Esq. in which he urges delinquents on the fund for the Daniel Boone Monument to pay up at once and earnestly solicits the help of

others as he hopes to begin work at an early day. Mr. Bryan is much interested in the enterprise, and he certainly deserves the aid of our people in its consummation. Please let him hear from you as soon as possible."[11]

A Very Pretty Piece of Work

As much as Bryan wanted people to think about Daniel Boone and the old trails he had followed through Watauga County, others had different ideas about how best to get around in the mountains of North Carolina. Indeed, the "good roads" movement was getting started and communities in western North Carolina were engaged in getting the attention and the dollars of state government involved. In late August, the North Carolina Good Roads Association, meeting in Asheville, adopted resolutions asking the state to support the building of good roads by committing $1 million a year for 20 years. It was a hopeful effort, and one that clearly staked out the economic benefits to communities which were connected by macadamized roads at tolerable grades.[12]

Concurrent with the focus on improving roads, Watauga County was pursuing railroad service. On Election Day, the citizens of the county were to be voting on a referendum to issue bonds for the construction of a railroad into Watauga County. The attention of the press and the citizenry was on the economic benefits of having rail transportation into Boone. What civic attention was not focused on that issue or on better roads was spent on holding the first Watauga County Fair. It was to be an exploratory effort to see if the citizens would support an annual showcase of agricultural fecundity and an assemblage of educational exhibits and amusements. All across Watauga County, community leaders and the citizens were looking to the future. But that did not discourage Bryan from his singular mission to honor the past. He continued to work diligently on his project, deciding to do it by himself, if need be—at least as best he could without his missing tools.

On September 12, the *Watauga Democrat* printed another letter from an exasperated William Bryan.

> September 12, 1912
> **"Read This**
> Someone has one of my small stone hammers. Also a small crowbar about 3 feet long made of a hartooth [?] bar also a large log chain. The party in possession of these articles are [sic] requested to bring them home for I need them and have needed them for some time and hope to have them returned at once. – W.L. Bryan"[13]

No doubt, Mr. Bryan wanted to have his Daniel Boone Monument completed in time for the Watauga County Fair. It would have been a fine exhibit to have available to attract the attention of all those visitors expected to flood into Boone. He might have even garnered some additional contributions to fund its construction. At the very least, it would help educate the citizens of Watauga County about their frontier heritage and the heroics of his famous relative, Daniel Boone.

Unfortunately, Bryan did not complete the monument in time for the fair. The exploratory fair was held for three days, Thursday through Saturday, September 26-28. By all accounts it was a resounding success as reflected by the editor's comments a week later.

> October 3, 1912
> "Early Thursday morning the people began to gather from all parts of the county on foot, in bug[g]ies, wagons, hacks, carriages,

etc., and by 10 o'clock the crowd was so large that the streets and sidewalks of the village from the post office to the A.T.S. [Appalachian Training School] had almost the appearance of a busy thoroughfare in some great center of trade, and the finest specimens of horse, cattle, sheep, hogs, poultry, etc., etc., were in evidence everywhere, that cannot be surpassed, in the opinion of many, by any county in the State."[14]

The following week, the community received a status report on Mr. Bryan's work. "The Daniel Boone Monument is nearing completion," read the October 10 item under local news, "and will be a thing of beauty when the finishing touches are put on." The supporters of Bryan's efforts could take dutiful pride in what he had accomplished so far. But others may not yet have taken notice. With the successful county fair only a few days behind them, the citizens were looking eagerly toward Election Day. Not only were they voting on floating a $100,000 bond for the construction of a railroad into the county, they were also voting for their elected officials, including governor. And, Locke Craig, gubernatorial candidate, was then coming to Boone to speak to the citizens. The fall of 1912 bristled with gossip, debate, political rhetoric, and anticipation. What little attention Mr. Bryan could garner from the community for his cabin monument project among all the competing events of the day was indeed dearly won.

The year 1912 was also a presidential election year and one of partic- ular note. Two U.S. presidents were competing for the office along with a new contender. The incumbent President Howard Taft was seeking re-election and ex-President Theodore Roosevelt was seeking a third term running as the candidate for the Bull Moose Party. He had decided that his Republican protégé Taft had not worked out as planned and he wanted to return to the White House. Indeed, another William Bryan, one better known all across the country than Boone's former mayor, had something to say on the matter. William Jennings Bryan, erstwhile presidential candidate himself in 1896, 1900, and 1908, said that President Taft is "a man who went into office with a million majority and who will go out by unanimous consent."[15]

The election was supposed to be decided at the ballot box, but on October 14, a lone gunman tried to influence the outcome. "As ex-President Theodore Roosevelt was leaving his hotel in Milwaukee, Wisconsin," announced the *Watauga Democrat* on October 17 to a shocked readership, "a New York anarchist fired on him, inflicting a flesh wound in the abdomen. The Colonel, under the protests of his physicians, went on and delivered his speech very much as if nothing had happened."[16]

President Roosevelt was a hero to many Americans. He had been commander of the Rough Riders charging up San Juan Hill in Cuba during the Spanish American War and later he hunted big game in the wilds of Africa. He orchestrated the U.S. effort in constructing the Panama Canal, first by assisting with a revolution that separated Panama from Colombia. His grand scheme for connecting east and west captured the imagination of Americans. It was a promise to link the distant Pacific Ocean with the eastern seaboard, a project whose value had been revealed so poignantly and most recently when the *USS Maine* sank in Havana Harbor in 1898. The replacement ship, coming from the west coast, took 67 days to steam around the tip of South America. Roosevelt was the president of the "Square Deal," Big Stick Diplomacy, and the creator of the Great White Fleet. All of that was brought to the minds of the citizens of Watauga County in the middle of October as they read about Roosevelt being shot. These readers were living in the exciting years early in the 20th century when

DANIEL BOONE CABIN MONUMENT
Erected by Colonel W. L. Bryan, October, 1912.

W.L. Bryan, Esquire, posing with the Boone Cabin Monument he built single-handedly in the fall of 1912.

from A *History of Watauga County* by John P. Arthur, 1915

progress was the theme. They had new heroes and more than a century of impressive national history to reflect on since Daniel Boone had trod across the Blue Ridge plateau hunting deer and living what the readers imagined was a near-subsistence lifestyle. To many in the community with their eyes on the coming railroad and with the prospects of better roads and thinking about all that could do for Watauga County, Daniel Boone's solo trailblazing and the grandly embellished accounts of his encounters with Indians and wild beasts may have seemed rather tiresome and quaint and entirely irrelevant in

1912. But William Lewis Bryan pressed on, undaunted by the discouragements that surrounded him and undistracted by current events with their clamoring and unrelenting urgency.

On the last day of October, the newspaper happily reported, "The Daniel Boone Monument has at last been completed and is indeed a very pretty piece of work. The proprietor, Mr. W.L. Bryan is to be congratulated upon carrying to success this, his pet project."[17] Beyond that public acknowledgement by the *Watauga Democrat*, no public celebration or unveiling occurred. Bryan would, in fact, receive public recognition for his effort, but that was a year away. In 1912, the monument was his alone. He had thought of it, had worked earnestly to rally the community to the cause, but had generally failed to raise money adequate for a notable monument's construction. But he persevered. He was a direct lineal descendant, he believed, from a brother of Rebecca Bryan Boone whom Daniel married in 1756. (Even after extensive investigation, Bryan Family genealogists cannot confirm W.L. Bryan's relationship to Rebecca Bryan.[18]) Mr. Bryan would not let this monument project languish. In the end, he just built the thing himself. He chiseled some commemorations in stones placed on the four faces of the monument. One, of course, paid tribute to "Daniel Boone, Pioneer and Hunter" and then gave dates for Boone's birth and death, dates which have since been revised by scholars. The other statements chiseled in stone were mostly personal. He acknowledged his parents by name and gave his own birthday as November 19, 1837. So it was in 1912 that W.L. Bryan had given himself a slightly early 75th birthday present. And, probably to leave a lasting "thumb in the eye" to all those who had not contributed any money or support, he chiseled in one stone the startlingly low cost of the monument, "$203.37."

This Great and Good Work

Good Western Mules

Mr. Bryan was convinced, of course, that his monument marked the site of the cabin where Daniel Boone frequently stayed while hunting on the plateau. It was a hunters' cabin, tradition held, a place for refuge open to anyone who found himself needing shelter for the night, be he hunter or herder. It was, of course, well known that Benjamin Howard pastured his cattle on the plateau and left his enslaved herders to the task. One of those enslaved was a man named Burrell, who in 1760 showed Daniel Boone and his hunting companion, Nathaniel Gist, a route through the mountains to the Holston Valley. (That route follows through today's Mountain City, Tennessee, Damascus and Abingdon, Virginia, the last a place Daniel Boone had first named Wolf Hills.)

"Colonel" William Lewis Bryan
courtesy of *Watauga County Public Library*

Bryan had heard the stories of the hunters, of course, and he regarded this cabin site as worthy of a shrine. Only the year before he built the cabin monument, the stones from the cabin's chimney had still stood there, John P. Arthur, noted historian, wrote in 1915, and some of those chimney stones were used in the building of the monument, others said.[19] But the study of history is a continual process of discovery and rediscovery. It is a peeling away of assumptions and traditions to get at the facts as they become more reliably known. So it was that later investigations and scholarship determined that indeed two cabins had been on the plateau. The Howard cabin was used by his herders. The hunters' cabin was north from Boone about six miles away on Meat Camp Creek. A young William Bryan may have known of this hunters' cabin because he lived his first two decades at Meat Camp. Or maybe it did not matter that much to him in his eagerness to promote the Town of Boone and the famous woodsman he claimed as family. Irrespective of the facts, in 1912 the Daniel Boone Cabin Monument prominently celebrated Bryan's pioneer hero with appropriate regard. Only later did its location come to be suspect.

William Bryan was probably fortunate to have completed the monument when he did at the end of October, even though no celebration was afforded his creation by the community. Election Day 1912 was soon upon the country and the attention of every citizen was on the future. President Taft was defeated, but so was former President Roosevelt. The two Republicans had been rebuffed by a sweeping country-wide swing to the Democratic Party. Woodrow Wilson was the president-elect. The editorial page of the *Watauga Democrat* declared, "The great Democratic victory throughout the United States last week is unprecedented in all political history." Moreover, the bond referendum had passed. Watauga County was to get a rail line built into the mountains to connect that community with the 20th century. Soon, the citizens hoped, Watauga County would no longer be one of the "Lost Provinces."

In November, the *Watauga Democrat* reprinted an article from the *Lenoir News* which reported, "Yadkin River Railway Company received another shipment of 48 good western mules yesterday direct from St. Louis. This is the third shipment of mules from the west for the work on constructing the line out from North Wilkesboro." The times were changing, of course, and progress was coming to Watauga County. But, W.L. Bryan, Esq. and a few others who could look back three quarters of a century probably could not help but crack a smile as they read that article, noting very clearly that a little bit of the old was still needed to bring in the new. And just as was William Lewis Bryan, a little bit of that old was notoriously stubborn.

Mrs. Lindsay Patterson
—Lady Bountiful

Although he had to build the Boone Cabin Monument by himself, William L. Bryan's passion for commemorating Daniel Boone was shared nevertheless by others. One, in particular, was fairly nearby and she had the personality and charisma to entice the willing support and participation of a large troop of allies and advocates for her project. Marking Daniel Boone's Trail would have been enough of an achievement in a career of civic service for most anyone. For the industrious Mrs. Lindsay Patterson, it was but one more bead of lustrous pearl added to a long string of skillfully wrought accom-

**Mrs. Lindsay Patterson
(Lucy Bramlette Patterson)**
from *DAR Magazine*, April 1914

Mrs. Lindsay Patterson—Lady Bountiful

plishments for the DAR, for her home community, for her adopted state, and for her country during a most remarkable life. To understand better the motivations and capabilities of this noteworthy leader, a look at her life preceding the 1912 project is most telling. In particular, her family history clearly reveals the origins of her deep, abiding interest in Daniel Boone's Trail.

The Beloved Road of Her Heart's Desire

Lucy Bramlette Patterson was truly blessed. She was Ulster Scot on both sides of her family. She came from a heritage of Philadelphia wealth and prominence and had the good fortune to be born in the South, in Tennessee, in the bosom of another well-to-do family. She also had the benefit of later marrying a Patterson, so she enjoyed the convenience of never having to change her name.

Both her father's and mother's families had ancestral homes in the upper Tennessee River Valley between the Powell and Clinch rivers. She was born during the aftermath of the Civil War on August 22, 1865, at the home of her maternal grandfather, General Hugh Graham, a man exiled from Ireland in his youth. The home was called *Castle Rock* (also *Castle Roche*) and sat in Tazewell, Tennessee, not so far from the Cumberland Gap. Some said Graham lived there like a feudal lord. His home was a self-contained village with flower gardens and groves in front of the home and sunken gardens of vegetables and fruits in the rear, all kept up, of course, with enslaved labor. It was a beautiful home with a promenade lined with blossoming locusts; and, the Grahams were known for their welcoming hospitality. They were also known for having the largest library in the South, it was said. Hugh Graham was a voracious reader, collecting books shipped from American and European publishers and subscribing to numerous magazines and newspapers. Unfortunately, the war took its toll on the

Castle Rock (*Roche*), the home of Colonel Hugh and Catherine Graham, where Mrs. Patterson was born, stood in Tazewell, Tennessee. (top)
from *Claiborne Progress*, Tazewell, TN

Castle Rock was dismantled in the 1950s and moved brick by brick to Knoxville, TN, where it was reconstructed. The portico was added from another family home. Today the house is known as *Speedwell*.

family and Union troops plundered *Castle Rock* in the spring of 1865. Having lived to the ripe old age of 81 without ever calling a physician, the family progenitor's health failed him then and he died in March only five months to the day before his granddaughter, Lucy, was born. He was laid to rest at the Irish Cemetery in Tazewell with the help of newly freed, former slaves of the family.[1]

Hugh Graham's wife was Catherine Nenny Graham, a woman of legendary beauty and graciousness. She was a secessionist as was her husband, but, curiously, she advocated the abolition of slavery. That duality amused some of her descendants who noted that she never waited upon herself a day in her life and depended completely on the attentions of the enslaved house workers. Still, after the war, the formerly enslaved servants remained to help attend to their beloved mistress.

Mrs. Lindsay Patterson—Lady Bountiful

25

Catherine Nenny was from Bedford County, Virginia, where lived her mother, Lucy Bramlette. This Lucy's father, William Bramlette, served during the Revolutionary War and later went into Kentucky with Daniel Boone. Family stories differed, but all agreed that Bramlette was murdered there, some say for his land, others that he was mistaken for an Indian. He was buried at Cumberland Gap, the story goes, along with two others. In time, it was said, a rock rolled off the mountain and fell on top of the graves.[2]

Lucy Bramlette Patterson's other grandfather, on her father's side, was the noted general, Robert Patterson of Philadelphia, a man who fought in three wars: War of 1812, the Mexican War, and the Civil War.[3] Major General Patterson was a founding member of the Aztec Club and served as its president from 1867 to his death in 1881. This was an association of officers from the Mexican War. Three of its members were elected to be presidents of the United States: Zachary Taylor, Franklin Pierce, and Ulysses S. Grant. The meetings of the Aztec Club were most often held at the Philadelphia home of the general, who was famous for his hospitality. Indeed, in his later years he hosted a veritable who's who of notable persons. Throughout her formative years, the young Miss Patterson was exposed to some of the most influential and powerful persons of the day. She later wrote about impressions made upon her by experiences at her grandfather's home.

Mrs. Patterson was also influenced by her grandfather's accounts of Cumberland Gap. In 1835, the general had traveled from Philadelphia to the Ohio River by way of the Cumberland Gap; he kept a journal of that experience. He reported in part:

"The scenery at Cumberland Gap is magnificent. On the one side lays spread out at your feet the rich valley of Kentucky stretching away as far as the eye will reach while on the other are the hills and valleys of East Tennessee. It was thro' this Gap, that Daniel Boon [*sic*] passed on this first visit to Kentucky and one can not but echo his expression when looking for the first time on the scene of his future triumphs that it was a country worth fighting for. ... My ride to day was quite romantic. Crossing the Cumberland river, at a point some 15 miles above Barbourville, I kept along its margin until I reach that town. I[t] had not been my intention to travel so far on that day but being mounted on a blooded mare of my brother's that walked faster than any animal I had ever ridden I felt some curiosity to try her power. I left Tazewell at [7:30]o'clock and reached Barbourville at 25 minutes after 6 o'clock, accomplishing without feeding or going out of a walk, 44 miles in eleven hours less five minutes., crossing on the route Cumberland Mountain and some difficult hills."[4]

Mrs. Patterson was influenced as well by childhood experiences with her maternal grandparents. Writing of herself in 1914 in the third person as chairman of the Boone Trail Committee, Mrs. Patterson fondly recalled her childhood visits in Tennessee during the 1870s:

"Her earliest childhood memories are of wandering through the beautiful box-bordered flower gardens of 'Castle Rock,' the home of her grandmother, Mrs. Hugh Graham, of east Tennessee, and listening to stories of the great-great-grandfather, William Bramlette, of Bedford Co. Va., who went to Kentucky with Boone and was killed at Cumberland Gap, where the great boulder that marked his grave, also, strangely enough, marked the spot where Virginia, Tennessee and Kentucky come together.[5] There, in the spring, after a course of sassafras tea to 'thin the blood,' another course of sulphur, molasses and cream of tartar to improve the complexion, the grandchildren were piled, four deep, on the back of fat, gentle old Bill to ride over Boone's Trail to the sulphur spring where the final touches were supposed to be given to the physical house-cleaning by its bubbling, evil-smelling water. That over with, the Trail was followed to the top of Cumberland Gap, for a refreshing look over into Kentucky and back over the green fields of Tennessee. Is it any wonder that locating the Trail was a labor of love with the chairman? Or that, back in her mind for many long years, has been the wish and intention some way, and some time, to mark the beloved road of her heart's desire?"[6]

After living in Philadelphia for a time, the young Miss Patterson's parents moved to the family home of her great-grandfather, the general's father. The home, called *Sycamore*, was near Patterson's Crossroads in Claiborne County, Tennessee, and consequently closer to the Cumberland Gap than was *Castle Rock*. It was there that her father, Colonel William Patterson, lived with her mother, Cornelia Graham Patterson. Their postal address was Cumberland Gap.

While living in Philadelphia, young Lucy had been exposed to cultured society under the tutelage of a family with a high regard for education. And when it came time for her secondary schooling in 1879, her parents sent her to a school they thought the most fit and proper for their daughter, the Salem Female Academy in Salem, North Carolina.

A young Miss Patterson arrived in Salem in the fall of 1879, enrolling on November 4 at Salem Female Academy at the age of 14. She completed her education at the academy, graduating after three years. (A 12th year of schooling for most students in public or private schools was not added until the early 1900s.) The last entry of her presence at the school was June 1882. She then returned to the nurture of her immediate and extended family in Tennessee and Philadelphia.

A Gentle, Persuasive Influence

Thirty years would pass in the life of Mrs. Lindsay Patterson before she undertook the marking of her "beloved road." Those were not idle years and indeed the fruits of her labors on several fronts before and after the marking of Daniel Boone's Trail contributed to a life which garnered her recognition at its end as a person of "rare genius and heroic mold." Although no telling of the story of the marking of Daniel Boone's Trail could be complete without mention of Mrs. Lindsay Patterson, a review of her entire biography is unnecessary. However, a recounting of events and projects leading across a decade preceding that notable and noble undertaking provide essential and interesting insights into the life and times of Mrs. Patterson and others involved in bringing about the successful marking of Daniel Boone's Trail.

After half-a-dozen years, which likely included travels around the country and perhaps abroad, Miss Patterson returned to North Carolina upon her marriage on September 6, 1888, to distant cousin J. Lindsay Patterson, a prominent attorney of Winston. (The town names, Winston and Salem, were officially joined in 1913; but, for years before, the two names had been joined by a hyphen and the pair called the Twin City, especially by the *Winston-Salem Journal*.)

Lindsay Patterson was the grandson of North Carolina Governor John M. Morehead (1841-45) and the great-grandson of William Lenoir, a hero of the Battle of Kings Mountain in 1780. Lenoir was also a founder of the University of North Carolina, chartered in 1789. The Pattersons, Lucy and Lindsay, built in Winston one of the most beautiful homes of the South. She named it *Bramlette*[7] and thereafter,

J. Lindsay and Lucy Bramlette Patterson built _Bramlette_, one of the most beautiful homes in the South, on Depot Street (later Patterson Avenue).

post card image courtesy of Molly Grogan Rawls

as befit the times, preferred to be known as Mrs. Lindsay Patterson. While in her 20s and 30s, she entertained at _Bramlette_ and engaged herself in the social life of the community. As she did so, and to make good use of the advantages with which she was blessed, she lent an eye toward the improvement and betterment of society. In all her projects, it was said, she advanced her cause with "a gentle, persuasive influence."[8]

Faith, and Strength, and Patience

Returning to Winston-Salem was generally agreeable to Mrs. Patterson, but she soon discovered that something was missing from her life. The fellowship of other women in the service of community was one of the enjoyable aspects of her life in Philadelphia that she found sorely lacking in the South. The women's club movement was not widely popular in the South although the movement was then 25 years old.[9] Mrs. Patterson took the initiative to remedy that situation in Winston-Salem, but she did so with great political savvy. Aware of social resistance at the time to women organizing into clubs, Mrs. Patterson chose to organize first an embroidery club, knowing that it was regarded purely as a feminine pursuit. Despite some misgivings by observers and invitees, she succeeded in bringing women together and forming this sewing club. To assuage further concerns about her club, she exhibited what was regarded as appropriate, womanly hospitality by preparing and serving elaborate refreshments.

Upon the success of the embroidery club and after some time, she was encouraged to organize a social gathering of young couples. She did so with the same grace and charm. Afterwards, she organized a card club which also achieved great popularity. With success in organizing several clubs in the Winston and Salem communities, Mrs. Patterson accepted the challenge to broaden her effort.

In 1902, Mrs. Patterson was in service to her alma mater. She was then president of the Salem Alumnae Association and was busily planning the centennial of Salem Female Academy, founded in 1802. (For 30 years prior, young women had been taught in an informal setting at the Academy through the efforts of dedicated Moravian women; hence, the school has roots back to 1772, roots which it proudly embraces today. However, in 1902, the school celebrated its founding upon the first calling of a headmaster, Rev. Samuel Kramsch, in 1802.[10])

Amidst this planning for Salem Female Academy's centennial event, the influential Mrs. Patterson was approached by the General Federation of Women's Clubs about forming women's clubs in North Carolina. The *Winston-Salem Journal* reported, in the quaint manner of the day, on May 21, 1902:

"Mrs. Lindsay Patterson has just received a letter from Miss Louise Poppenheim, president of the State Federation of Women's Club for South Carolina, expressing her earnest intention of attending the Centennial. ... She is naturally much interested in the federation organization of our Southern States, and has written to Mrs. Patterson to ask her assistance and co-operation in the matter. ... In furtherance of Miss Poppenheim's plans, Mrs. Patterson has requested Mrs. H. R. Starbuck to extend invitations to the presidents of the various clubs in the city and to others interested in this important matter .... Miss Poppenheim has heard much of our live and progressive clubs, and deems this a most favorable time and place for effecting this much to be desired federation."[11]

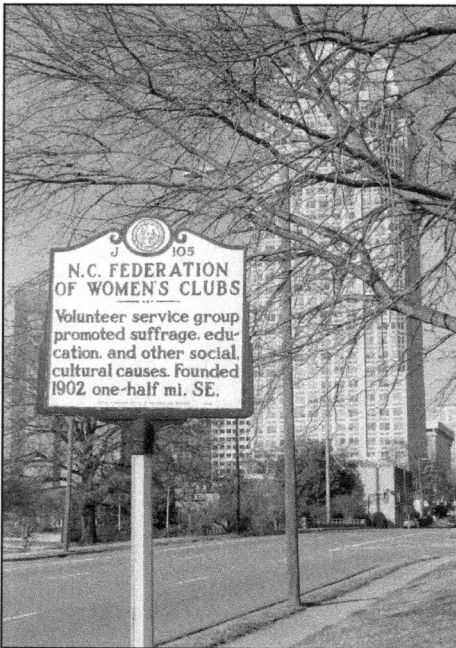

The women gathered on May 26, 1902, at the home of Mrs. Starbuck. After suitable discussions, the women created the North Carolina Federation of Women's Clubs, adopted a

Between the sites of the formerly separate Salem and Winston stands a historical marker commemorating the founding of the North Carolina Federation of Women's Clubs in 1902. The meeting occurred in today's Old Salem.

TRAILING DANIEL BOONE

constitution, and accepted an invitation to hold their first annual meeting in October in the Twin City. Before adjourning their first meeting, Mrs. Lindsay Patterson was elected president of the North Carolina Federation.[12]

Thirty-nine years later, Mrs. Patterson said of the effort:
"Once I had the skeleton of an organization I knew I could by hard work and perseverance, build the rest of it, if it took years. It did take two years of the hardest, most discouraging work I have ever done in my life, and over and over I felt that the only sensible thing to do was to drop it. Men censured the movement as unwomanly; club women in other towns refused to join or left letters unanswered. Pride kept me going, for I had made up my mind I would not be responsible for a failure. It required faith and strength and patience to keep on but the result today is worth every effort that was made in those pioneer days."[13]

Mrs. Patterson served as president of the Federation for three years during which time the club took on work in several areas of service to the community including education, library extension, village improvement, and state charities. Notably, they created 39 traveling libraries, a project regarded as furthering the education of women, especially those isolated on farms in rural communities. Her commitment to improving education in the state continued in other arenas as well. She served as assistant to Governor Charles Aycock's (1901-1905) crusade through the Southern Association of Improvements for Public Schools, visiting counties across the state by horse and buggy.[14] In 1905, after serving as president for three years, Mrs. Patterson asked to be relieved of the responsibilities of the presidency of the Federation. However, her service to education, literacy, and literature in North Carolina would continue through other efforts.

Mrs. Lindsay Patterson—Lady Bountiful

Salem Female Academy Centennial

The newspaper called it the "greatest event in the history of our towns."[15] The occasion was the centennial of the Salem Female Academy. Mrs. Patterson did not find the organizing of a federation of women's clubs in the midst of her centennial celebration any manner of distraction. She was more than capable, and in the spring of 1902, the execution of well-made plans continued as designed. As the president of the Salem Alumnae Association, she was deeply involved in the schedule of events for the week-long celebration ending with commencement ceremonies on Thursday, May 29. The festivities included extensive programs of music and orations, ceremonies, luncheons, receptions, and entertainments such as a "series of magnificent tableaux beautifully designed and brilliantly executed" to tell the story of North Carolina and Salem.

Plans for the notaable occasion—the 100th year of a school for women in America—had been under way for some time. Mrs. Patterson and Mrs. William Neal (Kate Bitting) Reynolds both served on the executive committee of the Alumnae Association. As part of the celebration, the alumnae proposed to support the building of a memorial chapel, a gathering place for community events and a means of making space in the other campus buildings available for classrooms and the pursuit of demanding subjects, including science. The cost was estimated at $16,000 and the centennial celebration was deemed an excellent time to raise funds for its eventual construction. They would on this occasion also lay the cornerstone for Alumnae Memorial Hall on Church Street across from Home Moravian Church.

In late November 1901, Salem Academy hosted a dinner for 125 people representing the "professional, business, and social interests of

Winston-Salem" to explain the plans for the special occasion. Mrs. Patterson reported on the plans for the event. She may have surprised some with her intentions for inviting speakers, but Mrs. Patterson did not shy away from opportunity. She, of course, intended to invite the governors from all the Southern states. She proposed as well to invite President Theodore Roosevelt to give the principal address and his wife to lay the cornerstone for memorial hall. She reported to the gathering at the dinner that she and a committee of ladies planned to travel to Washington, D.C., in two months to extend the invitation personally.[16]

Visit to Washington
The ladies arrived in Washington, D.C., on Tuesday, January 14, 1902, and at noon on Wednesday had their interview with President Roosevelt. Mrs. Patterson, Mrs. Reynolds, and Miss Adelaide Fries were escorted by Senators Furnifold Simmons and Jeter Pritchard and by Congressmen Blackburn and Kitchin. *The Academy* reported in its February issue:

"The President gave them a hearty and cordial welcome, and listened to their petition. He stated that it would give him great pleasure to be present, were it not that he had determined to accept no invitation which would take him away from Washington while Congress was in session, except the one to the Charleston Exposition, and that was semi-official. After some further conversation the party were [*sic*] invited to inspect the various rooms of the White House, and though they regretted the decision of the President, they at once determined to continue the work in other directions.

"Thursday they went to the Capitol, and under the escort of our Senators, they had interviews with a number of prominent men, and received the promise of Senator Clark, of Montana, to be present. The interest of others was assured, and they will, in a number of instances, attend."[17]

Most of the "assured interest" given to the Alumnae Association's invitations where couched in terms such as "unless unforeseen circumstances prevent my attendance," so even an acceptance was not a promise to attend. So, it must have been with some relief that a reassuring letter from the principal speaker was received in May.

"A letter has just been received from Senator Clark stating that he will be with us ... ," the *Winston-Salem Journal* reported. "Senator Clark is an able man, well informed and has taken quite an interest in our section and this specific occasion. We feel complimented that he comes from his distant State of Montana thus bringing the greetings of the far distant West to our school and community in the East."[18]

Montana's senator may have seemed a curious choice to some as the principal speaker for this special occasion in North Carolina. Senator William A. Clark, Sr. (b. 1839) was indeed a long way from home. He had become a wealthy businessman before he entered politics; and, he had his champions and his detractors. With profits from a venture into commerce, he moved into banking. He made his initial fortune by foreclosing on silver mines. He also operated smelters, power generators, and railroads. He was soon renowned as one of the three "Copper Kings" of Montana and in 1901 had personal wealth estimated at $50 million, making him one of the wealthiest men in the world. (In today's purchasing power, he was at least a billionaire.) One writer said of him that "never a dollar got away from him that didn't come back stuck to another... ."[19]

Mrs. Patterson had asked the senator in his speech to reflect on the condition of America as it was in 1802. He obliged. In addressing the state of affairs then, he harked back to the era of Daniel Boone. "The only means of communication with all those settlements west of the mountains," he said, "were two wagon roads through an almost unbroken line of forest. One of these led from Philadelphia to Pittsburg, the other from Virginia to Tennessee, with a branch through Cumberland Gap to Kentucky." Mrs. Patterson must have been delighted at this public mention of her childhood haunts, either by coincidence or by the graciousness of Senator Clark's speech writer.

Governor Charles Aycock spoke as well on the occasion. He was North Carolina's education governor and later Mrs. Patterson would work in support of his educational efforts. Mrs. Aycock helped lay the cornerstone for Memorial Hall, the new building which would grace the campus of the Academy. To help with the fundraising, Senator

The three-story Alumnae Memorial Hall (1907-1965) stood on Church Street behind the Inspector's House, which remains today in Old Salem.

post card image courtesy of Molly Grogan Rawls

Mrs. Lindsay Patterson—Lady Bountiful

Clark presented a gift for the building fund of $500 toward the cost of $16,000. (That gift would have equaled over $13,000 in 2010 dollars.) It was a substantial gift to a worthy cause, and one may ask if that gift had not been, perhaps, Mrs. Patterson's goal all along in inviting the wealthy senator to speak on such an important occasion.

Daughters of the American Revolution

In the spring of 1902, while Mrs. Patterson was engaged with organizing the North Carolina Federation of Women's Clubs and planning the centennial celebration as president of the Salem Alumnae Association, she was also helping organize a new chapter of a patriotic organization. She and 13 other women, including Mrs. William Neal Reynolds, organized a chapter of the Daughters of the American Revolution. The National Society had been founded only a dozen years before, in 1890. They initially named the new chapter the Salem Centennial Chapter because of the occasion coincident with their founding. The DAR chapter was formally organized nearly two years later and eventually became today's Colonel Joseph Winston Chapter. Mrs. Patterson was elected the chapter's first regent.[20]

As Mrs. Patterson relinquished her role as president of the Federation of Women's Clubs after three years, she took on even broader responsibilities with the Daughters of the American Revolution. In 1905, she was elected as Vice-President General of the National Society, Daughters of the American Revolution, and served two years. She was, of course, just then a young 40 years of age. Coincident with that service she continued as president of the Southern Woman's Interstate Association for the Betterment of Public Schools; vice-president, North Carolina Historical Society; and president, County Association for Betterment of Public Schools. Mrs. Patterson was a very busy person, influential in many circles of civic life.

Patterson Memorial Cup – Well Done in My Memory

During his life of study and scholarship, Mrs. Patterson's father, Colonel William Houston Patterson, was an avid champion of Southern literature, believing that it would rise again to its previous "rich fruition." His own library in Philadelphia was one of the most celebrated in the city and had afforded his daughter a rich opportunity for self-education. Colonel Patterson was an invalid for many years. He passed away in 1904 at age 72, after a most productive life as a writer, scholar, illustrator, and patron of letters.

As a memorial to her father, a man she admired and deeply cherished, and to encourage writing talent in North Carolina, Mrs. Patterson created an award named the William Houston Patterson Cup. In 1905, she had a massive gold cup manufactured and studded with 49 precious gems, all from the state of North Carolina.[21] Standing 16 inches tall and seven inches in diameter, the cup had three handles. At the

The William Houston Patterson Memorial Cup, displaying the family crest, was created in 1905 to encourage North Carolina writers.

The cup is in the possession of *North Carolina Department of Cultural Resources, Office of Archives and History.*

Mrs. Lindsay Patterson—Lady Bountiful

base of each handle was a crest. One was for North Carolina and a second for Pennsylvania. The third was the Patterson coat of arms. Below the engraved title of the cup was an attached shield declaring "cor cordium," (that is, "heart of hearts") with the dates "1832-1904." She gave the cup to the State Literary and Historical Association of North Carolina for awarding annually to the North Carolina author judged to have published the work of the highest literary skill and genius. Mrs. Patterson selected the panel of judges which included professors in history from the University of North Carolina and Trinity College (later Duke University) and professors of English at UNC, Davidson College, and Wake Forest College. The president of the North Carolina Literary and Historical Association also served. The names of annual recipients were engraved on the cup.[22] [23]

The first award was made in Raleigh on Wednesday, October 18, the evening before President Theodore Roosevelt was to arrive in Raleigh as part of his 1905 tour of the South. The award went to John Charles McNeill of the *Charlotte Observer* for the best literary work done by a North Carolinian in the prior year. Governor Robert B. Glenn, in presenting the cup, said:

"A devoted daughter, in kindly remembrance of an affectionate father has purchased this costly and exquisite cup, and has asked me to present for her as a token of progress either in poetry or prose to him or her who shall show such great merit. That woman, Mrs. Lindsay Patterson, is doing more than any other North Carolinian. This cup is made of pure gold and is studded with gems of the Old North State, even as it is with studied thoughts of greatness and worth. Mr. Patterson could not have given a thing more worthy, and could he be here tonight he could only say in this award: 'Daughter, well done in my name and in my memory.'"

The audience rose in a standing ovation to Mrs. Patterson.[24]

Later that same evening, shortly after midnight, the governor's brother, General James Dodge Glenn, who also served him as Secretary, passed away from "an attack of acute indigestion." The duties of greeting President Roosevelt later that morning fell to Lt. Governor Francis D. Winston. Roosevelt's visit would be brief as his train was to continue on that night to Roswell, Georgia, where his mother lived, and then on to Atlanta.[25]

President and Mrs. Roosevelt arrived in Raleigh by train at 9 o'clock that same morning and were greeted by a party of dignitaries including the lieutenant governor. The President was soon seated in a carriage for a procession into Capital City. "Along the line of march President Roosevelt saw thousands of smiling faces and cheering people," reported the *Winston-Salem Journal.* "Often he stood in his carriage and lifted his hat, responding to the shouts from houses and streets. Just as he turned from Martin into Fayetteville street, the first sunshine of the morning came peeping from the sky, and instantly the cheering increased to volume and vigor."

Shortly, the president arrived at the Senate chamber where a select party greeted him and each citizen was introduced to President Roosevelt and separately to Mrs. Roosevelt. "John Charles McNeill, winner of the Patterson Cup, got the heartiest greeting of his life," the *Journal* continued, "when he was introduced to the President. He had to stop for a moment to receive congratulations and when he was presented, Mr. Roosevelt's eyes twinkled. 'I have read after Mr. McNeill,' he said, 'and I have enjoyed his work.'"[26]

The Patterson Cup was awarded 14 times from 1905 through 1922. Its

Mrs. Lindsay Patterson—Lady Bountiful

41

President Theodore Roosevelt rode through Raleigh, North Carolina, on October 19, 1905, during a tour of southern states.

from *Raleigh News and Observer*
courtesy of *NC Dept. of Cultural Resources, State Archives*

recipients included Samuel A'Court Ashe, R.D.W. Connor, Archibald Henderson, and Josephus Daniels. Clarence Poe received it twice.[27] In 1905 during the election of association officers, Mrs. Patterson was elected secretary, Clarence Poe was elected treasurer, and Charles Brantley Aycock was elected president. Aycock had immediately preceded Glenn as North Carolina's governor, serving from 1901 to 1905.

Our Lady of Letters

Mrs. Patterson was an accomplished writer herself and was often called "Our Lady of Letters" within the literary circles of North Carolina. She was known as much for her selfless assistance offered to other writers and for her encouragements to struggling, young, creative writers. Every year she held a party at her home, *Bramlette*, to which she invited the authors of North Carolina, believing that the state's writers would benefit from knowing one another.

A biographical sketch of Mrs. Patterson, printed by the DAR in 1912, offered this assessment:

> "'Mrs. Patterson, young in years and younger in spirit, is wide
> awake in the interest of her adopted state. In the numerous essays
> that she has written no one can fail to have gathered therefrom
> much of the writer's personality. In these letters, so gay and so sad,
> so caustic and so gentle, so witty and so tender, so severe and so
> kind, one reads a many sided nature; a soul strong to stand for the
> right and combat the wrong, a charity that believeth all things, a
> pride of race [Scots-Irish] which is inherent; the deep love of blue
> skies and little children and singing birds and the tender blooms
> of life.' Endowed with such attributes she well deserves the appel-
> lation given her by a correspondent of the *Charlotte Observer* as
> 'Our Lady of Letters,' to which may be added 'Lady Bountiful.'"[28]

Two brief excerpts from one of Mrs. Patterson's writing pieces serve
to illustrate not only her accomplishments as a writer, but also reveal
more details about the social influences upon her as a child. In 1915,
she wrote a biographical essay about her grandfather, General Robert
Patterson, titled "The Old Patterson Mansion, the Master and His
Guests."

> "General Patterson was a Philadelphian whom few men equaled
> in the impress he made throughout an unusually long life. As a
> merchant, a man of affairs, a capitalist, a club man, a promoter, a
> veteran of the War of 1812, the Mexican, and the Civil War, in
> which he was a Major General, a host under whose roof-tree gath-
> ered the army, the navy, the volunteer service, the political, scien-
> tific, pioneer and social life not only of this country but of
> Europe, there was no phase in Philadelphia activity in which he
> did not play a part. From youth to old age there were few civic
> occasions of note, and certainly no military ones, in which he was

not foremost among the leaders.[29]...

"For fifty years the old home of my grandfather was a gathering place for men and women who represented in the old world and the new every phase of human activity in art, science, letters, law, the army and navy, politics and religion; from the plantations of the South, the factories of the North and the centres of the world's markets. ..."[30]

It bears noting that Robert Patterson was a wealthy, self-made man, coming to America as a child when his family was driven from Ireland during the United Irishmen Rebellion of 1798 as was the family of Hugh Graham. His father was an insurrectionist in the rebellion that was inspired against British rule by the American Revolution and against authoritarian rule by the French Revolution. A product of public schools in America, Patterson made his fortune in banking and textiles, owning 30 cotton mills and a sugar plantation in Louisiana. Consistent with that station in life, he was involved in politics. The only blemish on a successful military career came late in his life at the Battle of First Manassas (a.k.a. Bull Run). Given only vague orders from General Winfield Scott, Patterson, then 70 years old, failed to contain the advancement of Confederate reinforcements who then helped win the battle. Patterson was severely criticized and then relieved of command after only three months of service as the commander of Pennsylvania volunteers. He retired from service with an honorable discharge in July of that year and wrote his own account of the affair, *A Narrative of the Campaign in the Valley of the Shenandoah in 1861*, published four years later and coinciding with the birth of his granddaughter, Lucy Bramlette Patterson.[31]

Jamestown Historical Exposition, 1907

During 1906, Mrs. Patterson also served as chairman of the Jamestown Historical Commission, creating the state's exhibit for the History Building at the Jamestown Ter-Centennial Exposition. The event was to celebrate the 300th anniversary of the Jamestown settlement in 1607, the first permanent English settlement in North America. That pending anniversary had become the impetus for organizing an exposition in the area. History was selected as the appropriate theme to illustrate the progress that had taken place during three centuries. But, after the site of Jamestown was deemed inappropriate for handling the expected crowds, Norfolk was selected to host the Jamestown Exposition. At that point, the focus broadened from Virginia history to entice other participants, including other states and other countries. Thus did North Carolina rise to the challenge with an exhibit conserving its history. An account of its exhibit began, "The keynote of American life is progress—an excellent and most powerful characteristic; yet harm and ultimate ruin will surely follow in its trail unless safeguarded by conservatism."[32] Remembering the past and making it accessible to succeeding generations—conservatism— was a recurring theme in the projects championed and undertaken by Mrs. Patterson.

The Exposition of 1907 was another event in a string of world fairs held to commemorate the 400th anniversary of Columbus's arrival in the Americas. The other fairs, all considered great successes, included the 1893 World's Columbian Exposition in Chicago, the 1901 Pan-American Exposition in Buffalo, and the 1904 St. Louis World's Fair. (At the 1901 event in Buffalo, New York, President William McKinley was assassinated. Vice President Theodore Roosevelt became president on September 14.)

North Carolina's Historical Exhibit, directed by Mrs. Patterson, was recognized through the presenting of one of only three silver medals awarded for excellence. In the exhibit guide book, she wrote, "It has been the purpose of this exhibit to illustrate by portraits, maps, manuscripts, books, implements, and domestic utensils of all kinds the early history of North Carolina and her people." To that end, she presented copies of the 1580s paintings of John White prior to the Lost Colony and portraits of numerous notables across 300 years. She wrote, "Mrs. Beal's splendid picture of Charles I occupies the centre space, round which are grouped portraits of North Carolina worthies, among the number Penn and Hughes and Hooper, signers of the National Declaration of Independence from North Carolina." To pique visitor interest, she included the portrait of Theodosia Burr and related the story of the disappearance of Vice President Aaron Burr's daughter off the coast of North Carolina at the hands of pirates.

North Carolina's Historical Exhibit received one of three silver medals given for excellence at the Jamestown Ter-Centennial Exposition in 1907.

from *NC Historial Commission Bulletin No. 2*
courtesy of *North Carolina Department of Cultural Resources, Outer Banks History Center*

Playing to patriotism, she presented artifacts from the battles of Ramsour's Mill, Kings Mountain, and Guilford Courthouse. To emphasize North Carolina's early dissatisfaction with the King and initial rebellion during the colonial period, she presented artifacts from the Battle of Alamance, the Edenton Tea Party, and a copy of the reconstructed Mecklenburg Declaration of Independence. She presented seven cases of artifacts, maps, and documents, including one holding items loaned by Mrs. Ida Rodman of Washington, North Carolina. (Mrs. Rodman would later serve in 1915-16 as State Regent, North Carolina Society, DAR.) Ever loyal to her "dear Salem," Mrs. Patterson presented four cases of objects collected by the Wachovia Historical Society and used them to present a picture of life in the Moravian community. It was, in fact, the generosity of the Wachovia Historical Society which began Mrs. Patterson's collecting of relics for the exhibit. (Mrs. Patterson would later serve as president of the Wachovia Historical Society.)[33] [34]

Not every participating exhibitor offered such well-thought-out and efficient displays. Kentucky spent $40,000 to build a replica of Daniel Boone's fort at Boonesborough. Georgia also splurged, building a replica of *Bulloch Hall*, the Roswell home of Mitte Bulloch Roosevelt, the mother of President Roosevelt. Elsewhere the intentions of the exposition also faltered. Despite the focus on history to show "progress," historical accuracy was sometimes cast to the wind. The Powhatans had hoped to exhibit themselves as a modern people, but they were relegated to the "amusement area" and only allowed to reenact the rescue of Captain John Smith by Pocahontas, thus reinforcing the lingering public image of them as "savages." Elsewhere, a wild west show completed the insult by featuring tribes of the Great Plains in the roles the public found more "authentic."

Mrs. Lindsay Patterson—Lady Bountiful

Indeed, big and bold and showy seemed to be what most had in mind. The organizers focused on the military might of the United States Navy, it being less than a decade since the victory at sea wrought during the Spanish American War. Naval parades, mock battles, and a reenactment of the Civil War-era Battle of Hampton Roads between the Monitor and the Merrimac (*CSS Virginia*) were planned. Less attention was paid to the other exhibits and on April 26, 1907, at the opening of the Exposition, only a third of the buildings were built. Even by August, it was not complete and the fair closed November 30. A third fewer people attended the event than was projected and revenues were off by two-thirds. The event itself was generally regarded as "a financial fiasco, plagued by poor management, overly ambitious plans, insufficient resources, and tight deadlines." But in the end, although the fair defaulted on a $1 million loan from Congress, Norfolk had impressed the military and was rewarded with the commissioning of a naval base there. From Hampton Roads, Roosevelt launched his around-the-world voyage of the Great White Fleet on December 16, two weeks and two days after the end of the Jamestown Ter-Centennial Exposition.[35]

The critique of the event and its financial losses were probably sufficient to get the attention of almost anyone who was planning such similar events elsewhere. No doubt, Mrs. Patterson observed the debacle with some detachment, noting the colossal mess that was created by the men who had attempted to organize the matter. She may have taken some quiet pride, however, in the fact that North Carolina was one of only two states whose exhibits were organized entirely by women. Her co-custodians of the exhibit were Miss Rebecca Schenck of Greensboro and Miss Mary Hilliard Hinton of Raleigh. They had created an award-winning display occupying the allotted space of 28 feet by 22 feet, and had done so within the $2,000 budget provided them, refunding $6.39 unspent. Of the display, Miss Hinton wrote, "[The exhibit] was made with the people's money, by the people and for the people. ... As fashion and history repeat themselves, so again the daughters of Carolina have taken the lead and have done their duty in placing her where she justly belongs—in the front rank. Too much praise cannot be given Mrs. Lindsay Patterson, Vice-President General of the Daughters of the American Revolution, who first planned and arranged this exhibit."[36]

Spirit and Soul

Mrs. Lindsay (Lucy Bramlette Patterson) Patterson was a celebrated person of great accomplishment, a woman of generous heart and social grace. She was seldom if ever idle. One project or another—in literature, in education, in civic service, or some other enterprise—continually engaged her time, her interests and her creativity. She saw no project beyond the pale of possibility. She was at ease with presidents and governors and interested in the welfare of the least among the citizens of North Carolina. It was perhaps not long after the completion of the exhibit for that Jamestown Exposition, that she began to consider seriously a commemorative of some sort to honor the effort of Daniel Boone in opening for others passage through the Cumberland Mountain barrier and into the rich meadows and sylvan forests of Kentucky. What more suitable project could she have fashioned to honor her beloved Cumberland Gap than such a worthy effort? Such was the spirit and soul who gave birth in 1912 to the marking of Daniel Boone's Trail.

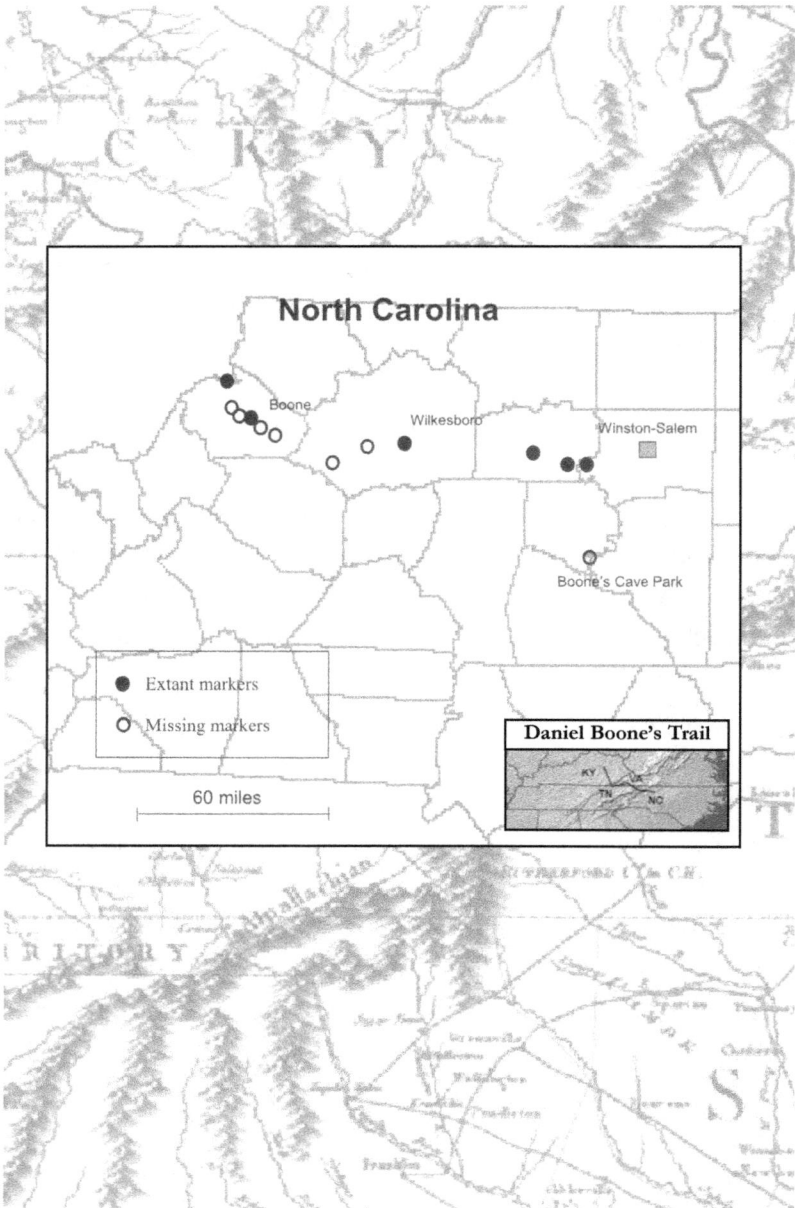

North Carolina

Boone

Wilkesboro

Winston-Salem

Boone's Cave Park

● Extant markers
○ Missing markers

60 miles

Daniel Boone's Trail

KY VA
TN
NC

North Carolina
—A Long and Weary Hunt

For the Present and Rising Generations

The idea for a Daniel Boone trail originated in North Carolina. The first evidence of the DAR's project for marking the trail came in the fall of 1912 in Asheville at the close of the 12th Annual State Conference of the National Society of the Daughters of the American Revolution in North Carolina. The meeting was hosted that November 6 and 7 by the Edward Buncombe Chapter, Asheville, North Carolina, one of western North Carolina's most active. The occasion was blessed with the attendance of President-General Mrs. Matthew T. Scott, leader of the National Society, Daughters of the American Revolution. The last item on the agenda was the Daughters singing together "The Old North State."[1] However, before the group adjourned, Mrs. Lindsay Patterson was invited to share with the Daughters then assembled her plans and progress for a project to mark Daniel Boone's Trail. She shared that the trail in North Carolina would be marked first, with Daughters in Tennessee, Virginia, and Kentucky joining in later. The minutes reported, "Mrs. Patterson is looking up the trail in the three States before the others begin their work." She proposed the placing of boulders in North Carolina with each DAR chapter being asked to pay for one and then placing that boulder with an appropriate ceremony.[2]

Mrs. Patterson's work on locating the North Carolina trail had engaged the help and interest of a number of people whom she would later recognize in subsequent presentations to the North Carolina Daughters. One of them, of course, was William L. Bryan of Boone. He was easily excited about projects that promised to promote and celebrate the heritage of Daniel Boone, and as Mrs. Patterson said prominently later, William Bryan was a genuine help in the effort. He may, however, have preempted Mrs. Patterson's announcement of the project with a postscript to his April 25, 1912, letter to the editor suggesting a Boone Cabin Monument. He wrote:

> "P.S. —I also want each county in N.C., Tenn., and Va. through which Daniel Boone passed on his way to Kentucky to build a monument on his pathway thro' the counties through which he passed to mark his trail through the wilderness as it was in those days. I want this for the benefit of the present and rising generations. – W.L.B."[3]

Maybe Bryan had already been working with Mrs. Patterson on determining Boone's route through the mountains and that work is what prompted him to suggest something special for the town of Boone, such as the cabin monument. If his enthusiasm overpowered his sense of protocol, his mention of the trail idea ahead of Mrs. Patterson's announcement was done most probably in honest earnestness. Of course, it is possible that the idea for a Daniel Boone trail originated with William Bryan, and Mrs. Patterson picked up on it through reading that particular copy of the *Watauga Democrat* perhaps brought back to Winston-Salem by her husband from a visit to Boone. The newspaper, reporting on the comings and goings of prominent visitors, had published under "Local News":

May 9, 1912

"Mr. Lindsay Patterson and little daughter, of Winston-Salem, are in the county of a few days. The contribution of $25 by Mr. Patterson to the Fair Association was highly appreciated by the management."[4] [The "daughter" was undoubtedly Mrs. Patterson's niece, Miss Margaret Beaufort Miller, as the Pattersons had no children of their own.]

Mrs. Patterson said on more than a few occasions that she had been working on the project "for years" before 1913, so marking the trail had been her intention all along. The newspaper story of May 9 probably only served to let her know that Bryan had "jumped the gun" and that his enthusiasm might have needed a little corralling. In any case, William Bryan and Mrs. Patterson seemed to work well together on the project and no evidence appeared of any competition for credit over the origins of the idea. By their subsequent actions, these two capable people seem to have been more interested in getting the trail marked than worrying about who would get credit. It was a wonderful idea whose timing was ripe for action.

In 1912 at the state conference, Mrs. Patterson was no stranger to the North Carolina Daughters or to the President General who joined them in their Asheville meeting. She had already served prominently as a Vice-president General for the National Society, and only that summer, the North Carolina Daughters had published their quarterly journal, *The North Carolina Booklet*, which included a most interesting biography titled, "Mrs. Lindsay Patterson."[5] The Daughters most assuredly looked to her for leadership on this project.

This New World Appian Way
During the following spring of 1913 at the DAR's 22nd Continental Congress in Washington, D.C., North Carolina State Regent Mrs.

William Neal (Kate Bitting) Reynolds alluded to the trail-marking project and to the support it was receiving. "Never has the State of North Carolina been so interested in her Revolutionary history as at the present time," she reported during the April 14-19 gathering. "Never has there been more activity in locating and marking historic spots and all work done by the D.A.R. has met with the heartiest co-operation from our citizens and public press."[6] (Mrs. Reynolds was past regent of the Salem Centennial Chapter, Winston-Salem. Her husband was a brother to Richard Joshua Reynolds and was part owner of R.J. Reynolds Tobacco Company. This arrangement afforded her great opportunity for civic service and philanthropy.[7])

State Regent Mrs. William Neal (Kate Bitting) Reynolds
from *DAR Magazine*, April 1914

In the fall of 1913, Mrs. Patterson shared more of the specifics of her project in her report in Charlotte to the North Carolina Daughters attending the State Conference. Her report was titled, "Marking Daniel Boone's Trail through North Carolina":

> "Daniel Boone's Trail through North Carolina, lost for more than a century, has, after two year's research and hard work, been accurately located and marked. The Trail begins at his home on the Yadkin River, near Salisbury, N.C., and enters Tennessee at Zionville, a distance of one hundred and fifty miles. It passes on through east Tennessee into Virginia, crossing Cumberland Gap

into Kentucky, and ends at Boonesboro.

"Not only was the trail through North Carolina lost, but even historians had forgotten her leading part in building this new-world Appian Way, over which our forefathers traveled in ever-increasing number to open up the great Northwest. With them went law and order, civilization and religion. Surely many a sturdy pioneer took courage, as watching his blazing campfires at night and cloudcapped Cumberland Mountains by day, he remembered how Israel's God had led His chosen people to the promised land by fire and cloud.

Mrs. Lindsay Patterson
from *The North Carolina Booklet*,
NCDAR, 1912

"So, remembering North Carolina's part in the past, it seems eminently fitting that she should, once more, take the initiative, in marking her part of the Trail, and in asking her sister states—Tennessee, Virginia, and Kentucky—to join her in continuing the work through their territory. Nothing that the North Carolina Daughters of the American Revolution have ever undertaken has met with such widespread enthusiasm and hearty support; no sooner had the Chairman suggested that Boone's Trail be marked than the different Chapters subscribed money to carry the work to a successful completion.

"Twelve boulders have been placed along the Trail, marked by tablets on which is inscribed 'Daniel Boone's Trail from North

Carolina to Kentucky. 1769. Erected by North Carolina Daughters of the American Revolution.' ..."

Mrs. Patterson described the process of identifying the trail in North Carolina, expressing gratitude for the assistance she received from several individuals of note. She also shared with a characteristic humor her dismay at the outset of the effort:

"Locating the trail through North Carolina was the real labor of the undertaking, as the Chairman found, to her speechless amazement, that no history or map had any record of it. Then began a long and weary hunt through old letters and ancient manuscripts, and still no results. Then the Chairman wished she had died when a baby, so she wouldn't have to explain to the Daughters that she had asked them to mark a trail that couldn't be found. But the old adage about its being darkest just before dawn held good, and all at once light came. Dr. Archibald Henderson of Chapel Hill, a descendant of Judge [Richard] Henderson, sent extracts from family papers; Mr. W[illiam] L. Bryan, of Boone, related to the Boones, and an encyclopedia of interesting information concerning him, gave valuable suggestions; while Mr. John P. Arthur, of Asheville, went over the entire trail, interviewing all the old inhabitants concerning it, and writing down all that they told him. Mr. P.M. Wilson, of Washington, sent government maps, while the State Regent and Daughters were tireless in their efforts. With all this valuable and most appreciated assistance, locating the long-lost trail became a matter of careful comparison of authorities; and, when they agreed, following the trail and marking it.

"It seems strange that the Wilderness Road, naturally one of the most beautiful in the world, and historically one of the most interesting, should have been so long 'unhonored and unsung.' Its marking should be a matter of special interest, not only to the States through which it runs, but also to the Western Daughters, whose ancestors traveled over it with high hopes and brave hearts."[8]

Again at their state conference the North Carolina Daughters were blessed with the attendance of the President General. In the fall of 1913, this was Mrs. William Cummings (Daisy Allen) Story. In her remarks to the Daughters, she alluded to the project begun in North Carolina to expand westward and to an apparent counterpart effort farther west commemorating perhaps the environs if not the events of the latter days of Daniel Boone's life. "Coming from Missouri, where the Chapters are accomplishing such wonderful work in the marking of historic trails and scenes of Revolutionary history," she declared, "it is with joy that I perceive in North Carolina an equal activity, with the two extremes fairly marching into each other's arms with the promotion of this work."[9]

The Trail in North Carolina
Mrs. Patterson listed for the Daughters, at the state conference in 1913, twelve tablets placed on boulders in North Carolina so that "the reader may follow the trail across the State."

Boone's Cabin
"His cabin on the Yadkin was on a beautiful bluff," Mrs. Patterson continued in her presentation, "overlooking the horseshoe bend of the river, and is almost as wild and isolated as when the hardy pioneer made it his home." Here Mrs. Patterson was referring to what is today called Boone's Cave Park in Davidson County. The site was embraced and championed by local admirers in 1909 as the homesite of Daniel Boone early in his life in North Carolina, which extended from 1752

to 1773. (Some historians cite earlier beginning dates of 1750 and 1751.) The local promoters were successful in getting the North Carolina General Assembly to incorporate the Daniel Boone Memorial Association in 1909. On April 30, 1910, a replica cabin and a 15-foot granite arrowhead monument with a plaque commemorating Daniel Boone were dedicated at the Yadkin River site near Lexington, erroneously referred to as "Holman's Ford" in a *New York Times* article. However, to the delight of the memorial association, the article did declare: "These promise to become a mecca for patriotic pilgrims."[10] With the efforts of the Daniel Boone Memorial Association already under way to celebrate the site at the time of Mrs. Patterson's efforts, it was logical that this site would be noted and included as the easternmost site on Daniel Boone's Trail.

The dedication of the DAR's Daniel Boone's Trail marker took place on November 1, 1913, after being postponed for a week "on account of the rain and the mud," the *Lexington Dispatch* reported on October 29. The remoteness of the site prompted such prudence, and even in an account of the ceremonies, reporters felt compelled to mention the difficulty posed by the roads. "Five automobiles made the trip to the monument, passing over several stretches of road that have not been improved since Boone's day."[11] Another account reported that other

TRAILING DANIEL BOONE

visitors came in wagons and buggies along the rough roads.[12]

Nov. 5, 1913

"Celebration in Boone [township].

Beginning of Daniel Boone's Journey Across Mountains to Kentucky Fittingly Marked.

"Saturday afternoon a small company of men and women gathered at Boone's Cave on the Yadkin river, in Boone township, and there unveiled a bronze tablet marking the spot where began Daniel Boone's history-making trail that led him finally to the banks of the Missouri river, where he died, after spending a long and eventful life preparing the way for civilization in the wilds of new America.

"The national organization of the Daughters of the American Revolution, interested in preserving the history of our country, started a movement for marking a number of historic trails and the trail of Daniel Boone from his cabin on the Yadkin to Kentucky, was one of those taken up. The state organization had practically completed its work in North Carolina and the state organizations of Virginia and Kentucky will carry the work on through to the end.

"The exercises Saturday were in [the] charge of the General William Davidson chapter of the D.A.R of this city, which defrayed the expense of providing and placing the tablet, and Mrs. S.W. Finch, regent of the chapter, presided. On behalf of the chapter, Mr. S.W. Finch made the speech of introduction and presentation, placing the memorial tablet in the keeping of the Daniel Boone Memorial Association. It was very fitting indeed that Mr. J. Ray McCrary, president of the association and the man who has done more than any other man in the state to preserve the traditions and legends that cluster around the great pioneer, should receive the tablet on behalf of this association. Both speeches were eloquent and greatly pleased the little company of about 40 men, women, boys, and girls, who heard them.

"Mrs. W.N. Reynolds of Winston-Salem, state regent of the D.A.R., was called on for a speech and she responded with a very graceful and charming little talk. Mrs. Lindsay Patterson, also of Winston-Salem, was asked to speak and she told of her struggles to locate Boone's trail through North Carolina which began several years ago and ended only recently in success. When she undertook the work all the information available in books of history started Boone's trail in Tennessee and she acknowledged with grateful appreciation, the help of Mr. J.R. McCrary, who was first to offer encouragement.

"There were a score or more of the students of Churchland High School present and they furnished patriotic songs. The unveiling was done by two little girls and two little boys, who ranged themselves on each side of the beautiful Daniel Boone arrowhead monument, to whose base the tablet was affixed, and at a given signal let fall the American flag that covered it. These children were Alexander Springs of Lexington, and T.J. Farriah, Jr. of Winston-Salem, and Sarah Holland Springs of Lexington and Norena Sowers of Boone township.

"After the exercises were over[,] the crowd broke up and wandered over the grounds, visiting the Boone cabin, rebuilt on the spot where the original cabin stood, Boone's Cave, Devil's Den,

and other points of interest on the grounds. The property, comprising five acres, belongs to the Daniel Boone Memorial Association and was a gift from Mr. Phillip Sowers, a good citizen of that section, who is approaching his 90th birthday. ..."[13]

The *Salisbury Evening Post* published an account on November 3 titled "Marker is Unveiled at the Boone Cabin." It reported substantially the same account, but with one interesting variation:

"... Mrs. Lindsay Patterson, also of Winston-Salem, spoke interestingly of her struggles in establishing and locating Boone's trail. Mrs. Patterson has done more than any other person in the state to preserve the traditions that cluster around this famous pioneer and it was a great privilege to hear her own story of the work which was recently culminated in

A plaque placed in the heart of Lexington, NC, in 1918 commemorates Daniel Boone's presence in the lower Yadkin River valley at mid-18th century.

North Carolina—A Long and Weary Hunt

the marking of the trail ..."[14]

For many years, the site served as a state historic site; but, in the 1960s the state discontinued the status of "state historic site" noting that no documentation could be found that showed that the Boones had ever owned that property. A controversy erupted over the matter as many local residents cited the long tradition that acknowledged Boone's presence at the site. The site was retained as a state park from 1971 to 2002. Since 2002, Davidson County has owned and operated the site as a county recreational and environmental park with a Boone-heritage theme. Other memorials to Daniel Boone were erected at the site over the years and replica cabins have twice been consumed by fires of suspicious origins. The DAR's tablet placed in 1913 is no longer there. However, in 1918 another commemorative marker was erected, this one in Lexington at the corner of W. Center Street and N. Main Street. The marker commemorates Boone's presence on the Yadkin River at Boone's Ford after 1750. It was erected by the North Carolina Historical Commission and the Board of Commissioners of Davidson County. Today, Boone's Cave Park has again received the attention of stalwart citizens and a supportive county government. It is a site in the Davidson County Parks and Recreation system and part of the Blueway System offering a canoe trail along the Yadkin River.

Shallowford

"The next marker," Mrs. Patterson shared with the Daughters at the 1913 state conference, "is at the Shallowford, where [General Lord Charles] Cornwallis crossed on his way to fight [General Nathanael] Greene; and later still made famous by Winston Churchill, in his book, 'The Crossing.'" Mrs. Patterson appreciated and promoted good literature throughout her life. She, no doubt, had read Churchill's novel written in 1904, which may have helped inspire her interest in mark-

The North Carolina Daughters placed one marker along the approach road to Shallowford from the east side. The old roadbed is now eroded. The site is on private property in Forsyth County.

ing Daniel Boone's Trail. [American novelist Winston Churchill of New Hampshire (1871-1947) should not be confused with British statesman Winston Spencer Churchill (1874-1965).]

> "We crossed the Yadkin at a ford, and climbing the hills to the south of it we went down over stony traces, down and down through rain and sun; stopping at rude cabins or taverns, until we came into the valley of another river." – from *The Crossing* by Winston Churchill, 1904

Mrs. Patterson may also have been informed and inspired by the 1902 biography *Daniel Boone* by Reuben Gold Thwaites. Based on the manuscripts of Lyman C. Draper, Boone's 19th century biographer. It was at the time, the most up-to-date and comprehensive biography on Boone.

A marker was placed on the eastern side of the shallow ford of the

Yadkin River. The tablet was mounted onto a boulder in a draw that rises up from the famous ford at a prominent rock outcrop. Runoff from plowed fields and erosion over the years may have deepened the old roadbed into a rugged, rocky, impassable streambed today. In 1913, as in the 1700s, this depression was likely the obvious and most approachable access to crossing the Yadkin River on foot, by wagon, or by automobile during the era before a bridge was built over the river. Indeed, speaking of herself in the third person, Mrs. Patterson recounted, "The tireless State Regent and the Chairman went in their cars, and with invited guests followed the trail, attending and participating in all the exercises, and afterward serving picnic lunches."[15] The marker is on private property today.

Huntsville

The North Carolina Daughters erected the first of their Boone Trail markers in Huntsville along the Mulberry Road at High Street, opposite the Kelly Tavern. High Street is not a paved road today, but a road remnant passing behind homes facing east along Courtney-Huntsville

The marker at Huntsville was the first marker dedicated along Daniel Boone's Trail. It faces the old roadbed for what was High Street and is adjacent to Mulberry Road.

Road. The Kelly Tavern is dilapidated beyond repair, roofless and collapsing, but not yet gone. It is well hidden in a tangle of vines and undergrowth. Mulberry Road led travelers to the Shallowford from the west running from Mulberry Fields in what is today Wilkesboro. In 1913, crossing the Yadkin River was still accomplished by ford and ferry. The Mulberry Road near the DAR marker was the site of the Battle of Shallowford, fought October 14, 1780, just a week after the consequential Battle of Kings Mountain.

The Daughters of the General Joseph Winston Chapter met in Winston-Salem on Saturday, October 4, 1913, at the home of Miss Edna Maslin on West Fourth Street, reported the *Winston-Salem Journal* in its Society column. "During the business session, the 'Boone Trail' was discussed and plans were made to go to Huntsville on next Friday in automobiles where the Boone Trail tablet will be unveiled. Dr. Archibald Henderson of Chapel Hill will be the orator upon this occasion."[16]

The actual ceremony was concluded a little differently. Repeating a story taken from the *Statesville Landmark* and one that may have been a week older by then, the *Lexington Dispatch* reported on October 22:

"The unveiling of the first of these tablets was in the center of Huntsville, Yadkin county, last Friday by the members of the chapter. When the audience had gathered around the stone bearing the memorial tablet, over which was spread the North Carolina state flag, all joined in singing "Carolina." Mrs. Lindsay Patterson briefly told of the efforts for the D.A.R. to establish the Boone trail and explained the significance of the occasion. She introduced Mr. Patterson, who spoke for some time on the notable achievements of the pioneer in whose honor the tablet was erected. Mrs. W.R. [*sic*] Reynolds of Winston-Salem, a native

of Yadkin, presented the tablet. —*Statesville Landmark*."[17]

Yadkinville

On October 29 at 11:30, the marker in Yadkinville was dedicated at a ceremony attended by the teachers and students of Yadkinville Normal School. The tablet was presented by Mrs. Margaret Kelly Abernethy on behalf of the Mecklenburg Chapter, Charlotte; it was received on behalf of the town by Mr. W.E. Rutledge, editor of the *Yadkin Ripple*. The students then sang "America" and "Carolina." Two students who helped unveil the marker were related to Daniel Boone. Of course, Mrs. Patterson and Mrs. Reynolds attended, and they were joined by the North Carolina Society's secretary, Mrs. Edwin Overman, of Salisbury.[18] Today, the DAR marker in Yadkinville stands at the courthouse along Main Street (old US Hwy 421) which runs through Yadkinville. The marker is between US Hwy 601 and Jackson Street.

When Daniel Boone lived in this area, it was known as Rowan County, which was the parent of Surry County, the parent of Yadkin County. Daniel Boone's grandfather-in-law, Morgan Bryan, was an early settler in the Forks of the Yadkin and owned massive amounts of land all along the Yadkin River. When Daniel married Rebecca Bryan in 1756, they moved to land in the Bryan Settlement along the modern border of Yadkin and Davie counties. They built a cabin in the forks of Sugar Tree Creek. (The cabin site is on private property. Some local residents say they can point to the exact spot where the cabin stood; others declare the site is lost to history.) The Morgan Bryan home was along South Deep Creek, a stream which flowed into the Yadkin River just upstream of the Shallow Ford. Nothing remains of the Morgan Bryan home, but it would have been southeast of today's Shacktown in Yadkin County, south of US Hwy 421.

Wilkesboro

In September 1913, *The Wilkes Patriot* reported that the DAR had asked for permission from the county commissioners in Wilkes County to place a marker on the "courthouse green." The local news item referred to Daniel Boone as "that famous and intrepid hunter, frontiersman and patriot." On November 27, the newspaper reported in detail the plans for unveiling the marker at a ceremony on December 2, a Tuesday, at 1:00 p.m.:

"The Elizabeth Maxwell Steele Chapter D.A.R. will unveil one of the Daniel Boone Trail markers on the courthouse square in Wilkesboro, on Tuesday, December 2nd, 1913. The exercises will begin at one o'clock p.m. and will be of a patriotic nature and interesting. The following ladies will deliver addresses: Mrs. Wm. Reynolds, State Regent, Winston-Salem, N.C., Mrs. Lindsay Patterson, Chairman North Carolina Branch Daniel Boone Trail Markers National Society D.A.R., and Mrs. Edwin R. Overman of Salisbury will present the marker for the Elizabeth Maxwell Steele Chapter D.A.Rs, and Mr. F.B. Hendren will make the address for Wilkes County. Miss Rose Addie Allen, the grand-daughter of Richard Allen who was Wilkes County's first sheriff and who held that office from 1778 to 1790 and again from 1798 to 1804,

The old courthouse square in Wilkesboro, now home to the Wilkes Heritage Museum, is also home to the Daniel Boone's Trail marker.

whose home is near Roaring River, has been invited to unveil the marker. School children from the two towns will sing patriotic songs.

"The occasion ought to be exceedingly instructive and interesting. Let the people from all over the county come out and hear something about the most illustrious citizen that ever lived in the county. It will pay you."[19]

Although Mrs. Patterson had already reported to the North Carolina Daughters in the fall that the markers had all been placed, she may have meant that all the marker sites had been "located." Certainly, all of them had not yet been dedicated. The December 18 *Wilkes Patriot* reported that the unveiling had been postponed and that it would be rescheduled for the spring. Unfortunately, no copies of *The Wilkes Patriot* survive for the first six months of 1914. Perhaps the eventual ceremony was conducted exactly as planned, but no record of the exercises has yet been found.

The DAR marker in Wilkesboro was placed in the lawn of the courthouse built in 1902. Today that building is the home of the Wilkes Heritage Museum. The marker is on the southeast corner of the courthouse block at the corner of East Main Street and Broad Street. Daniel Boone lived in what is now Wilkes County from 1766 to 1773 and built three cabins there for his family. Today, the city of Wilkesboro occupies the site where Christopher Gist lived in the 1750s. His house was shown on the Jefferson-Frye map of 1752 as a solitary residence on the sparsely settled Carolina frontier. Boone knew the Gists well and frequently hunted with Nathaniel Gist, a son.

Holman's Ford
One of the cabins Daniel Boone built for his family was along the Yadkin River at Holman's Ford. That site is now submerged beneath W. Kerr Scott Reservoir. An exhibit in the Corps of Engineers visitor assistance center at the dam provides some information. Two other Boone cabin sites in the Yadkin River valley were along Beaver Creek. A replica of the Daniel Boone Cabin along Beaver Creek stands as an exhibit at Whippoorwill Academy and Village along NC Hwy 268 near Ferguson. The whereabouts of the DAR marker placed at Holman's Ford in 1913 is unknown, but it was probably destroyed during the flood of 1916. (See Elkville, page 71.)

A replica of Daniel Boone's cabin, like the ones at Holman's Ford and along Beaver Creek, is part of the collection of historic buildings at Whippoorwill Academy and Village near Ferguson on NC Hwy 268.

North Carolina—A Long and Weary Hunt

Crossing the Blue Ridge

In his *History of Western North Carolina*, John Preston Arthur offered information about several possible routes Daniel Boone might have followed in his many sojourns through the Blue Ridge Mountains. Because Boone was an explorer, it is likely that he followed them all from time to time and others as well. Moreover, there is credible evidence in reports made by local residents to Arthur in 1909 and in traditional accounts to support these several routes. The challenge for Mrs. Patterson was to find one route the DAR could mark with some authority. For the markers to be placed through Watauga County, she relied on John Preston Arthur and William Lewis Bryan in selecting the sites.

On page 82 of his *History*, Arthur offered this passage:

"They went up the ridge between Elk creek and Stony Fork creek, following a well-known Indian trail, passed through what is now called Cook's Gap, and on by Three Forks church to what is now Boone. ... and having reached the town of Boone or Howard's cabin, his most direct route would have been through Hodge's gap, down Brushy Fork creek two miles, and then crossing the Grave Yard gap to Dog Skin creek; then along the base of Rich mountain, crossing what was then Sharp's creek (now Silverstone) to the gap between what is now Zionville in North Carolina and Trade in Tennessee. He would then have been at the head of Roan's creek, down which he is known to have passed as far as what is now known as Shoun's Cross Roads."[20]

It would appear that Mrs. Patterson decided, or persuaded the Daughters, to mark that route.

Elkville

One of the routes Daniel Boone followed from the Upper Yadkin River (that is, from Holman's Ford) into the Blue Ridge Mountains was along Elk Creek. The creek entered the Yadkin River near the Wilkes-Caldwell county line. A marker was erected in 1913 in Elkville, which lies near the confluence of Elk Creek with the Yadkin River. Elkville also lies along today's NC Hwy 268.

That marker, however, did not survive long. In mid-July 1916, a massive flood ripped through the Upper Yadkin River valley destroying homes, barns, and bridges, and scouring the river channel. *The Wilkes Patriot* reported on July 20: "At Ferguson on the W&YRR [Watauga and Yadkin River Railroad], the outgoing train was swamped. One car was washed away and the engine was pushed down the track a long distance by the high water. Sanders' dwelling, the depot, and W.V. Williams' warehouse were washed away. C.D. Coffey lost all of his lumber and tanbark at that place. … Many of the farms were greatly damaged and the crops ruined."[21]

The *Winston-Salem Journal* reported extensively on the destruction as news of the catastrophe made its way slowly out of the valley. On July 21, it reported, "The Watauga and Yadkin River Railroad running to Grandin, in Caldwell County is obliterated. The two engines are standing in the Yadkin River and two coaches are lodged in a sea of mud."[22] (Grandin is only a couple of miles upstream of Elkville.) The DAR markers at Elkville and Holman's Ford were, no doubt, destroyed or at least buried. Mrs. Patterson and Mrs. Reynolds must have read those accounts with shock and dismay for the fate of the markers, but probably more so with great concern for the welfare of the people they had met just three years before in dedicating those markers along the Yadkin River. A flood relief fund was begun in Winston-Salem. The

Reynolds family was an early contributor. The extent of the expanding catastrophe was revealed with more news from *The Wilkes Patriot* a week later: "There has not a day passed since the flood twelve days ago that soaking rains have not fallen here ... . Now that we are facing a very serious problem in the matter of food for man and beast during the coming Winter and Spring, everything possible must be grown to take the place of the crops that have been destroyed."[23]

Cook's Gap

John Preston Arthur mentioned on page 32 of *A History of Watauga County* that the North Carolina Daughters placed a marker at Cook's Gap, one of six erected in Watauga County during October 1913. Curiously, neither Mrs. Patterson nor Mrs. Reynolds mentioned placing a marker at Cook's Gap in their accounts of the project. However, the *Watauga Democrat* noted on November 18, 1913, "The last marker for the Daniel Boone trail through Watauga has been shipped to Lenoir by Mrs. Lindsay Patterson, and will be attached to a suitable boulder at Cook's Gap as soon as it can be gotten from the depot. This will make six on the historic trail through the county." Apparently the marker at Cook's Gap was an afterthought in the DAR's planning and accounted for a 13th marker erected in the state on Daniel Boone's Trail. On May 7, 1914, the *Watauga Democrat* reported the placing of the marker:

"The Last Boone Marker

At the request of Mrs. Lindsay Patterson, chairman of the Boone Trail Committee of the D.A.R., Mr. W.L. Bryan sent Mr. W.A. Miller to Cook's Gap Saturday for the purpose of placing the last marker on the trail of Daniel Boone in this State. He was assisted by the following public spirited citizens of that locality: Thomas L. Critcher, R.A. Green, Richard Green, C.L. Cook, and a worthy colored man named Jack Grimes. These would accept nothing for

Near Cook's Gap on the Blue Ridge Parkway is a pull-out called Boone's Trace. One of the 1913 DAR markers was moved there in 1963, but has since been stolen.
image of marker attached to boulder c1998 courtesy of E. Gary Marshall

their labor in helping to place the heavy boulder in position, and in addition, Mr. Critcher furnished dinner to the visitors from Boone, and provided all the tools which were required to complete the job."[24]

The marker was placed without apparent public ceremony but not without public approval and pride. During the week before, on April 30, the *Watauga Democrat* reported on a scheme that had been suggested for who would look after these markers after they were placed. The citizens seemed to think that making the children of the Sunday school classes from a church nearest each marker was an idea with merit. Thus did the duties for protection and maintenance fall to the "watchful guardians in the boys and girls" in Mt. Gilead Church and Three Forks Church and whatever churches were near three other named markers. The "marker at Boone will be the care of every child in this town." One citizen at Cook's Gap remarked sternly (and one hopes with hyperbole), "If any man should injure a marker on Boone's trail, he would be lynched."[25]

Whatever events befell the marker or those who "injured" it, the Boone Trail marker was certainly missing from Cook's Gap in 1963

North Carolina—A Long and Weary Hunt

when another of the DAR markers was moved there as a replacement marker to serve along the Blue Ridge Parkway. (See Three Forks Church.)

Three Forks Church

For the times that Daniel Boone ascended the Blue Ridge Mountains along Elk Creek, he reached the crest of the plateau at Cook's Gap and then descended to a ford across the New River near where three branches of the river converged. At that historic ford in later years, a Baptist congregation formed. The founders included two of Daniel Boone's nephews, Jesse and Jonathan, the sons of his brother Israel, who died of consumption in 1756. Married in August that same year, Daniel's new bride of 17, Rebecca, took on the task of rearing this instant family.

At the site of the Three Forks Church, the Daughters placed one of the tablets. The church later moved a half mile north to face the main road, US Hwy 421. The marker remained in place adjacent to the church's old graveyard until 1963. In that year, the DAR marker was moved to the Blue Ridge Parkway near Cook's Gap as part of the state's celebration of its 300th birthday, the Carolina Charter Tercentenary. On June 28, 1963, a celebration and ceremony was held at the reinstalled marker as part of "Daniel Boone's Crossing the Blue Ridge Mountains." On June 12, 1964, a group of conscientious citizens placed a wooden sign at the Three Forks site. It included the same wording which had been on the bronze tablet and was placed "to keep intact the original route" Boone traveled through the area.[26]

The bronze tablet that had been moved to Cook's Gap was stolen from its mountings along the Blue Ridge Parkway sometime around 2002. The site of the original Three Forks Baptist church and grave-

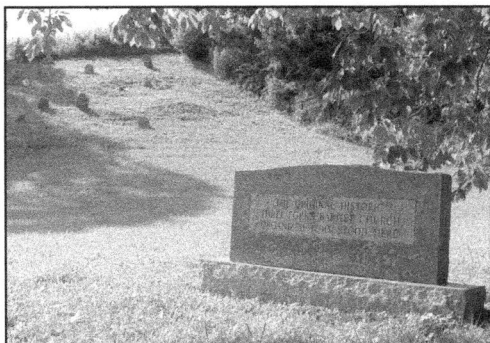

The original site of Three Forks Baptist Church and graveyard was the site where the DAR erected one of the markers for Daniel Boone's Trail in 1913.

yard where the DAR marker was placed in 1913 is marked with a stone marker along New River Hills Road (also called Charlie Hollar Road) a half mile south from US 421 where it crosses the New River. The wooden sign placed in 1964 is gone.

Watauga Courthouse

The Boone Trail marker placed at the Watauga Courthouse in Boone was dedicated with great ceremony under the sponsorship of the Edward Buncomb Chapter, Asheville, there being no local DAR chapter at the time.[27] It was unveiled on October 23, 1913, and accompanied by patriotic singing and addresses and the reading of a ritual by Mrs. William N. Reynolds, State Regent, with responses from the large audience. John Preston Arthur, who delivered one of the addresses, reported in a later history of Watauga County both that "the county court house was filled" and that "short addresses were made in the open air to the people who had gathered around the marker … ."[28]

A recounting of the actual ceremony was reported in the following two issues of the *Watauga Democrat*. Unfortunately, only the November 6 issue survives and includes only the second part of John Preston Arthur's lengthy address about the life of Daniel Boone. However, the plans for the ceremony were reported a week before and probably relate with some reliability what transpired on the 23rd:

October 16, 1913

"Unveiling the Boone Marker

The Edward Buncombe Chapter, D.A.R. will unveil this tablet at the court house in Boone on Thursday, Oct. 23rd 1913. The exercises will commence promptly at 9 o'clock a.m. in order not to interfere with the Masonic picnic. The gallery will be reserved for the faculty and the students of the Appalachian Training School, and the bar for the visiting Ladies, the Confederate Veterans, the Masonic Lodges and those taking part in the exercises. The Invocation will be by Rev. J.J.L. Sherwood, provided he can be there. There will be speaking and singing, and the Delegates of the Daughters of the American Revolution will give their ritual. The tablet will be unveiled by little Margaret Linney, Alice Councill and the small niece of Mrs. Lindsay Patterson. Mrs. Reynolds, the state Regent, and Mrs. Theodore D. Morrison, the Regent of the E.B. Chapter, with other delegates, are expected to arrive in Boone on the afternoon of the 22nd."[29]

During the week after the 1913 marker dedication in Boone, the *Lexington Dispatch* ran a piece from the *Watauga Democrat* on the day of the event, October 23. It recounted some of the preparations taken for a series of dedications in Watauga County:

Nov. 5, 1913

"Marking the Trail of Boone.

Mr. C.L. Newman, manager of the Winston Stone Company, is in the county putting in place the boulders and attaching thereto the tablets which mark the trail of Daniel Boone through Watauga county in 1869 [*sic*]. There will be five in the county as follows: Three Forks church, Boone, Hodges' Gap, Grave Yard Gap, and Zionville. The stone here is a massive one, a moss-covered granite weighing probably more than two tons. It occupies a very prominent place on the courthouse square, and its rough appearance is in close contrast with the rugged nature of the grand old pioneer. The tablet will be unveiled today with fitting ceremonies.—*Watauga Democrat*"[30]

Arthur wrote in his 1915 book, *A History of Watauga County*, his account of the dedication ceremony and in particular mentioned the recognition given William L. Bryan on that occasion for his building of the Boone Cabin Monument 12 months before:

"When the trail was marked at Boone court house in October, 1913, E. S. Coffey, Esq., a distinguished member of the Boone

bar, presented a resolution of thanks to Colonel Bryan for his services in having this spot [the Boone cabin] so appropriately and permanently marked. The resolution was adopted by a rising vote of the large audience which packed the court house to the dome."[31]

At last, the community thanked the "colonel" for the effort he had made to bring recognition and notoriety to the town for its pioneer history.

College students in 1923 gather at the marker for Daniel Boone's Trail in front of the 1904 courthouse.
courtesy of *University Archives, Appalachian State University*

North Carolina—A Long and Weary Hunt

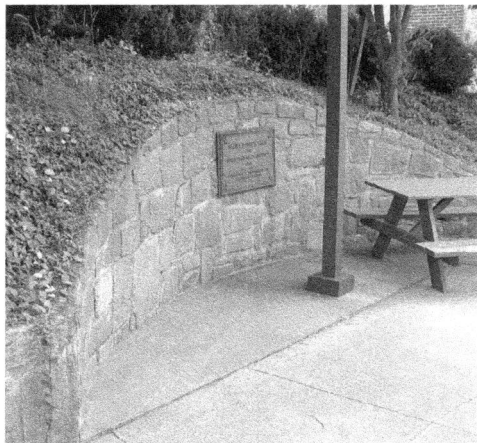

At the current Watauga Courthouse in Boone, the DAR marker from 1913 has been attached to a stone wall.

Arthur continued his account of the ceremony, declaring that Bryan "originated and inspired the idea of marking the trail through this county and it is not too much to say that if the Daughters of the American Revolution had not marked it, he would have done it himself. He did, in fact, help place every marker in the county."[32] Arthur, at least, must have been of the opinion that Bryan's mention in April 1912 of marking a Daniel Boone trail was the impetus for the eventual project. Be that as it may, Mrs. Lindsay Patterson and the Daughters of the American Revolution put it into action with the generous assistance of W.L. Bryan. Arthur noted that Mrs. Patterson did, in fact, place every marker in Watauga County as recommended by Bryan. He then acknowledged the cooperation and contributions of the two: "It is not too much to say that but for Mrs. Patterson the trail would not have been marked till it was too late to locate it with any degree of certainty, and posterity will give both Colonel Bryan and Mrs. Patterson their full measure of gratitude for their patriotic work."[33]

Arthur reported that five little girls, all with Revolutionary War ancestors, participated in unveiling the marker. One was "little Margaret Beaufort Miller," a niece of Mrs. Patterson. Mrs. Lindsay Patterson spoke at the ceremony as did Mrs. Reynolds as State Regent, and the

Regent of the Edward Buncombe Chapter from Asheville. Professor B.B. Dougherty, President of Appalachian Training School delivered an address as did John Preston Arthur.[34]

Today the marker has been removed from its original mounting on the massive, rough boulder placed on the grounds of the 1904 courthouse and is encased in a stone wall at a landing along stairs leading to the newer courthouse from the street-level sidewalk. The reinstalled marker was rededicated in 1982, the marker's 69th anniversary year. The ceremony was attended by two women who as little girls had participated in the unveiling: Margaret Linney Coffey and Neil Coffey Linney.[35]

Hodges Gap

Two miles west of the Watauga Courthouse in Boone, another marker was placed at the crest of the road in Hodges Gap. Today that road is known as Old Bristol Road and the high point of the road through the gap is 150 feet west of Hub Brown Road. No marker remains today on this residential street which parallels US Hwy 421 on the bluff above the commercial buildings along US Hwy 421. Hub Brown Road is 0.4 miles east along Old Bristol Road from its intersection with US Hwy 421. Old Bristol Road is opposite and north from NC Bypass 105 at US Hwy 421. (Curiously, modern maps locate Hodges Gap a few miles farther south at the intersection of NC Bypass 105 and NC Hwy 105. However, in 1913, this crest along Old Bristol Road

The marker placed here at Hodges Gap on Old Bristol Road at Hub Brown Road has disappeared. View is looking east toward the courthouse.

North Carolina—A Long and Weary Hunt

was clearly called Hodges Gap.) One can follow sections of Old Bristol Road today and imagine the stalwart Mrs. Patterson and Mrs. Reynolds motoring along that serpentine route in 1913 earnestly seeking to place the markers that commemorated the travels of Daniel Boone through this same mountainous terrain 144 years before. He traveled the narrow paths on foot or horseback at best and with packhorses most likely, but certainly with no wagons, as later Boone commemorators would suggest so earnestly.

Straddle Gap or Graveyard Gap

Yet another marker was placed in Watauga County at the recommendation of William L. Bryan, as were five others. Mrs. Patterson had relied on the counsel and advice of Bryan as well as that of John Preston Arthur in choosing the sites to place the markers. These men had traveled about the county, interviewing some of the longtime residents and gathering recollections of facts and stories that had been passed down in their families about the old paths through the mountains. In fact, Arthur declared, "A straight line between Holman's Ford [North Carolina] and Roan's Creek [Tennessee] would pass nearer to the points named by the DAR than to any other points Boone is known to have been in this locality. A well-defined and much traveled Indian trail also marked this identical route, and Boone doubtless followed it into Tennessee."[36]

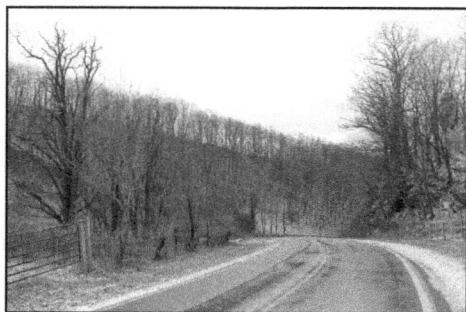

The marker placed at Straddle Gap (or Graveyard Gap) on Linville Creek Road is missing. View is looking north toward Zionville from crest in road.

This marker stood at Straddle Gap, also known as Graveyard Gap. It was only a couple miles west of the Hodges Gap marker. Today, that gap lies along Linville Creek Road 0.6 miles north from US Hwy 421 and a few dozen yards north of the intersection with Incline Road. No marker remains there today, but local residents recall moving the marker on its boulder and then returning it after a road widening project. The marker was cracked and thus removed for repair; unfortunately, no one ever saw the marker again.[37]

Zionville

On page 40 of his *A History of Western North Carolina*, Arthur wrote, "This, in all probability, is the gap through which Daniel Boone and his party had passed in 1769 on their way to Kentucky. It is between Zionville, N.C. and Trade, Tenn., and the gap is so low that one is not conscious of passing over the top of a high mountain. Tradition says that an Indian trail went through the same gap, and traces of it are still visible to the north of the present turnpike."[38]

The marker erected in Zionville was placed on private property in the curve along Emory Greer Road at John's Lane. This site is about 200 feet east of the intersection of Old 421 Road and Emory Greer Road, an intersection, in turn, about 0.4 mile south from US Hwy 421 along Old 421 Road. The site of the marker was along the "Old Buffalo Trail" which passed through Watauga County about six miles north of Boone. It crossed Meat Camp Creek where a hunters' cabin existed during Boone's visits. The Buffalo Trail continued southeasterly toward Deep Gap. The route is readily visible from atop Rich Mountain. The location and history of the Buffalo Trail has been researched and documented by Watauga County scholar Brian Fannon.[39]

The marker at Zionville is in the yard of a private home on Emory Greer Road at John's Lane. It also marks the Buffalo Trail.

William L. Bryan was involved in more than just locating the sites. His letter to the editor in the November 13, 1913 issue of the *Watauga Democrat* shows how he helped install the markers:

"On last Thursday morning I went to Zionville to put up the last marker on the Daniel Boone trail from North Carolina to Kentucky in 1769, the other four having been previously placed. The boulder was at the head of Cove Creek, and, after a splendid dinner at Cicero Greer's, with Will Profit's cattle and Greer's horses, it was hauled to this place before dark... . Early Friday morning we went to work on the marker, which we finished before noon having cemented and painted it, in which Mr. Philip did the fine work gratuitously. I had no trouble in getting all the help I needed without charge. Mr. Willett Adams painted the tablet and cemented the same to the stone, without charge. The marker stands in front of his work shop and in fine view of the road. The people at Zionville were kind to us, and seemed to be very proud of the marker, which they say they will keep in good condition. ... After dinner we went to Mr. Thomas Bingham's and painted the marker we had placed in Straddle gap a few days before... . His sons and Mr. Moody helped us greatly in placing that marker.

Passing the newly painted Brushy Fork Baptist church we painted the marker in Hodges gap and cemented it to the boulder."[40]

The Boone Trail Highway

In the fall of 1913, Mrs. Patterson reported to the North Carolina Daughters at the State conference in Charlotte the progress made in marking Daniel Boone's Trail in North Carolina. What remained then was to engage and motivate the Daughters in the other three states to mark their respective sections of the Trail. With that done, the DAR could then proudly claim to have accomplished something of lasting value, something worth doing, and something that no one else had dared to do. That singular effort for a grand scheme was theirs alone. But, before the Daughters could get their long-planned project completed, others got involved.

The trail-marking efforts of Mrs. Patterson and Mrs. William N. Reynolds had garnered scant notice in the hometown newspaper except for mention of one actual dedication ceremony. Any other occasional mention was relegated to the society column along with news of all the social clubs and circles. But on December 14, 1913, the *Winston-Salem Journal* covered most of the front page of its Sunday feature section with an article titled "The Boone Trail Highway." Unfortunately, the article was not written by Mrs. Patterson or by any knowledgeable Daughter; it was written by J. Hampton Rich. He touted the work of his newly established association, The Boone Trail Highway and Memorial Association, a group formed "on the porch of the home of P.H. Hanes in Winston-Salem" in consultation with him and A.J. Eller. The group officially formed in North Wilkesboro on October 13, 1913 and later was chartered by the state of North Carolina.[41] "The Boone Trail Highway Association," he wrote in the December article, "following in the pathway of Mrs. Patterson and

Mrs. William Reynolds are [*sic*] seeking to commemorate the work of Daniel Boone by promoting the building of a great highway along or near his trail." Rich continued in his article plugging the participation of highway men in North Carolina, Tennessee, and Kentucky who were planning to link up with this road. He then wrote at great length in this inaugural article and in two subsequent and likewise lengthy articles about the history of Daniel Boone and the likely routes Boone had taken through the mountains. To his credit, Rich did acknowledge, Mrs. Lindsay Patterson for her "collation of many of the facts, which we will write in this and subsequent articles."[42] Unfortunately, Hampton Rich was no historian and inaccuracies were no strangers to his written accounts or to his understanding of Boone's life; but he was enthusiastic and that counted for something. (See *Rich Man: Daniel Boone* by Everett G. Marshall, 2003.)

An interest in better roads across the country was already prevalent when Mrs. Patterson had proposed her trail-marking project to the North Carolina Daughters the year before. Demonstration projects had been built already. One of them, an object-lesson road, was built through Cumberland Gap in 1908. Each state had groups of "public spirited businessmen" actively promoting better roads as tools of commerce and economic development. North Carolina certainly had its own association, the North Carolina Good Roads Association, which met in Asheville. In support of that effort, Governor Locke Craig had proclaimed November 5 and 6, 1913 as "Good Roads Days" in North Carolina, "calling upon all patriotic people through-out the State to work upon the public roads of the State on these days."[43] Mayors and county commissioners followed suit and issued their own proclamations in support of the governor. In some commu-nities, schools were let out so teachers and students could participate in the civic effort.

So it was that State Regent Mrs. Reynolds (probably in concert with Mrs. Patterson, who was a master of the art of leadership) had seen opportunity earlier in the fall. They instinctively understood one of the key principles of leading and they put it into practice. They knew that one can get people to do most anything one wants, if one lets the others think it is their idea.

In the November 12 issue of the *Davie Record* (Mocksville), H.W. Horton enthusiastically wrote[44] from North Wilkesboro:

"The Trail of Boone is being traced and tablets set up at principal points along the trail and this scheme, which is being put through by the Daughters of the American Revolution, with Mrs. Lindsay Patterson of Winston-Salem as one of the moving spirits and Mrs. Wm. Reynolds. The State Regent gave berth [*sic*] to a new idea which the men have taken up and hope to put through, following the marking of The Trail. That idea is the building of a graded highway called the "Boone Trail Highway," following the route the old Pioneer traveled as nearly as the character of the country will permit, and to be a fit memorial to the brave man who blazed the way for civilization up through the great resourse- ful [*sic*] northwestern section of North Carolina, East Tennessee and Kentucy [*sic*].

"... This highway would enable travel from the central and eastern sections of the State to go directly into the heart of the mountains for outings and vacations ... .

"The tentative route of the trail ig [*sic*] beginning at Salisbury then through Mocksville, Farmington, Huntsville, Yadkinville, Wilkesboro, Boone and on into Tennessee and Kentucky. It means much

North Carolina—A Long and Weary Hunt

and should receive the hearty support of every citizen."[45]

A year after beginning the trail-marking effort, the Daughters of the American Revolution had allies in their commemoration project and they seemed to welcome it. The interest of "the men" in building better roads did lend moral support to the Daughters' commemorating efforts. Besides, Mrs. Patterson had plenty enough to occupy her time and her creative mind. In fact, she had been away recently, in Richmond, Virginia, immediately after the North Carolina Daughters' state conference. She had been appointed on November 18 by Governor Locke Craig as a delegate from North Carolina to the convention on December 3 and 4 for "the Celebration of the One Hundred Years of Peace Between the English Speaking Peoples under the Treaty of Ghent." [The Treaty of Ghent (1814) ended the War of 1812, one of the three wars in which Mrs. Patterson's grandfather had fought. The war, sometimes called the Second War for American Independence, was fought between Great Britain and the United States.] Who else could have represented North Carolina with such knowledge and grace? Where Hampton Rich had latched onto a single idea (erecting markers to Daniel Boone) that he would ride unrelentingly for the next 25 years, the multi-talented Mrs. Patterson with her variety of interests and capabilities was already engaged in other matters even before her current pet project, the marking of Daniel Boone's Trail, was even completed. Mrs. Lindsay Patterson moved ahead. Indeed, her participation in the Richmond conference may well have been the reason for the postponement in the dedication of the Wilkesboro marker which had been planned for December 2.

Aside from her service in matters of historical interest, the dedicated work of Mrs. Patterson for the betterment of her community in other arenas had manifested itself already that fall. Alumunae Memorial Hall at Salem College, the building for which she had so skillfully begun raising funds in 1902, had been completed in 1907. In the fall of 1913 just before the DAR state conference in Charlotte, the hall's presence enabled the city of Winston-Salem to host as a speaker "the most wonderful woman of our age." The *Winston-Salem Journal* reported on the October 6 lecture:

"Helen Keller ... spoke last night in Memorial Hall, Salem College, to a packed house of interested and sympathetic listeners. ... There was something thrilling about this woman who possesses neither the sense of seeing or hearing. Her voice was not entirely natural, but when one remembers the tremendous obstacles overcome by her in learning to speak, the accomplishment is nothing short of marvelous. And as she poured out to her hearers the tender and beautiful thoughts often times with outstretched hands and arms in her darkness, there came with her struggling words all the power and personality of a powerful and heroic soul.

Alumnae Memorial Hall (1907-1965) at Salem College from whose stage Helen Keller addressed the community on October 6, 1913.
courtesy of *Forsyth County Public Library Photography Collection*

North Carolina—A Long and Weary Hunt

"… The work of [her teacher, Mrs. Anne Sullivan Macy,] aside from being a lifelong labor of love and devotion is a great educational triumph. … She has accomplished what is considered the miracle of the century and has shown the world something, at least, of what may be accomplished with a human being if only someone has the infinite patience and care to lead the young mind."[46]

The fruits of Mrs. Patterson's untiring efforts would continue to benefit her community, her state, her country, and the world at-large.

The Leading Part Played by North Carolina

In spring 1914, the North Carolina Daughters and their original Daniel Boone trail-marking project received national attention, at least among the National Society, DAR. The report that Mrs. Lindsay Patterson gave at the state conference in Charlotte appeared the following spring as an article in the April issue of *Daughters of the American Revolution Magazine*. The announcement to a national audience of Daughters that North Carolina had already completed its marking of Daniel Boone's Trail no doubt motivated the Daughters in Virginia, Tennessee, and Kentucky to complete their portions as well. The article included a photograph of Mrs. Patterson, Mrs. William Reynolds, Miss Maslin and three young girls posing with one of the tablets to be placed. They selected a setting for the photograph significant to Mrs. Patterson. The stone pedestal supporting the weight of the tablet which was propped up for the photograph was part of the steps at Salem Female Academy campus erected as a memorial from the Class of 1896. Those steps, now on the Salem College campus, are adjacent today to the north side of the Rondthaler Science Building, built in 1950. The tablet was not installed there.[47]

Posing with a North Carolina Daniel Boone's Trail tablet at Salem Female Academy. Adults (from left) are Mrs. Lindsay Patterson, Mrs. William N. Reynolds, and Miss Edna Maslin. Children (from left) are Elizabeth Shelton, Margaret Miller, and Martha Maslin.
courtesy of *Forsyth County Public Library Photography Collection*

In that article, Mrs. Patterson made it clear that the help of others was so essential to the achievement of marking the trail in North Carolina.

"And because the State regent has been so tireless in her help, and practical in her sympathy with the undertaking, that a successful outcome was assured from the beginning, it is fitting that her assistance, as well as that of the other enthusiastic Daughters should be specially acknowledged, as they are deeply appreciated."

The magazine article appeared in the same month that the Daughters gathered in Washington, D.C., for their 23rd Continental Congress during April 20-25, 1914. State Regent Mrs. William N. Reynolds gave her report on the national stage sharing with great pride in the accomplishment of the North Carolina Daughters. She noted most especially the Daniel Boone's Trail project, reporting:

North Carolina—A Long and Weary Hunt

"Tablets have been placed on boulders, with this inscription ... :
Daniel Boone's Trail
From North Carolina to Kentucky
1769
Erected by the North Carolina
Daughters of the American Revolution.

"The D.A.R. have never undertaken a work that has met with such enthusiastic support. The expense of marking the Trail was borne by the different chapters in the State. After the Trail had been located, and the tablets placed on the boulders, the members of the chapters came from all parts of the State for the unveiling of the tablets. The school children attended in a body, singing patriotic songs and taking active part in the exercises; patriotic addresses were made, and the country people came for miles to be present at the exercises. The Chairman of the Boone Trail Committee, Mrs. Lindsay Patterson, and the State regent of North Carolina, with invited guests, traveled in their cars from point to point along the route, and in spite of the rough mountain roads, and sometimes stormy weather, each tablet was unveiled at the appointed time. ... The interest aroused among all classes and ages has been remarkable, and the D.A.R. feel more than repaid for their efforts to set forth the leading part played by North Carolina in the opening of the great Northwest."[48]

The North Carolina Daughters selected the date of 1769 to place on their markers for good reason. "It was on the first of May, in the year 1769, that I resigned my domestic happiness for a time, and left my family and peaceable habitation on the Yadkin River, in North Carolina, to wander through the wilderness of America, in quest of the country of Kentucke ...,"[49] wrote John Filson in the voice of

Daniel Boone in 1784. Some believe that Judge Richard Henderson was behind Boone's 1769 exploration, which led to Boone's marking of the Boone Trace in 1775. Hence, North Carolina's role in that historic route which began at Long Island of the Holston River in today's Kingsport, Tennessee, finds its origins six years earlier and nearly 200 miles farther east.

During the following fall at the state conference in Durham on November 3 and 4, 1914, Mrs. Patterson gave her report on the Boone Trail, telling of "her pride and delight in knowing that North Carolina finished her part of the Boone Trail first." Looking toward completion of the trail, she asked the North Carolina Daughters to contribute $100 from the state treasury as its share of the cost of the joint monument planned for Cumberland Gap. [50]

TRAILING DANIEL BOONE

Magic City

The Cumberland Gap Mrs. Lindsay Patterson had known as a child and the Cumberland Gap she encountered in the second decade of the 20th century, were remarkably different, But, they were not as different as they might have been. Few people visiting the area today could possibly imagine the history of this area in the late 19th century. Progress is not always a steady march, it seems. Sometimes it moves in fits and starts, and some of those starts are really more wayward outbursts than true beginnings.

The Race for the Prize

By 1887, the flora of Cumberland Gap had recovered from the battle scars and events that shook its tranquility during the Civil War. The slopes of the gap and the face of the Pinnacle were soon to be again covered with trees and undergrowth. The area was again a quiet pass for the travelers sojourning from one side of the Cumberland Mountain barrier to the other. But it was the natural resources rather than the native natural beauty of the area that first attracted the attention of investors. The preeminent champion of these untapped resources was Alexander Alan Arthur, a Scotsman and a distant cousin of the recent U.S. president, Chester A. Arthur (1881-85). After making his own tour of the Cumberland Gap in June 1886, A.A. Arthur garnered the interest and investments of some young men of Eastern wealth whom he met in Asheville, North Carolina. He took them to the Gap. The night they camped in the saddle of the gap, August 31, 1886, they felt the earth shake beneath them for several minutes, discovering later that Charleston, South Carolina, had been wracked and devastated by a monstrous earthquake. Their own unfolding plans could easily have wrought the same to the Cumberland Gap area.

Alexander Alan Arthur, "The Duke of Cumberland"
courtesy of *Carnegie-Vincent Library, Lincoln Memorial University*

Arthur parlayed the interest and initial capital of these Easterners into substantial investments from banks and steel men in Great Britain. These investors intended to harvest the rich timberlands and to mine the region for coal and iron ore. They built railroads into the area, extending the Louisville & Nashville Railroad south from Pineville, Kentucky, into the Yellow Creek valley. The Knoxville, Cumberland Gap & Louisville Railway, was built north from Knoxville. Another 10 railroads, it was said, were under construction or planned, all vying to serve the interests of businesses who would surely come to profit from exploiting the Southern highlands.[1]

Geologists, politicians, writers for trade publications, attorneys, and investors came to see the area for themselves. One writer described in his January 1889 *Harper's* article the experience of traveling through the Yellow Creek valley. He followed the route, through marshes and canebrakes, Daniel Boone and countless settlers had followed a century and a quarter before:

> "We drove from Pineville to Cumberland Gap, thirteen miles, over the now neglected Wilderness Road, the two mules of the wagon unable to pull us faster than two miles an hour. The road had every variety of badness conceivable—loose stones, ledges of rock, bowlders, sloughs, holes, mud, sand, deep fords. ... Settlements were few—only occasional poor shanties. ... We climbed up to the top of the mountain over a winding road of ledges, bowlders, and deep gullies, rising to an extended pleasing prospect of mountains and valleys. The pass ... is a narrow, a deep road between overhanging rocks."[2]

The Duke of Cumberland

In the summer of 1888, Arthur laid out the town of Middlesboro in the Yellow Creek valley intending to build a town suitable for a quarter-million people. He and his business associates originally named it Middlesborough after the industrial town in England (Middlesbrough) whose success they hoped to match in this American version. Engineers arrogantly constructed channels to drain the low areas and to address the flooding local residents had warned of. The streets running east and west were given English names, the main street named Cumberland and others, Winchester, Exeter, and Manchester. More train track was laid around the perimeter of the town. Lots were sold and a commercial district erupted at the site becoming a boomtown created to prosper from the promised mining, smelting and timbering activities, none of which had actually begun. Capturing the scene perfectly, Dr. Robert Kincaid, chronicler of the Cumberland Gap in his 1947 book *The Wilderness Road*, wrote: "The quiet of the forest was broken by the clank of steel, the ring of hammers, the whir of saws, the shriek of steam whistles and the shouts of legions."[3] Greed and ambition, unbridled and carelessly inflamed, had descended upon the

Cumberland Gap.

Dr. Kincaid further described the activity surrounding the enterprise: "By the middle of 1889, his tent city was a surging congeries, digging, building, sawing and trading. Shanties and temporary frame structures grew by magic. The wide streets were churned into bogs of mud. Sawmills were located along the streams. Coal seams were tapped and tipples built. Business houses rose rapidly to fill in the pattern laid out on the blueprints."[4]

A tunnel was dug beneath the gap from the east and from the west, with the two crews breaking through on August 8, 1889, after 18 months of drilling. Wild celebration ensued. In a few more weeks, the engines of two trains, from north and south, nosed together. With the sale of lots by auction in October 1889, the town soon surged to a population of 5,000. A coal mine was open and operating, two blast furnaces and a tannery were under construction, as were power plants for providing heat and electricity to the town and the growing indus-

A great fire burned throughout Middlesboro on May 31, 1890.
courtesy of *Bell County Historical Society*

trial complex. A 150-room hotel was nearing completion. All this was tangible evidence of the $10 million invested during the prior 18 months into building the town. They called it "Magic City." But in the spring of 1890, the first problems arose. A series of fires erupted in the town. Businesses and homes were destroyed; but, the ever optimistic Arthur, already frequently away to New York and elsewhere promoting the entire project, sailed to London and secured another $8 million from investors. Rebuilding began.

Ever the showman, Arthur invited over 300 investors and economic experts to visit the site and to see it for themselves. They came from England, France, and Germany, interested in the future of their steel enterprises. Arthur entertained them at the hotels which had sprung up, and he received glowing reports from these men about the prospects for the whole venture. Called by others the "Duke of Cumberland," Arthur expanded his vision beyond the industrial and began to promote the area for its beauty and health-sustaining potential. Soon a 700-room Four Seasons hotel was erected and nearby a

The Four Seasons Hotel was built in 1892 and sold for salvage three years later after the Panic of 1893. The sanatorium is in the left background and serves today as Grant-Lee Hall, residential housing for students at Lincoln Memorial University.
courtesy of *Carnegie-Vincent Library, Lincoln Memorial University*

Magic City

As seen in the hotel lobby, the furnishngs of the Four Seasons were overly grand and ostentatious.
courtesy of *Carnegie-Vincent Library, Lincoln Memorial University*

sanatorium arose as well. At the hotel's opening in April 1892, it bustled for two weeks with 400 of New York's wealthiest socialites. They had chartered a train together to celebrate in the Southern Highlands in the most ostentatious fashion with elaborate dinners, dances, polo, lawn tennis, and a grand ball inside the Cumberland Gap Cave. After their departure, the expected multitudes of guests never arrived.

But trouble for Arthur's plans had already begun to surface. In November 1890, the London bank of Baring Brothers had failed. It had been one of the principal routes for channeling capital to Arthur's venture. The investment began to sour. Little of the $20 million invested had been spent on developing productive assets. The value of shares tumbled from £40 to £1.5 in six months. In January 1891, Arthur was dismissed as president and general manager of the enterprises, although local residents thought him unjustifiably blamed. The momentum of the undertaking already built up in the towns continued their survival for a little while and another auction of lots infused the town with investments from Kentucky speculators and northern industrialists. But the economic panic of 1893 in America doomed the enterprise. The development of Middlesboro, Harrogate, and the Town of Cumberland Gap as centers of industrial commerce was thwarted. Through 1894 and 1895 banks and railroads and real estate developments failed. Properties were sold for less than a penny on the dollar. The Four Seasons Hotel, only three years old and built at a cost of $1.5 million, was sold for salvage at $9,000 and torn down. A few of the industries were too far along in construction to stop and went into operation anyway, but they failed before the end of the century.[5] The promising economic boom had come to woeful bust.

Arthur tried his hand at other ventures, which came to nothing. In poor health, he returned to Cumberland Gap, a place where he had seen success at one time. He sat on the porch of his modest home in Middlesboro and watched the town slowly recover under the efforts of others. Across the mountain, Harrogate prospered with the establishment and development of Lincoln Memorial University. Arthur

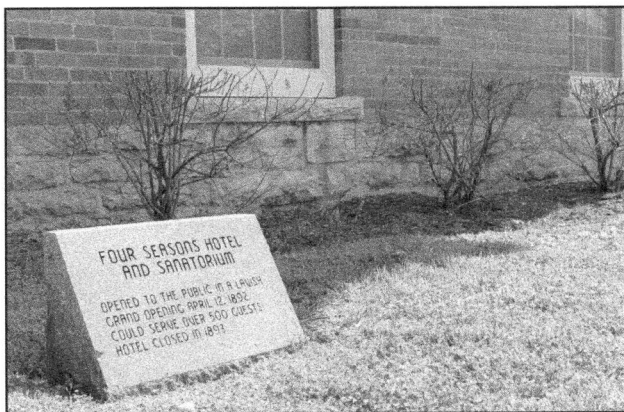

Avery Hall on the LMU campus is built on the site of the Four Seasons Hotel and sits on foundation stones taken from the demolished hotel.

Magic City

Lincoln Memorial University was chartered in 1897 to fulfill a desire expressed by Abraham Lincoln made during the Civil War for a university to serve the people of this region.

witnessed this all with some content and some wistful recollections of his earlier days until he passed away in March 1912, the month before another visionary for a scheme of decidedly less grand scale of construction, wrote his letter to the citizens of Boone, North Carolina. A.A. Arthur was buried in Middlesboro and was honored by the people who remembered well what he had tried to do.

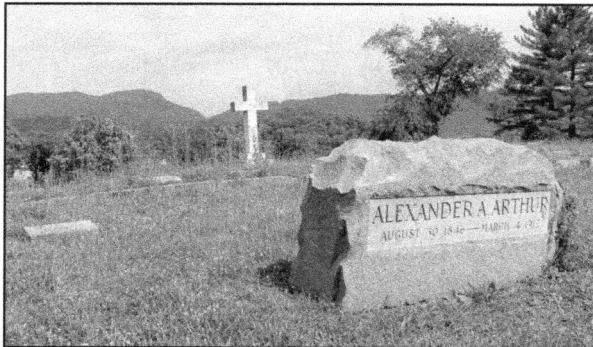

The hilltop grave of Alexander Arthur in Middesboro Cemetery affords a view of Cumberland Gap from the northwest.

Magic City

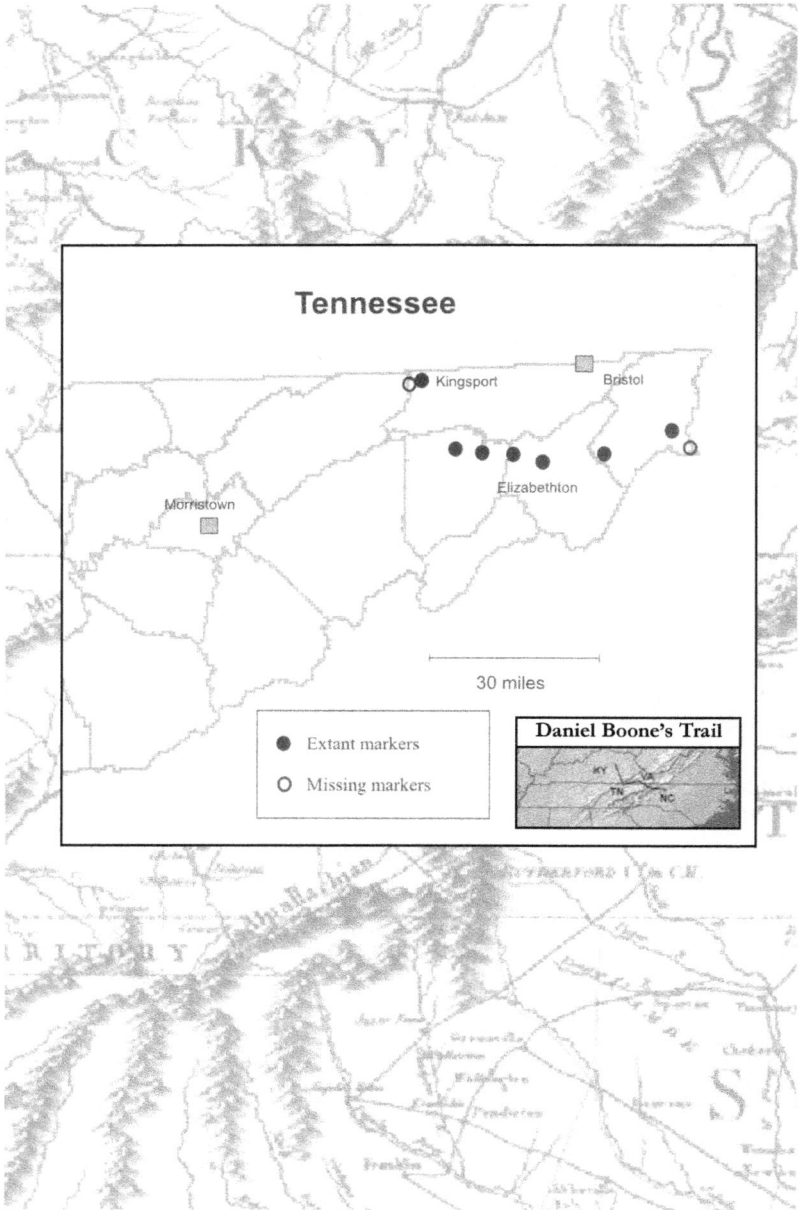

Tennessee

Kingsport Bristol

Elizabethton

Morristown

30 miles

● Extant markers

○ Missing markers

Daniel Boone's Trail

Tennessee–Something Worthwhile

The letter North Carolina's State Regent, Mrs. Reynolds, wrote in the fall of 1912 inviting the Daughters from three other states to join in the trail-marking project must have struck an immediate and cooperative chord in Tennessee. By the fall of 1913, the Tennessee Daughters were heartily engaged in marking Daniel Boone's Trail. The particulars of how Tennessee DAR came to be involved are lost to history, but one can readily surmise a likely account from knowing who was involved.

Mary Boyce Temple

Miss Mary Boyce Temple chaired Tennessee's trail-marking efforts. Miss Temple was the organizing Regent of the Bonny Kate Chapter in Knoxville on October 7, 1893, and had served as Vice-President General of the National Society, DAR, during its first decade, filling that roll during 1898 and 1899. She was Tennessee's State Regent during 1906-07 (and again during 1920-21). Miss Temple was educated at Vassar College, graduating 1877, after having immersed herself as a child in the private library of her father, Judge Oliver Perry Temple, one of the founders of the University of Tennessee. She travelled broadly and was invited by the governor to represent the State of Tennessee at the Exposition Universelle in 1900 in Paris, and at expositions in Stockholm and Rio de Janeiro.[1] In 1904 at the St. Louis

World's Fair, she was the only woman on a jury of higher education. Miss Temple also helped organize Knoxville's National Conservation Exposition in 1913 to promote conservation primarily among the Southeastern states.[2] It was during the exposition's run from September 1 to November 1 that Mrs. Patterson was in Knoxville discussing plans for marking Daniel Boone's Trail in Tennessee.

Miss Mary Boyce Temple
from *Tennessee State History of the DAR*
by Kate K. White, 1930

Miss Temple and Mrs. Patterson had much in common in several areas of service to their communities, and they probably knew each other through their mutual involvements. As was Mrs. Patterson, Miss Temple was active in the women's club movement of the day. She was the first president of Knoxville's Ossoli Circle[3] and the first Secretary of the General Federated Woman's Clubs of Tennessee. Miss Temple was nine years older than Mrs. Patterson and one can imagine that she might have played a generous and helpful role as mentor and compatriot to Mrs. Patterson in perhaps more than one of their mutual endeavors.[4]

On October 18, 1913, Mrs. Patterson wrote from Knoxville to the Virginia Daughters inviting them to participate. (See Chapter:

Virginia—Such Rapid and Thorough Work). She was, undoubtedly, visiting with Miss Temple at her home, *Melrose*, an antebellum, Italianate mansion and one of the most prominent homes in Knoxville. It was named for the Scottish abbey where Miss Temple's grandmother was born.[5] Mrs. Patterson could have been in Knoxville for any number of reasons: to help the Bonny Kate Chapter celebrate its 20th anniversary, to join Miss Temple in attending, perhaps, a Tennessee Daughters' state conference usually held in the fall, or maybe to attend the National Conservation Exposition. Because it could well have been any or all of these events—all involving the remarkable Miss Temple—the trail-marking project in Tennessee was most fortunate to have such a well-educated, well-read, prominent, and effective leader as Miss Temple as its champion and chairman.

In the Dilemma of War

World events sometimes imposed themselves on the public's attention as the Daughters engaged in their numerous projects promoting patriotism. So it was in late April 1914, during the 23rd National Congress in Washington, D.C., and, following the Tampico Affair on April 9. At the time of that gathering of Daughters, President Woodrow Wilson had offered for Congressional action his policy toward Mexico's Huerta government. Mexico's unpopular leader (whom the U.S. had only recently helped install) was embroiled in a revolution with two different rebel factions and the U.S. had decided to prevent the delivery of weapons to the government's military by way of Germany.[6] At Continental Hall, the *Knoxville Journal and Tribune* reported, "a spirited demonstration followed the announcement of Mrs. William Cummings Story, President-General, that war with Mexico virtually had been declared."[7] The Daughters voted a resolution of approval for President Wilson's Mexico policy and pledged the members of the organization "to hold themselves in readiness for any service which may be required in the dilemma of war." The next day, April 22, brought headlines: "First Americans Are Killed at Vera Cruz, Mexico."[8]

Although U.S. troops did occupy Vera Cruz for six months, a full-scale war was avoided and life for the country and the Daughters resumed its peace-time pace. In the spring of 1914, only three weeks after the National Congress, the Bonny Kate Chapter held its last meeting of the club year in Knoxville. During that May 14 meeting, Miss Temple reported to the chapter that she had conferred with three gentlemen–judges Henderson, Allison and Kyle–with regard to which of four possible routes through Tennessee the Daughters were to mark as Daniel Boone's Trail. The bronze markers would be placed during the summer. She also shared that the date for the dedication of the joint monument at Cumberland Gap had been changed from October 13 to the following spring. They selected a date near the end of term for Lincoln Memorial University. "The hotel there has signified its desire to entertain the D.A.R. members at that time," she reported, "and the occasion with the university will be the time of the attendance of a number of distinguished guests."[9]

Daniel Boone's Trail in Tennesssee

The details of when the Tennessee Daughters dedicated each of the nine markers they placed are unknown except for three markers, whose ceremonies were reported in *The Bristol Herald Courier* and *The Comet* (Johnson City). Given Miss Temple's involvement in the project, it is likely that all the markers were placed with the same attention to ceremony and engagement of the public.

In 1915, the *New York Times* published an article about Daniel Boone's Trail, listing the Tennessee markers:

"The Tennessee part of the trail traverses the four eastern counties of the State—Johnson, Carter, Washington, and Sullivan. Over the first part of this trail there rested much uncertainty, but through the efforts of the Tennessee State Chairman, Miss Mary Temple, the trail was established. From Sycamore Shoals, where the great treaty with the Indians was signed [Transylvania Purchase, 1775], to Cumberland Gap lies the historically best known portion of the trail.

"The first marker on Tennessee soil is at Trade, one mile from Zionville. The second is at Shoun's, nine miles due north through a wild and picturesque gorge along Roan Creek. The third is at Butler, southwest fourteen miles from Shoun's and at the junction of Roan Creek and the Watauga River. At Butler there is now living a lineal descendant of Daniel Boone, one Finley Curtis, whose great-great-great-grandmother was Daniel Boone's daughter Anne.

"The fourth marker is about nineteen miles due north [*sic,* west], at Elizabethton; the fifth at Watauga, Carter County, eleven miles northwest; the sixth is placed at Austin Springs, Washington County, six miles distant; the seventh marker is at Boone's Tree, Washington County, four miles away; the eighth is at Old Fort, south end of Long Island, Sullivan County. The ninth is eighteen miles away at beautiful Kingsport, opposite the centre of Long Island, where Boone gathered his men to start for Kentucky while the treaty with the Indians was being consummated. From this point it is two miles distant to the Virginia line."[10]

Although the listing of sites is helpful to historians, the directions and distances given are not all correct and some are misleading.

Tennessee—Something Worthwhile

Trade

The marker at Trade cannot be located and is probably the victim of development and road construction over the century. However, the marker placed there in 1914 could possibly be the one later placed at the cemetery of the Pleasant Grove Baptist Church on TN Hwy 167 in Maymead. That marker has since been moved. (See Butler, next page). Along US Hwy 421 near TN Hwy 67 today is a highway historical marker explaining the history of The Trading Ground and Daniel Boone's use of the gap in his travels.

From Trade, US Hwy 421 follows closely along Roan Creek toward Mountain City for about 11 miles. About five or six miles into that route going northwest, Old Hwy 421 departs from modern US Hwy 421 about a mile past Midway. A drive along Old Hwy 421, running snuggly against the base of the mountains and out of the floodplain of Town Creek, affords modern travelers a sense of the driving experience of early 20th century automobilers, but without the problematic and ubiquitous mud and ruts of that era.

The DAR marker is missing at Trade, but a Tennessee highway historical marker mentions the importance of the Trading Ground.

The tablet on the DAR marker at Shoun's Crossroads has oxidized into a distinctive and colorful reddish hue.

Shouns (Crossroads)

Where Old Hwy 421 (Crossroads Drive) intersects TN Hwy 167 stands the DAR marker placed in 1914. It is reachable more immediately from the intersection of US Hwy 421 and TN Hwy 167, which is a quarter mile west of the marker. A drive north along Crossroads Drive from the marker follows Old Hwy 421 for a couple of miles into Mountain City. Again, this route affords the modern traveler a sense of the driving experience of the Tennessee Daughters in 1914.

The marker was paid for by the Samuel Doak Chapter, Morristown, organized in January 1911. An impressive 62 members joined at that initial organizing under the leadership of Mrs. T.M. (Lucy Michaux) McConnell.[11] This chapter of Tennessee Daughters was the closest to the homesteads of Mrs. Patterson's family. One can imagine the role she played in encouraging them to sponsor a marker of the trail.

Butler

From Shouns (Shoun's), the Trail descended the valley along Roan Creek to the southwest using the roads known today as TN Hwy 167 and Little Dry Run Road, arriving at the confluence of Roan Creek with the Watauga River. There in the community of Butler in 1914, the citizens gathered at the church yard to dedicate the DAR monument for Daniel Boone's Trail. (Because a photograph shows a cere-

A tablet was erected in Butler in 1914, but disappeared during subsequent floods. Woman at left may be Miss Mary Boyce Temple.

courtesy of *Butler Museum*

mony participant believed to be Miss Temple, this ceremony was held probably a few days after the August 15 ceremony in Elizabethton, and may well have been the next day, a Sunday.)

Local historians report that the extreme floods of 1924 and 1940 likely washed away the original marker. In fact, such flooding prompted the Tennessee Valley Authority (TVA) to begin planning in 1942 for a flood control dam. Although work on the dam was interrupted by World War II, the project resumed in 1946 and the dam was completed late in 1948. The town was to be submerged, so TVA relocated the entire community, moving Butler to the north a few miles. The town's original site, where the DAR monument was erected, sits about 300 feet below the surface of Lake Watauga.

Touting itself at "the town that wouldn't drown," the relocated community of Butler proudly tells its history at the Butler Museum. Standing just as proudly at the entrance to the museum is a DAR marker pronouncing "Daniel Boone's Trail." The marker in "new"

A 1914 DAR marker stands in front of the Butler Museum in the town relocated by the Tennessee Valley Authority in 1948.

Butler was moved there, as a Ruritan project, from the cemetery of the Pleasant Grove Baptist Church near Maymead, along TN Hwy 167 between Shouns and Butler. Residents remember that marker standing in the cemetery and may have assumed that the DAR placed it there, but the DAR mentioned no such placement in 1914.[12] In the 1960s, that marker was moved from Pleasant Grove Baptist Church to the Baptist church in "new" Butler, and then subsequently to the Butler Museum around 2000. The marker may have been moved from "old" Butler for safekeeping and not lost in a flood after all. Noting that all the bases for the Tennessee markers are so different, the current marker looks too much like the one dedicated in 1914 to be otherwise.

Elizabethton

The marker at Elizabethton is due west from Butler, not north as suggested by the *New York Times* article. The marker is along East Elk Avenue at East Doe Avenue in the lawn of Harvest Baptist Church. At the opposite, east end of East Elk Avenue, in a traffic circle, is the

Tennessee—Something Worthwhile

veterans monument and
nearby is a monument for
Watauga Old Fields, placed by the DAR in 1923. Watauga Old Fields
was the site of the 1772 gathering of pioneering, overmountain settlers to form the Watauga Association. It was, as the plaque declares,
"the first place west of the Alleghenies where men joined together in
a written compact for civil government and for the preservation of
their ideals of Liberty." Daniel Boone was no stranger to the Watauga
community and was known to many of the men who signed the compact.

On the afternoon of Saturday, August 15, 1914, Miss Mary Temple
was joined by Mrs. W.C. (Carrie M.) Clemens, Regent of the John

Elizabethton's DAR marker, erected in 1914, stands along East Elk
Avenue at East Doe Avenue in the lawn of Harvest Baptist Church.

TRAILING DANIEL BOONE

Carter Chapter of Elizabethton, for the dedication of the Daniel Boone's Trail marker in Elizabethton. Unfortunately, just as the ceremony was to begin, a rainstorm blew in and the participants moved to the porch of the Lynnwood Hotel where they held the ceremony nonetheless. "Miss Templeton [*sic*] made a very excellent address and told of the originating of this work to memorialize the noted pioneer and hunter who roamed over the hills and through the forests of Tennessee and Kentucky," reported the *Bristol Herald Courier*. "The address at Elizabethton was made by Hon. W.R. Allen, who in a short and concise manner gave an account of the wanderings of Daniel Boone." Because of the rain, the unveiling of the marker was omitted. Several descendants of John Carter, for whom the DAR chapter was named, were there to participate in that part of the ceremony.[13]

The location of this marker in Elizabethton is interesting because of its proximity to Sycamore Shoals and the site of Fort Watauga, a site already commemorated by the DAR in 1909. It was at the fort and surrounding meadows in 1775 that Richard Henderson treated with the

Cherokee leaders for the Transylvania Purchase. After gathering the chiefs together at the request of Richard Henderson, Daniel Boone departed that treaty and celebration while it was still active. He rendezvoused at the Long Island

Tennessee Daughters erected a monument in 1909 to commemorate the site of Fort Watauga. It stands on West G Street near Sycamore Shoals State Historic Area on West Elk Avenue.

Tennessee—Something Worthwhile

of the Holston with 30 axmen to begin marking the trail for Henderson and others to follow. Thus began Boone's Trace. The 1909 monument was placed jointly by the John Sevier, Bonny Kate, and Sycamore Shoals chapters.[14]

Visitors to Elizabethton can visit the DAR's 1909 monument on West G Street and explore the pioneer period's history at the nearby Sycamore Shoals State Historic Area on Elk Street (US Hwy 321/TN Hwy 67) to the west of Elizabethton. A visitor center, museum, replica fort, seasonal outdoor drama, hiking trails, wayside exhibits, and scheduled reenactments help interpret the history of early East Tennessee when it was the "Overmountain region" of North Carolina.

Watauga
West-northwest of Elizabethton is the community of Watauga. It sits in the extreme northwest corner of Carter County near the Washington County line. The Tennessee Daughters erected a marker there in 1914. Today it stands along TN Hwy 400 (West Fourth Avenue) in the lawn of City Hall and the police department at South

Mary Boyce Temple dedicated the marker in Watauga on the evening of August 15, 1914. It stands in front of City Hall today.

Fourth Street. The site is on a high knob well above the floodplain of the Watauga River running just to the south and west of Watauga. The marker faces the road right at the curb line; visitors should be careful of traffic when viewing the marker.

Automobile traffic might not have been such a problem when the marker was installed. News from around the region was reported in the *Bristol Herald Courier* three days after the event:

"Watauga, Tenn. – Aug. 17

Saturday was a red letter day at Watauga. Several Sunday schools picnicked here. Persons were here from three counties: Sullivan, Carter, and Washington.

"A large crowd was present in the evening. Miss Mary Boyce Temple of Knoxville, Regent of the Bonny Kate Chapter of the D.A.R. and Mrs. E. Muncy [Munsey] Slack, of Johnson City, came to dedicate and unveil the marker of the Boone Trail at this place."[15]

Undaunted by the rain showers in Elizabethton that afternoon, Miss Temple simply moved on to Watauga for another dedication ceremony that evening.

Austin Springs

Farther west along the Watauga River is the community of Austin Springs. A DAR marker, mounted in a pedestal of river stones stands on the north side of Austin Springs Road about 0.15 miles south of Riverview Road. This marker is along the south side of Watauga River, the route Boone would have likely followed on his way from the Transylvania Purchase treaty at Sycamore Shoals in March 1775 to Long Island of the Holston from which he began to mark Boone's

The Tennessee Daughters erected this marker at Austin Springs along the Watauga River, a route Daniel Boone took going west.

Trace toward the Cumberland Gap.

Nearby this site, only a mile downstream and along the Bristol Highway (US Hwy 11E/19W), is today's Winged Deer Park, a Washington County recreation facility with ball fields for organized team play. At the northeast end of the complex is the Massengill monument honoring the pioneer families of East Tennessee. (This 1937 monument was relocated to the park in 1990.) Adjacent to the monument is the twice-relocated, 1770s cabin of Robert Young, the overmountain militiaman who is credited with shooting the commanding British officer, Major Patrick Ferguson, from his horse at the Battle of Kings Mountain in 1780. Young was 62 years old at the time. That battle was a turning point of the American Revolution in the Southern Campaign. (See book, *Before They Were Heroes at King's Mountain*, 2011.)

Only a couple of miles north from Winged Deer Park along US Hwy 11E/19W is Rocky Mount Museum State Historic Site, featuring living history interpretations and an excellent museum about pioneer life in early East Tennessee. Rocky Mount Museum is in Piney Flats. In August 1914, Piney Flats was the scene of a large county fair. All the community's attention, at least that recorded by the newspapers, seems to have favored the fair in lieu of other events such as the dedication of the Boone Trail marker at Austin Springs. No account of the dedication has been found, though it was most likely conducted while Mary Boyce Temple and Mrs. E. Munsey Slack were in the area dedicating other markers in mid-August.

Boone's Tree
Tradition has it that in 1760 Daniel Boone carved in a tree along Reedy Creek in Washington County his name and an account of his killing a bear. (This creek should not to be confused with Reedy Creek in Sullivan County where in 1775 Boone also carved his name on a tree.) The DAR placed a marker at that 1760 tree in August 1914.

The John Sevier Chapter, Johnson City, hosted the ceremony with Mrs. E. Munsey Slack, Chapter Regent, in charge. Mary Boyce Temple delivered the dedicatory address. An account of the event appeared on the front page of the August 13 issue of *The Comet*, published in Johnson City, Tennessee.

> **"Boone Trail Marker Is Formally Dedicated,**
> *The Famous Boone Tree Upon Which Daniel Boone, Pioneer and Hunter, Killed a Bear in 1760 is Used to Mark Trail*
> About 400 patriotic admirers of Daniel Boone, pioneer and hunter, attended the unveiling of the monument erected on the Daniel Boone trail at the Boone tree, seven miles north of Johnson City. ...

> "The giant beech on which is carved 'D. Boone cilled a bar in

1760,' may fall to the ground, but the granite boulders which have been laid in cement will not soon yield to the gnawing tooth of time. The marker is five feet high, four feet wide and two feet thick. Embedded in the western front is a marble tablet two feet square, on which is letter[ed]: 'Daniel Boone Trail, 1769.'"[16]

The article further explained that the Boone Tree was a beech tree about three feet in diameter and 100 feet tall, leaning about 15 degrees from vertical. The letters carved on the tree, the newspaper said, were "almost obliterated by the corroding of time," but "the tree marks in the bark made by Bruin[']s claws are still visible." Expressing the pride of the community in their special artifact of Boone's life, the article concluded, "It will pay any one to travel miles and miles to see this famous tree."[17] Reportedly, the tree was felled in a windstorm in 1928.

John Preston Arthur was one of the vocal critics of the day regarding the authenticity of this tree's carvings as evidence of Boone's presence there in 1760. He cited a lack of documentation, the degree of protracted unrest between the Cherokees and the settlers at the time, and principally "that the letters were then legible, which could not have

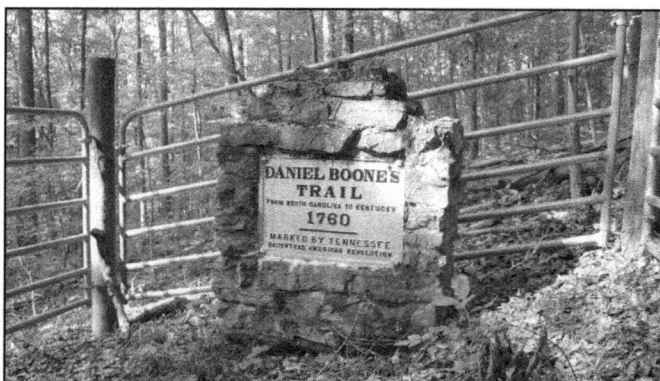

The marker at the site of the Daniel Boone Tree was unadvisedly defaced at some time to change the date from 1769 to 1760.

TRAILING DANIEL BOONE

been the case if they had been put there in 1760."[18] Regardless of such controversy, the Tennessee Daughters used that spot to commemorate Daniel Boone and placed a tablet there.

The newspaper article mentioned a "marble tablet two-feet square," but the marker erected was undoubtedly one of the bronze tablets placed at all the other sites. Moreover, the reporter is a poor estimator of dimensions, as the stone monument is a little smaller than described. At some point since its placement, the original tablet erected by the Tennessee Daughters in 1914 appears to have been augmented, changing the date from "1769" to "1760." The change was probably made by someone believing the marker should somehow be dated to the time of the tree-carving episode. Others may regard the change, however well intentioned, as actually defacing the DAR marker, which was erected as part of a set of nine identical markers along a well-conceived, commemorative route through East Tennessee. Had those persons attempted such augmentation near Cook's Gap in North Carolina, there might have been different consequences.

The Boone Tree marker is on private property along Reedy Creek about a third of a mile upstream (south) from Old Gray Station Road. (At this writing, respectful visitors have been welcomed and walking access to the marker has been marked.) The marker is east of the stream and up a moderately steep and wooded slope. The marker is surrounded by fencing to protect it. Access is easiest in late fall to early spring; a footbridge crosses the stream near the marker.

Tennessee—Something Worthwhile

Old Fort

The eighth marker placed by the Tennessee Daughters was erected at the site of "Old Fort." In 1776, Virginia patriot militia mustered under Colonel William Christian to attack and chastise the Overhill Cherokees for aggression against the settlers in the overmountain region of North Carolina. This attack was coordinated with Rutherford's Expedition from the east against the Cherokees of the Middle and Valley towns. (These overmountain settlements were violations of prior treaties, so "aggression" is a matter of perspective. The Cherokees were protecting their homeland from trespassers. See book, *Before They Were Heroes at King's Mountain*, 2011.) As the Virginia militiamen gathered at the Long Island of the Holston, they built a fort opposite the southeastern, or upper, end of Long Island. Believing at the time that area was still in Virginia, they named the fort in honor of Virginia's governor, calling it Fort Patrick Henry.

To accommodate the construction and operation of the Eastman Chemical Company in Kingsport during the 20th century, engineers altered the channels and the landform of the island at the upper (southeast) end.[19] The exact site of the fort was lost within the con-

A view along the Long Island of the Holston River, 1920.
from *The Wilderness Road into Kentucky* by Willam A. Pusey, 1921

This marker for the Wexler Bend Pilot Plant for making RDX explosives during WWII is a reasonable proxy for the location of Fort Patrick Henry opposite the southeast end of Long Island.

struction of the plant. The bridge for TN Hwy 93 crosses the Holston River at the southeast end of Long Island and is certainly in the general vicinity of the site of Fort Patrick Henry. A marker for Eastman Chemical Company commemorating its role as a producer of RDX explosives during World War II is a reasonable proxy for the general location of "the southeast end of Long Island of the Holston." That marker is located at the foot of the exit ramp for Riverside Drive off TN Hwy 93 (John B. Dennis Highway) on the east side of Kingsport.

A century ago, however, the location of historic "Old Fort" was confusing to some. In his 1921 book, William Pusey declared that "Old Fort," the site from which Boone and his men began to mark the trail to Boonesborough, he said, was much farther west at the confluence of the South Fork and North Fork of the Holston River.[20] That site was actually the location of Fort Robinson, built in 1761 and also called "old fort" by some. A marker was placed at that site in 1931. In any case, in 1914 the Daughters of the Chickamauga and Bonny Kate chapters erected the eighth marker in Tennessee for Daniel Boone's Trail at the site of Fort Patrick Henry, the "old fort." That marker and its base are missing today.

Tennessee—Something Worthwhile

A monument for Fort Robinson, built in 1761 at confluence of North Fork and South Fork Holston River, was dedicated in 1931. The tablet was stolen from the stone base in the last decade.

Image at right shows Fort Robinson marker before 1946.
from *Kingsport, the Planned Industrial City,*
Kingsport Rotary Club, 1946

Kingsport

The ninth and final marker on Daniel Boone's Trail in Tennessee stands prominently at the heart of Kingsport on Church Circle at Watauga Street. Its placement is opposite the center of Long Island from which Daniel Boone left on March 17, 1775, with his party of 30 axmen to mark a trail for others to follow. His recently married 14-year-old daughter, Susannah, went along as a camp keeper, cooking for the corps of adventurers, who, over the next three weeks, marked Boone's Trace to the site of what would become Fort Boonesborough.

The Kingsport newspapers did not begin until 1916, so no contemporary accounts of the marker's dedication have been found.

Honored Guests of the Occasion
The fall of 1914 was a busy time for the women of Knoxville, including the Tennessee Daughters. The city would host the state conference

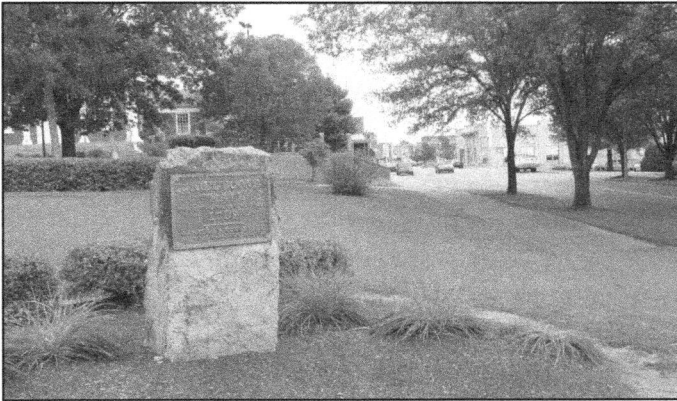

Standing today on Church Circle at Watauga Street, in the heart of Kingsport, is the 1914 marker; but, it may have been moved here from its original, unknown location.

of the Women's Christian Temperance Union and a meeting of the National Congress of Mothers. At the end of October, the city would also host the state conference of Suffragists, whose national conference would follow in Nashville in mid-November. "The equal suffrage advocates of Tennessee are going to 'whoop 'em up' this fall," reported the *Knoxville Journal and Tribune.* ... [O]ne thing is certain, and that is there is going to be some suffrage agitation in Tennessee this fall."[21] Some thought Tennessee and Kentucky would be the first of the Southern states to enact equal suffrage and to grant women the right to vote.

The American Highway Association also was meeting in November, in Atlanta, and one day was dedicated to a meeting of the newly created women's department "to discuss the whole subject of roads and woman's work for their betterment." Women from the East Tennessee region were expected to attend.[22] Another "good roads" meeting was planned for Bristol as well, this one for the Southern Appalachian Good Roads Association. With all those meetings and conferences

Tennessee—Something Worthwhile

taking place in and around Knoxville, it is not surprising that the state conference of the Tennessee Society, NSDAR, was scheduled for that city as well. Planning for that would begin in earnest, but only after the beginning of the club year.

Miss Temple called the first meeting of the Bonny Kate Chapter for the new club year in due course. By tradition, their first meeting was their annual celebration of the Battle of Kings Mountain, the date of that chapter's founding in 1893. This gathering at the home of Miss Temple was a grand occasion for the members and invited guests. "The honor[ed] guests of the occasion," reported the *Knoxville Journal & Tribune*, "will be Mrs. Reynolds, of North Carolina, regent of the D.A.R. in that state, and Mrs. Lindsay Patterson, also of North Carolina, former regent [*sic*] for the state. [She was former Vice-president General for the National Society.] These two ladies arrived in the city Wednesday and are the guests of Miss Temple."[23] Also joining the gathering was Mrs. Scott Glore, State Regent, Kentucky Society, NSDAR.

"Mrs. Patterson gave a vivid sketch of the battle of King's Mountain, with all its historical settings, and a description of the battlefield and of the men who participated," reported the newspaper after the meeting. "Mrs. Reynolds told about the Boone trail, which the D.A.R. society is marking with tablets placed at intervals of about ten miles. ... Mrs. Glore also spoke commending the work of the society in marking this trail ..."[24]

As was the practice of the day, the newspaper described the hospitality offered at the gathering: "At the close of the very interesting program, the guests were ushered into the dining room, where an elaborate picture table was arranged and delicious refreshments served. The room, as well as the parlors, where the exercises took place, was decorated with autumn flowers and foliage. The affair was one of the most elaborate and enjoyable in the history of Bonny Kate Chapter."[25]

After this gathering, Mrs. Patterson, Mrs. Reynolds, Miss Temple, and Mrs. Glore went to Cumberland Gap to select a site for the joint monument to be placed in the spring of 1915.

A Movement with Much To Commend Itself
Mrs. Martha White Baxter, State Regent, had been away in Europe for a few months. Her return was uneventful but not necessarily without some anxiety. The Great War had begun in Europe during her visit abroad, with the assassination of Archduke Franz Ferdinand on June 28, 1914, and a month later the invasions of Serbia, Belgium, Luxembourg, and France. The *Journal and Tribune* reported on September 17: "Mrs. George White Baxter and Miss Eleanor Baxter, who spent the summer in Europe arrive in New York Saturday on board the *La France*, having been most fortunate in securing cabin passage on that splendid vessel. Mrs. Baxter and Miss Baxter, leaving the dock at Havre [on the English Channel], saw the *Tennessee* ladened [*sic*] with Americans on their way to safety in England. During the voyage across the Atlantic the *La France* was protected by British cruisers. ... After their recent experiences in the war zone Mrs. Baxter and her daughter are more than ever enthusiastic in their praise of America."[26]

As would likely have been the case for any overseas passenger of the era, Mrs. Baxter may have experienced some heightened anxiety sailing across the Atlantic just two years after the tragic loss of the *Titanic* in April 1912. She no doubt would further count her blessing to be back home when on May 7, 1915, the *Lusitania* would be sunk off the coast of Ireland by a German torpedo.

After her return from France, Mrs. Baxter attended a meeting in Washington, D.C., of the board of the National Society, DAR, and then returned to Knoxville to help plan the state conference. During that time she would also address the gathering of Suffragists as the State Regent of the Tennessee Daughters.

The Bonny Kate chapter hosted the DAR state conference November 9-11. The principal event of the opening day was the dedication of a marker to Captain David Campbell at Campbell's Station, with a host of Daughters motoring out to the site for the ceremony. The unveiling enjoyed the participation of six former and current Tennessee State Regents. Twenty-two chapters from across Tennessee were represented and up to 100 delegates attended the event which featured receptions, luncheons, speeches, ceremonies, and business meetings.

The second day included a welcome from host chapter Regent Miss Mary Boyce Temple:

"After six years the Tennessee division of the national D.A.R is again the guests of the Bonny Kate Chapter. Out of love for Mrs. Baxter, our state regent, we one and all have tried to arrange for your comfort, pleasure and profit, and for the success of this your ninth convention. We welcome you to our city and first and foremost we welcome you to beautiful historic East Tennessee."[27]

That afternoon, Daniel Boone's Trail received notable attention. Mrs. Baxter preceded a report by Miss Temple with some remarks:

"... [W]e are to be congratulated upon having accomplished something worthwhile. This trail refers to the first well-defined path into the wilderness becoming forever famous as the

Wilderness Road, or Boone Trail. To Mrs. Lindsay Patterson, now of North Carolina, but whose early life was spent in Tennessee, belongs the distinction of inspiring the great work of re-discovering the Boone trail. Mrs. Reynolds, regent of North Carolina, has greatly helped her, and now the states of Tennessee, Virginia and Kentucky are nobly assisting in the achievement of marking the road and making history."[28]

Miss Mary Boyce Temple spoke at some length about the marking of the Boone Trail in Tennessee. It was a topic of particular interest to the Tennessee Daughters. The *Knoxville Journal & Tribune* reported:
"Miss Temple said that Tennessee has placed nine markers in all. They are of bronze 19 by 28 inches, and are being manufactured by a Knoxville concern. They bear the inscription:
Daniel Boone's Trail
From North Carolina to Kentucky
1769
Marked by the Tennessee Daughters of
the American Revolution.

The trail passed through four states, North Carolina, Virginia, Tennessee and Kentucky, and covers a distance of 150 [*sic*, 400] miles."[29]

A later historian of the Tennessee Daughters remarked on Miss Temple's presentation, calling it "one of the most interesting of the conference and [one which] was greatly enjoyed by all present." In 1914, the marking of Daniel Boone's Trail was a "movement [that had] much to commend itself and [was] a permanent monument to Tennessee D.A.R.'s pride in her early history and her wish to perpetuate it ..."[30]

Virginia

30 miles

Cumberland
Gap

Gate City

Bristol

- Extant markers
- Missing markers

Daniel Boone's Trail

Virginia
–Such Rapid and Thorough Work

Virginia's efforts to mark the Daniel Boone Trail began in earnest in early 1914. At the 23rd Continental Congress in Washington, D.C., held April 20-25, State Regent Mrs. James S. (Edmonia F. Tomlin) Maupin reported, "The location and marking of the Old Trails Roads has appealed strongly to our Daughters. The location of the Daniel Boone Trail from Tennessee to Kentucky through Virginia had been established since January and seven boulders as markers will be erected during the year."[1] But much had happened before this occasion to bring the project to this point.

If You Know a Good D.A.R.

In the fall of 1912, the Virginia Daughters held their 16th State Conference on the Eastern Shore in Onancock in early October. During the meeting, the State Regent read to the assembly a letter she had received from the State Regent of North Carolina, Mrs. William N. Reynolds. In the letter, Mrs. Reynolds invited the Virginia Daughters to join in a collective effort with Daughters from her state, from Tennessee, and from Kentucky to mark the Daniel Boone Trail through their four states. Although interested in the project, the Virginia Daughters wanted more information; they deferred the matter to their spring meeting held concurrently with the Continental

Congress in Washington, D.C. However, it appears the Daughters took no action on the opportunity at that meeting.[2]

During the following fall at the 17th Virginia State Conference (Richmond, November 12 & 13, 1913), the State Regent read to the Daughters a letter from Mrs. Lindsay Patterson, signed Lucy Bramlette Patterson. Her letter, dated October 18, 1913, was skillfully constructed, revealing that the project was well under way, that neighboring states were already making progress, and requesting only that Virginia provide the name of someone to chair the project for the State.

"If you know a good D.A.R. in Bristol," Mrs. Patterson wrote, "I would suggest that locality as she would be near enough to be familiar with Scott and Lee Counties, through which the Trail runs, and she and the Tennessee chairman could consult together about details that I am too far away to be familiar with."[3]

As it happened, one of the stalwart Daughters of the state was from Bristol. Mrs. Robert (Elizabeth Preston) Gray was the current State Secretary. She was a descendant of the prominent William Preston family in Fincastle County, which until the end of 1776 included what is today Kentucky. (In summer 1774, Colonel William Preston had asked for a "good hand" to venture into Kentucky to warn the surveyors known to be there of pending Indian attacks. Daniel Boone and Michael Stoner covered 800 miles in 65 days, reaching the Falls of the Ohio and returning safely.)

It probably did not take much persuasion of Mrs. Gray by the State Regent to accept the appointment. So by the end of January 1914, Mrs. Gray also wore the hat of Virginia's Chairman, Boone Trail Committee. Undoubtedly, Mrs. Patterson was pleased with that much being accomplished, but she would not rely solely on that chairperson to infuse the Daughters with enthusiasm for the project. It was too important and time was short.

When Virginia Daughters convened in the spring of 1914 as part of the Continental Congress, Mrs. Patterson came to their meeting to report on the progress. The minutes recount the occasion: "At the conclusion of the roll call Mrs. Patterson of North Carolina, was introduced to the assembled delegates and made a most interesting report of the work accomplished by her State in locating and marking that portion of the old Boone Trail which is within the boundaries of North Carolina. Mrs. Patterson declared this trail equal in historic interest to the famous roads of an earlier civilization—the Roman Appian Way or the Grecian Highway to the Acropolis—urged upon Virginia the desirability of speedily finishing her part in marking this highway over which civilization and religion were borne to the great Western Wilderness."[4]

Unfortunately, Mrs. Gray was absent from that meeting, but the State Regent made a report sharing "that the Boone Trail within the confines of Virginia had been located and that the chairman [Mrs. Gray] recommended the erection of seven granite boulders at designated places along its length." She estimated the cost of each installed boulder marker at $25 and mentioned "that a great Interstate Celebration had been planned to be held at Cumberland Gap on the completion of that work." Two chapters (Margaret Lyn Lewis and Great Bridge) immediately volunteered to cover the cost of one marker each. Thus did the Virginia Daughters embrace the Boone Trail project.

At the 18th Virginia state conference in Alexandria, October 27-28, 1914, State Regent Maupin shared with the Daughters in her Regent's

Address about progress on the project. She offered a most encouraging report: "Remarkable work has been accomplished, "she said, "by the Daniel Boone Trail Committee, which was not appointed till January last. The trail has been located, both going and returning, and as it runs through a portion of Virginia near Bristol, a member of the Sycamore Shoals Chapter was appointed chairman of the committee. To her is due the credit for such rapid and thorough work, and she hopes soon to have her markers in place. A joint celebration of the completion of the marking of Daniel Boone Trail by the four States through which this trail runs—North Carolina, Tennessee, Virginia and Kentucky—is proposed by Mrs. Lindsay Patterson, National Chairman of the Daniel Boone Trail Committee, to be held at Cumberland Gap, Kentucky, in May, 1915."[5]

Mrs. Maupin's praise for her fellow state officer was not misplaced. Mrs. Gray had done a great much work, but in her report Mrs. Gray focused most readily on what remained to be done, the actual placing of the markers. She said, "I have to report that very little has yet been done on the work of marking the Boone Trail through Virginia. ... I expect to have the markers in place before the first of May." In her report, however, Mrs. Gray did emphasize the importance of the Trail to Virginians. "Boone passed through a very small corner of Virginia," she said, "and yet he probably suffered more in that little corner than on his long tour from North Carolina to Boonesborough, Ky." She shared the story of the attack on the party that resulted in his son James Boone's death and the stopping of the Boone family's emigration to Kentucky. She presented a map of the route and marked the places where she recommended the markers be placed. Along with the trail markers, Mrs. Gray recommended that they "erect a standard D.A.R. gravestone" at the gravesite of James Boone. [6]

Despite suggesting that she had done "very little," Mrs. Gray had, in fact, researched the matter in great detail, as she would report the following year, relying on the letters of Arthur Campbell and Richard Henderson. From that effort she concluded that Virginia should mark the route Boone took in 1773 in his ill-fated first effort to emigrate with this family from North Carolina to Kentucky. She acknowledged another route Boone had previously taken, perhaps more often in fact, in his sojourns to Kentucky through the Cumberland Gap beginning in 1769. That route followed "the waters of New River, to Ingles Ferry, and from thence follow[ed] the line of forts—Fort Chiswell, Royal Oak Fort, Kilmacrankie Fort, Black's Fort, Fort Blackmore, Fort Scott, and over the grand mountain pass," Cumberland Gap. Others would later champion Boone having followed as well another route from the Blue Ridge Plateau in North Carolina and into the Holston River valley near Abingdon, Virginia, by way of a pass through the Iron Mountains at today's Damascus. But in 1914, the Virginia Daughters selected a route through the Clinch and Powell river valleys between Moccasin Gap and Cumberland Gap, a route she learned was known in the mountains of southwest Virginia as "Boone Path."[7] Passage along that same route is commemorated and interpreted today by the Daniel Boone Wilderness Trail Association, Inc. with a well-marked driving route of interest to heritage tourists. (See *www.danielboonetrail.com.*)

A Tramp Across the Country

In her efforts to establish the authority of that route, Mrs. Gray spent weeks "among the good people" of the area, she said. "We found the people along the way very much interested and in many cases very well informed on the subject. Young boys, under twenty, and old men over eighty, were all ready with suggestions and information gained, the former from reading or from fireside tradition, the latter, from personal knowledge of remains clearly to be seen in the days of their youth." She mentioned the help of one man of 90 years in age, a Judge Duncan, whose grandfather, he said, was with Daniel Boone at Fort Blackmore.

"At last the time came," she reported in the fall of 1915, "when the data collected seemed ripe to put on paper, so a practical engineer went with me on a tramp across the country to really locate the route, and determine the proper locations for the monuments."

The Virginia DAR erected seven iron tablets along "Boone Path" and erected two more special tablets along the way. "The tablets which mark Virginia's part of the Trail," Mrs. Gray reported, "are truly Virginian. They were made by the Iron City Foundry of Bristol, Virginia, of Virginia iron, with Virginia coal, and by Virginia workmen; they are twenty-one inches wide, twenty-seven inches long, and one inch thick, with the letters raised ... ."[8] The whole of the effort was accomplished with the expenditure of $148 with contributions from 11 state chapters, although five chapters from Bristol, Lynchburg, Emporia, Norfolk, and Roanoke accounted for $118 of that. Nevertheless, the effort was truly a project of the state's Daughters.

The entire route in Virginia ran through only two counties, Scott and Lee. It ran from one gap to another, beginning at Moccasin and continuing to Cumberland.

Moccasin Gap

For Moccasin Gap, the DAR placed a marker in Gate City, bolting a tablet to the front wall of the county courthouse. In 1914, that route was known as the Bristol-to-Lexington Highway. Today it is US

The Virginia Daughters placed a marker on the front of the Scott County Courthouse in Gate City.

Business Hwy 23/421, also called West Jackson Street. The courthouse sits at the corner of W. Jackson Street and Manville Road.

Clinchport
"Boone Path," as determined by Mrs. Gray then "pass[ed] over Moccasin Ridge and along the water of Cooper Creek" (probably crossing the ridge along Burnt Cabin Branch) to Clinchport, "a thriving little village built just where Boone and his party reached the Clinch River." Today, travelers follow US Hwy 23/58/421 along the railroad route to VA Hwy 65, Clinch River Highway, which leads a half-mile to Clinchport. The tablet was "built into the wall of the new $30,000 High School," she reported.[9]

That school building was a two-story red brick structure and was for a time a high school and later a grade school through 7th grade. It stood between Clinch River Road and Mustang Avenue at Minton Avenue adjacent to Little Stock Creek. In April 1977, the Clinch River flooded the town and damaged the school which was still in use; the school was abandoned and classes for the remainder of the semester were held in churches in Duffield and Gate City. The Tennessee Valley Authority bought all the damaged structures and they were torn down and removed from the floodplain. No effort was made in the removal

Virginia—Such Rapid and Thorough Work

135

The school building in Clinchport to which the DAR attached a tablet in 1914 was razed after the flood of 1977. The marker is lost. courtesy of *Scott County Historical Society*

to resettle collectively the residents of Clinchport as had been done at Butler, Tennessee, 30 years earlier.[10] The fate of the DAR marker is unknown, but in the loss of the town, it probably was simply carried off as rubble in the razing of the school building.

Images of the Clinchport school building are included in the Library of Virginia online digital collection, but neither of two photos from 1939 show the DAR marker from the perspective at which the photographs were made. However, at least one area resident who was a student at the school recalls the plaque attached to the building wall to the right of the steps at the front entrance.[11]

Natural Tunnel

Mrs. Gray was informed by the helpful Judge Duncan that Boone's party camped at a point near the Natural Tunnel not so far from Clinchport. She shared that information with the railroad company and reported later, "When the General Manager of the Virginia and Southwestern Railroad heard that the Trail led so very near the Natural

Tunnel, Virginia's greatest natural wonder, he graciously volunteered to erect a tablet on the granite wall at the entrance of the tunnel. So Daughters of Virginia, we are indebted to Mr. J.H. McCue, for the presence of one of our tablets on this wonderful natural wall."[12] The tablet may have been erected at some point, but no record of that fact has yet been uncovered.[13] It may simply have been a well-intentioned promise that went unfulfilled, or perhaps the tablet was stolen after some time. In any case, no DAR marker is present today at Natural Tunnel. Local author and geologist Tony Scales has walked the entire length of the tunnel many times and assures that he has never seen a tablet or any evidence of one being attached to the tunnel wall.[14]

Duffield

From the camp mentioned by Judge Duncan, the Boone party then proceeded up Stock Creek, crossing Purchase Ridge and then descending into the Clinch River valley, "a charming little valley where is now situated the village of Duffield," Mrs. Gray wrote. "Here we found grandchildren and great-grandchildren of pioneers who had given aid to Boone and his party," she added. About their own reception, she remarked that the inhabitants were "gracious and generous in the true old-fashioned way." The meadow where Duffield now sits

The Ruritan's Daniel Boone Trail marker (left) is at US Hwy 23 and US Hwy 58. The DAR's marker (right) is on Railroad Avenue at US Hwy 23, replacing the one destroyed by an automobile accident in the 1950s.

was known as Little Flat Lick. It was a "commonplace marshy field where there [was] a spring,"[15]

The DAR erected a third tablet in Duffield, "between the post office and the railroad station, right on the side of the Highway, and in plain view of all who pass this way." In Duffield today, a marker stands at the intersection of US Hwy 23 and US Hwy 58/421. That is not the DAR marker, but one erected later by the Ruritan Club to take advantage of the "plain view of all who pass this way" afforded such a marker at the intersection of these improved roads. The Ruritan pedestal and tablet look very much like some of the ones erected elsewhere by the Virginia Daughters. The 1915 DAR tablet and current pedestal are 0.4 mile farther north on US Hwy 23 on the west side of the highway at Railroad Avenue. The original DAR marker was installed a quarter-mile north of this site along the alignment that is now Railroad Avenue, but was about 20 feet lower in elevation at the grade across the valley floor where the train tracks now run. The marker included a tall pipe with an eagle mounted on top. In the 1950s, according to local accounts, an automobile driver missed the curve, crashing into the marker. During the 1960s, the Ruritan Club erected its marker, apparently using the eagle and part of the pipe from the wrecked DAR marker.[16] The current Duffield pedestal, which displays the original DAR tablet, has been reconstructed with fieldstone and appears to have been well cared for. When this restored marker was erected is unknown, but given the excellent condition of the tablet and monument, it could have been only a few years ago.

Mrs. Gray continued her report to the Virginia Daughters, describing the terrain she found during her 1914 visit: "Standing in the little Duffield Valley, one is surrounded by grand wooded mountains, with apparently only two outlets; one through which a small stream runs, and which at the time in question [Boone's era] must have been a boggy canebrake; the other leads through a high mountain gap called Kane's Gap. Through this gap Boone led his party (there are still signs of the trail). Just over this ridge, nestled in the shelter of a cove in Powell's Mountain, was the old pioneer fort known as Scott's Fort."

Kane's Gap as viewed from Duffield across US Hwy 23 at Mechanic Street.

It was through Kane's Gap (also Kane and Kanes) that James Boone and Henry Russell, along with their small party, passed on

October 9, 1773, on their way to catch up with the larger party of Daniel Boone. After descending into Wallen Creek valley, these two young men, in their 16th years, were jumped by a party of Shawnees accompanied by a few Delawares and Cherokees just before dawn somewhere along Wallen Creek. (The location of the Oct. 10 attack has been contended by historians and history buffs for decades.)

Kane's Gap is accessible on foot today along a marked trail from a trailhead near Duffield. The trailhead is 0.4 mile west on Fraley Road off Boone Trail Road., 0.6 miles north of US Hwy 58. Boone Trail Road is about a quarter mile west of US Hwy 23 along Duff-Patt Road (US Hwy 58/421). Allow at least two hours for hiking uphill at a brisk pace and returning. Proper footwear, seasonally appropriate clothing, and water are essential.

Scott's Fort

"Just over this ridge, nestled in the shelter of a cove in Powell's Mountain," wrote Mrs. Gray, "was the old pioneer fort known as Scott's Fort. ... On the site of this old fort, alongside the highway, was erected our fourth marker, for it is very clear that the Boone Trail led over Kane's Gap and by Scott's Fort." This "fort" was the pioneer home of Archibald Scott and his intrepid wife, Frances "Fannie"

Virginia highway historical markers in Stickleyville tell the separate stories of attacks on Daniel Boone's son in 1773 and on Scott's fort in 1785.

Dickenson. (A highway historical marker in Stickleyville tells of her story.) In June of 1785, a band of 13 renegades attacked the Scott log home (not a palisaded fort but a reinforced or "forted" cabin), killing Archibald Scott, his four children, and another young man. The Indians took his wife, Fannie, into captivity; but, through her own craftiness, she later escaped and made her way through the wilderness to safety.[17]

The DAR marker placed at Scott's Fort is lost to a century, but it was undoubtedly close to the Duff Cemetery along State Route 612, called Kane Gap Road. This route follows along Wallen Creek and is close to "the Kentucky Road," which ran west from Kane's Gap. The cemetery is just east of Scott Branch near where it enters Wallen Creek. Driving from Stickleyville, follow Kane Gap Road (also called Wallen Creek Loop) off US Hwy 58 three miles east through Powell Valley toward Kane's Gap. The cemetery is on the left beside Mispah Independent Church, next to Scott's Branch Road.

The headwaters of Wallen Creek, three miles upstream from Stickleyville, offer beautiful views of Kane's Gap.

Virginia—Such Rapid and Thorough Work

Duff Cemetery next to Mispah Independent Church is likely near the site of Scott's Fort where the DAR placed a marker in 1914.

Local accounts attest that a store once stood on the north side of the present road between the cemetery and Scott Branch. That store stood along the old roadbed, which can be seen running adjacent to the cemetery on its north side. That road could be a farmer's field road or it could have been the road the Daughters found so convenient for their use in 1914. It most certainly is not the Wilderness Road, but if it were the prominent road through the valley at the beginning of the 20th century, Mrs. Gray could certainly have chosen to place the marker where it would be seen.[18] The old store at Scott Branch burned down many years ago and perhaps in that conflagration the DAR marker disappeared. Another store, now deeply weathered and worn, was built adjacent to the branch and to the Kane Gap Road. Visitors will certainly regard it as "an old country store."

In any event, the cemetery is an appropriate place from which to view the Wallen Creek valley and to consider the tragic experiences of the Boones and the Scotts during the 1770s and 1780s. No proof of a DAR marker placed at the site of Scott's Fort could be found, but evidence abounds as to its probable general location.

Jonesville

From Scott's Fort, Mrs. Gray determined Boone's route lay "directly across Lee County to Jonesville, the county seat." Such a route could follow Wallen Creek and today's State Road 612 west to the Powell River or perhaps cross Wallen Ridge near Stickleyville as does today's US Hwy 58 and then descend the Powell River to Jonesville. Indeed, the quandary over which of these two routes to mark concerned the Virginia Daughters at their 1914 state conference in Alexandria. "You will see from the accompanying map of the Bristol to Lexington (Ky.) Highway," said Mrs. Gray, "that the highway follows almost entirely the Boone trail, which proves that Boone selected the best location for a road. One detour is made. In Lee County the Boone trail goes a little to the south of Jonesville, but had the highway followed the trail here it would have skipped the county seat, and passed through an almost unsettled area for the two or three miles."[19] Mrs. Gray

The Virginia Daughters placed a marker in Jonesville, embedded in the retaining wall of the Lee County Courthouse.

asked the Daughters to consider placing two markers on either side of Jonesville or to place one marker in Jonesville. "If we place the marker in Jonesville," she offered, "we may secure aid from the Lee County people in marking the trail." After due consideration, the Virginia Daughters placed their fifth tablet in Jonesville at the county courthouse. It is embedded in the retaining wall along East Main Street about 100 feet west from Church Street.

Boone's Path

"From Jonesville," Mrs. Gray recounted, "following the line of the Louisville and Nashville [L&N] Railroad and the Bristol-to-Lexington Highway, we came to Boone's Path, a little post office and store, where there is no difficulty in discovering the traces of the old trail. Here for more than a hundred years has been maintained a post office bearing the name of the dauntless explorer, and here at the junction of two important county roads, was erected the sixth and last regular marker."[20]

Unfortunately, much development has occurred in the century since Mrs. Gray's visit and has obscured the "traces of the old trail." The exact location of the town of Boone's Path (also Boon's Path and Boone Path) and where the marker was placed are left to conjecture although evidence is offered. The Boone's Path post office was in Baylor's Store from 1873 to 1902, not "a hundred years" but rather three decades. That community was most likely at the intersection of Old Highway 58 and State Road 667, called Old Nursery Road.

The road into Rose Hill from Boone's Path in 1920.
from *The Wilderness Road to Kentucky* by William A. Pusey, 1921

The Boone's Path post office was for a time in the Baylor/Beaty Store.

(Others, in error this writer believes, place Boone's Path at the intersection of US Hwy 58 and Dr. Thomas Walker Road.) The (Charles E.) Baylor Store became the Beatty Store and another store opened in Rose Hill, the town to the west which arose because that is where the L&N Railroad built its depot. Because the railroad bypassed Boone's Path, the post office moved to Rose Hill in 1902 to Leonard Bales's store. So, during Mrs. Gray's visit in 1914, the "Boone's Path" post office was not actually in Boone's Path, but in Rose Hill.

The local gentleman who was advising Mrs. Gray, the Reverend Isaac Anderson, was a longtime resident of the area and may simply have continued to refer to the Baylor/Beatty store in Boone's Path as having a post office. It was across the street from the Boone's Path State Bank. (The community had been substantial in the late 1800s, but nothing of it remains today.) Moreover, the *New York Times* reported, in part, on August 1, 1915: "… and the seventh [marker was placed] at Boone Path Post Office, above Rose Hill, at a point where the trail crosses the Bristol to Lexington Highway." With confidence, one can conclude that the marker was placed along what is now the alignment of US Hwy 58 at the intersection with Old Nursery Road, State Road

Virginia—Such Rapid and Thorough Work

667. The Daniel Boone Wilderness Trail Association has marked SR667 and US Hwy 58 as its commemorative (and historically correct) trail route as well.

As interesting as some may find this issue of the location of the Boone's Path post office, where the marker was placed, it becomes irrelevant. At some point the Virginia Daughters' marker was most probably moved to Old Highway 58 on the west side of Rose Hill. This may have been a move to protect and preserve the monument and tablet during the widening and development of US Hwy 58, which bypasses Rose Hill. A Daniel Boone's Trail tablet mounted in a stone pedestal with an eagle atop a pipe stands on the west side of Rose Hill, but the DAR did not mention one at that location and specifically mentioned placing its last regular trail tablet (going from east to west) at Boone's Path. The moving of the marker has not been confirmed, but those who are searching for the Boone's Path DAR marker can most confidently satisfy their curiosity by visiting the tablet and pedestal on Old Highway 58 (Dr. Thomas Walker Road) near its

The DAR marker erected at Boone's Path has likely been moved west of Rose Hill to this spot on US Business 58.

intersection with Clearfield Drive about two-and-a-quarter miles west of the center of Rose Hill.. Wilderness Road State Park near Caylor interprets the history of Martin's Station, including Daniel Boone's presence there in 1769 and 1775, It was sited at today's Rose Hill.

Mrs. Gray was generous in her praise of Rev. Anderson, calling him "a man filled with patriotism, generosity and good works." She thanked him for providing the land on which to erect the marker and for the shaft, the stone pedestal, on which the tablet was mounted. He provided as well books and old maps and "time cheerfully given to conduct your Chairman over the route through Lee County," she wrote.[21]

Special Markers

The Virginia Daughters erected two additional tablets during the 1914 trail-marking project related to Boone's 1773 trek through Southwest Virginia. Both tablets were the same size as the regular Trail tablets, but each had different wording on it.

On October 10, 1773, Daniel and Rebecca Boone's oldest son was murdered along the trail in the Wallen Creek valley. He and his party were attacked just before dawn as they camped along the Creek. Two young men, James Boone (b. 1757) and Henry Russell, also 16, were tortured to death by a party of Cherokee, Shawnee, and Delaware Indians. All but one of the others in the James Boone party were either killed or escaped wounded. The exact location of this massacre has long been a contested issue, but in 1914, the Virginia Daughters were persuaded to choose one site over any others. As was reported in 1915 in the *New York Times*, "... local tradition and history pointed to a place between Ewing and Wheeler's Station in Lee County, and here were found two rudely marked graves, so here was erected a tablet to the memory of James the eldest son of Daniel Boone."

Local resident James Wheeler provided the land and financial assistance in placing the cast iron tablet which read:

"Near this spot

James Boone aged 18 years

Eldest son of Daniel Boone

Was killed by Indians.

October 10, 1773

Erected by

Virginia D.A.R."

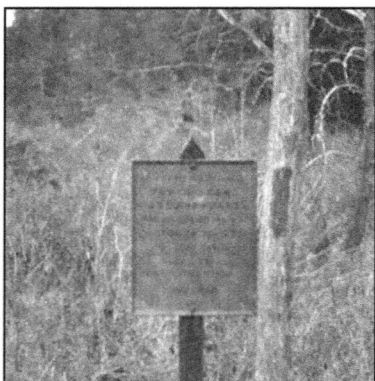

Special marker placed by DAR at supposed site of James Boone's death.
from *The Wilderness Road into Kentucky* by William A. Pusey, 1921

The whereabouts of this tablet is unknown today. Neither is it clear where it was erected or if a "standard DAR gravestone" was placed as proposed earlier. However, a private marker titled "Pioneer Graves" was erected in 1951 by M. Wheeler Kesterson. It claims to testify to the general location of the massacre, but it was erected on Indian Creek, well west of the sites with credible stories supporting their claims. Researchers continue to support locations farther east and upstream of the "Pioneer Graves" marker, sites located at the ford over the Powell River at the mouth of Wallen Creek and at Fannon Springs near Stickleyville.[22] The Virginia Department of Historical Resources at one time erected identical highway historical markers along US Hwy 58, one near Ewing Station and another in Stickleyville; only the one at Stickleyville remains today. The "Pioneer

A private marker in Caylor offers an inviting, if historically inaccurate, setting from which to consider the massacre of James Boone and Henry Russell in October 1773.

PIONEER GRAVES

Graves" marker is on VA 684 in Caylor only 300 yards off US Hwy 58.

The second special marker erected by the Virginia Daughters in 1914 was at Fort Blackmore. It was there that Daniel Boone, his wife, and travel party repaired to recover after stopping their journey upon their son's death. The tablet is mounted in a stone pedestal in Scott County about 10 miles northeast of Gate City at a bridge on VA Hwy 72 over the Clinch River.

The tablet reads:

"This tablet marks the site of
Fort Blackmore
where Daniel Boone and his party
rested from
October 1773
to
March 1775.
Erected by
Daughters of the American Revolution
in Virginia"

Virginia—Such Rapid and Thorough Work

Virginia Daughters placed a special marker at the site of Fort Blackmore on Clinch River.

A Joint Monument

In the fall of 1914, Mrs. Patterson had written the State Regents with her suggestions on conducting a dedication ceremony at Cumberland Gap in May 1915, "subject of course," she wrote with great political skill, "to the wishes of the States." She proposed a "four-sided monument with each side inscribed with the name of one State and names of places where tablets were placed, thus showing the Trail from beginning to end." She added that President Wilson would be invited to make the speech and other distinguished guests, "including our noble State Regents" would be expected to speak as well on the occasion. Mrs. Patterson also informed the Daughters that each state would need to contribute $100 to cover the cost of the joint monument and ceremony.[23]

The Virginia Daughters were much enthused about the project at this point and voted to accept the invitation and to contribute their share of the cost for the joint monument.

As the Virginia Daughters met in Washington, D.C., in the spring of 1915, on April 20, Mrs. Maupin, as State Regent, read a letter from Mrs. Gray reporting on the status of their Daniel Boone Trail and taking some pride on behalf of the Virginia Daughters for the effort. Mrs. Gray's letter reported "that the markers had all been placed and paid for, this work having been accomplished in one year; North Carolina had taken about two years, Tennessee quite as long, but did not know about Kentucky. The markers are all in place, and also the base of the monument at Cumberland Gap, and all are ready for the unveiling, ..."[24]

At this auspicious moment, Mrs. Patterson appeared with a contingent of visiting State Regents to address the Virginia Daughters. She was introduced as the National Chairman of the Boone Trail Committee and with her were Kentucky's State Regent, Mrs. Glore, and Tennessee's State Regent, Mrs. Baxter. Mrs. Patterson "gave a short sketch of the work," noting that everything was paid for and that all was ready for the dedication ceremony then planned for sometime between June 25 and June 30. "It is hoped that the governors of the four States can be present," she reported, adding "they had also hoped that President Wilson or Mr. [William Jennings] Bryan [Secretary of State] would be present, but, on account of the unsettled conditions of the whole world, neither of these two could make any engagements ahead or be more than two hours distant from Washington."[25]

With Mrs. Patterson present, Mrs. Maupin, in the name of the Virginia Daughters, "very gracefully thanked [Mrs. Patterson] for the good work she had done in connection with the marking of this trail."[26]

A Virginia First Lady

The consideration given to inviting President Wilson to the event warrants a look at his circumstances at the time. Elected in 1912 after serving as president of Princeton University (1902-1910) and as Governor of New Jersey (1911-1913), President Woodrow Wilson successfully advocated progressive legislation during his term. Unfortunately, his wife of 29 years, First Lady Ellen Axson Wilson, died in August 1914 of kidney disease, leaving a widowed president and a mourning White House. Such were his circumstances when Mrs. Patterson was considering inviting him to speak at Cumberland Gap.

Surprising some people but delighting others, President Wilson remarried 16 months later, in December 1915. He married Edith Bolling Galt, a Washington, D.C., widow originally from Wytheville, Virginia. She served as First Lady for the next five years during difficult times for the country. In April 1917, Wilson asked Congress to declare war on the Axis Powers. The First Lady modeled support for the federal rationing program observing "gasless Sundays," "meatless Mondays," and "wheat-less Wednesdays." After the president suffered a stroke on October 2, 1919, his wife became his constant attendant and controlled what matters came to his attention. Historians and investigative reporters have looked closely at accounts of this period and come to differing conclusions.[27] Some labeled this Southwest Virginia First Lady "the Secret President" and regarded her as the "first woman to run the government." Her own 1938 memoirs challenged such assertions.

First Lady Ellen Axson Wilson.
Library of Congress

Former First Lady Edith Bolling Galt Wilson lived a long life, attending the inaugural ceremony in 1961 of President John F. Kennedy. She passed away at age 89 on December 28, 1961, a date that would have been President Wilson's 105th birthday. [28]

President Woodrow Wilson and First Lady Edith Bolling Galt Wilson in 1920 after his stroke.

Library of Congress

One Man's Journey, Everyman's Dream

"Stand at Cumberland Gap and watch the procession of civilization, marching single file - the buffalo following the trail to the salt springs, the Indian, the fur-trader and hunter, the cattle-raiser, the pioneer farmer - and the frontier has passed by."

- Frederick Jackson Turner

Caintuck

The challenges of traversing the rugged landscape crossed by the hardy pioneers who followed Daniel Boone are difficult to imagine today. Their technology was based in mechanical advantage and on muscle power—both human and animal. The terrain they dared to

One Man's Journey, Everyman's Dream

enter was completely natural, untouched by bridge or ferry or by any road beyond a buffalo track or a deer trail. Coming from the well-settled areas to the east, they faced what to them were poorly marked tracks, but these same were known well to the ancient keepers of this forest—recently the Shawnees and Cherokees after the predecessor people who had occupied these lands. Those settlers who ventured westward endured freezing wind, rain, and snow, swollen rivers they had to swim, unruly and uncooperative beasts of burden, attacks by wild animals, uncertain food supplies, and the constant fear, if not the fact, of hostile acts by those people of another culture who were trying desperately to protect their hunting lands from invading trespassers. Yet these pioneers dared to go, and they did so for meager opportunity—the mere promise of a chance to build a better life.

In 1775, Judge Richard Henderson hired Daniel Boone to mark a trail for these hardy souls to follow. It ran from the east side of the Appalachian Mountains, through the Cumberland Gap, and then on to the lands of "Caintuck," which Henderson had leased from the Cherokees. He had treated with the

TRAILING DANIEL BOONE

Cherokees at Sycamore Shoals during March and concluded what was called the Transylvania Purchase, including the "Great Grant" and the "Path Deed," the latter providing for unmolested passage through the Cherokees' lands to the Cumberland Gap. Not all the Cherokee leaders approved. Tsi'yu-gunsini (called Dragging Canoe), declared, tradition holds, that the "Virginians" had bought "the bloody Ground," one that would be "dark and difficult to settle." Boone left the treaty while it was still in progress, and on March 17, with a group of men who joined him at the Long Island of the Holston, he began to mark what became known as Boone's Trace. Henderson and additional settlers would follow along in only a few days. Hundreds of thousands would follow in the next 20 years and countless numbers more after the building of the Wilderness Road.

In that spring of 1775, Daniel Boone and party made their way across the Cumberland Gap and on to the Kentucky River. There, they planned to establish a settlement that others named Fort

Boonesborough in his honor. Boone's party included 30 axmen marking trees and clearing a path suitable for travel by foot and by horseback. The party of workers were fed by two women working as camp keepers, a black woman enslaved by Richard Callaway and Boone's recently married daughter, Susannah, age 14. The party ran into no trouble until they were about a day away from their destination. Just before dawn on March 25, a party of Shawnees attacked the camp, determined to dissuade further settlement of Ken-te-ke,

One Man's Journey, Everyman's Dream

their hunting lands. Some men of Boone's party were killed; others were seriously wounded. Captain William Twetty (Twitty) was shot through both legs. Felix Walker was seriously wounded. Boone's party hurriedly built small protective cabins, ones they dubbed Twetty's Fort. Three days passed, when Twetty died. On April 1, Boone sent word back in a letter to Henderson of the attack. The men waited anxiously another few days for Walker to recover sufficiently to be carried forward in a sling. The party then moved on toward the Kentucky River, down Otter Creek, arriving around April 6 at the site where they would build the fort and settlement. Thus had they completed marking Boone's Trace in the spring of 1775.

William Calk

The lure of Kentucky was intoxicating. Men of an enterprising sort were eager to join in the expedition into this transmountain frontier, to be the early settlers and to gain the best lands. One of those men was William Calk [Caulk] of Prince William County. He lived in the

northeast corner of Virginia touching the Potomac River, nearly as far from Kentucky as a Virginian could be. He left his home on March 13, 1775, with a party of friends and associates intending to join with Richard Henderson's party in its first sojourn along Boone's Trace.

William Calk kept a journal of his experience. It has remained in the possession of his descendants. Two centuries later, in 1975, Kentucky historian Neal Hammon transcribed the journal, retaining

the spelling and punctuation of the original manuscript. Hammon's transcription is presented here with only short annotations of where along Boone's Trace Calk's account probably took place. Calk's journal, though brief, reveals in first-hand fashion the range of difficult challenges faced by those who followed Boone's Trace in the early years, challenges which would have turned back less hardy stock.[1]

"13 March 1775, Monday
I set out from Prince Wm. [County] to travel to Caintuck. On Tuesday Night our company all got together at Wm Prises on Rapadan [River], which was Abraham Hanks, Philip Drake, Eanack Smith, Robert Whirledge and my Self. Thear Abrams Dogs leg got Broke by Drake's Dog. ..."

Over the next three weeks, the party of men made their way across Virginia striving to reach Martin's Station where they expected to join with Henderson's party. They reached the Powell Valley and proceeded on past the station where they met up with Henderson along what is today called Boone's Path. As this party approached Cumberland Gap, Boone's party had already been attacked on March 25, but word of that incident had not yet reached Henderson. When it did, some of those less stout of heart, turned back. William Calk pressed on.

"5 April 1775, Wednesday [Powell Valley]
Breaks away fair & we go on down the valey and camp on Indian Creek. We had this creek to cross maney times and very Bad Banks. Abrams Saddle turn'd & the load all fell in. We go out this Eavening & kill two Deer.

"6 April 1775. Thursday
Henderson & company to come up. They come up about 12 o'clock & we join with them and camp there till this night waiting

One Man's Journey, Everyman's Dream

for some part of the compancy that had their horses ran away with their packs.

"7 April 1775, Friday
This morning is a very hard snowey morning & we still continue at Camp Being in number about 40 men & some Neagros. This Eaveng Comes a letter from Capt Boone at caintuck of the indians doing mischief and some turn back.

"8 April 1775, Saturday [Cumberland Gap and Yellow Creek]
We all pack up & Started Crost Cumberland gap about one oclock this Day. We Met a great maney people turning Back for fear of the indians but our Company goes on Still with good courage. We come to a very ugly Creek with steep Banks & have it to Cross Several times on this Creek. We camp this night.

"9 April 1775, Sunday [Yellow Creek and the Narrows/ Cumberland Ford]
This morning we wait at camp for the cattel to Be drove up to kill a Beef. Tis late Before they come & people makes out a little snack and agree to go on till Night. We git to Cumberland River & there we camp. Meet 2 more men turn Back.

"10 April 1775, Monday [Narrows/Cumberland Ford]
This is a lowry morning and very like for Rain & we keep at Camp this day and some goes out a hunting and I & two more goes up a very large mountain [Pine Mountain]; near the tops we saw the tracks of two indians & whear they lain under some Rocks. Some of the company went over the River a bufelo hunting but found None. At night Capt Hart comes up with his packs & there they hide some of thier lead to lighten thier packs that they may travel

faster.

"11 April 1775, Tuesday [Cumberland Ford and Flat Lick on Stinking Creek]

This a very lowry morning & like for Rain But we all agree to start Early, we Cross Cumberland River and travel Down it 10 miles through some turrabel cainbrakes. As we went down Abram s mair Ran into the River with Her load and swam over. He followed her & got her & made her swim back again. It is a very raney Eavening, we take up camp near Richland Creek. They kill a beef. Mr Drake Bakes Bread without washing his hands. We Keep Sentry this Night for fear of the indians.

"12 April 1775. Wednesday [Richland Creek north of Barbourville to Bailey's Switch]

This is a Raney morning But we pack up & go on. We come to Richland Creek, it is high, we tote our packs over on a tree & swim our horses over & there We meet another Company going Back. They tell such News [that] Abram and Drake is afraid to go aney farther. There we camp this night—

"13 April 1775, Thursday [Laurel River and Levi Jackson Wilderness Road State Park]

This morning the weather Seems to Brake & Be fair. Abram and Drake turn Back; we go on & git to loral River. We come to a creek Before wheare we are able to unload & to take our packs over on a log. This day we meet about 20 more turning Back. We are obliged to toat our packs over loral river & swim our Horses. One horse ran in with his pack & lost it in the river & they got it again.

One Man's Journey, Everyman's Dream

"14 April 1775, Friday [Raccoon Springs?]
This is a clear morning with a smart frost; we go on and have a very miry Road and camp this night on a creek of loral river & are surprised at camp by a wolf.

"15 April 1775, Saturday [Hazel Patch and Rockcastle River]
Clear with a Small frost, we start Early; we meet Some men that turns & goes With us. We travel this Day through the plais Caled the Bresh & cross Rockcass[tle] River & camp ther this Night & have fine food for our horses.

"16 April 1775. Sunday [Roundstone Creek, Boone's Gap, and Berea]
Cloudy & warm; we Start Early & go on about 2 miles down the River and then turn up a creek that we crost about 50 times. Some very bad foards with a great Deal of very good land on it. In the Eavening we git to the Waters of Caintuck & go a little Down the creek & there we camp. We keep sentel the fore part of the night; Rains very har[d] all night.

"17 April 1775, Monday [north of Berea]
Started, About 3 o'clock prevented by Rain. Travel's 7 Miles. This is a very rany morning But breaks about 11 oclock & we go on and camp this Night in several companeys on some of the creeks of Caintuck.

"18 April 1775, Tuesday [north of Berea]
Fair & cool and we go on, about 11 oclock we meet 4 men from Boons camp that caim to cunduck [conduct] us on. We camp this night just on the Beginning of the good land near the Blue Lick. They kill 2 bufelos this Eavening.

"19 April 1775, Wednesday [Twetty's Fort and Otter Creek]
Smart frost this morning; they kill 3 bufelos about 11 oclock we
come to where the indians fired on Boons Company and killed 2
men & a dog and wounded one man in the thigh. We campt this
night on oter creek.

"20 April 1775, Thursday [site of Fort Boonesborough]
This morning is Clear and Cool. We start Early & git Down to
caintuck to Boons foart about 12 oclock where we stop; they
come out to meet us & welcom us in with a voley of guns.

"21 April 1775, Friday
Warm this Day; they begin laying off lots in the town and preparing for the people to go to work to make corn."

When the Kentucky Daughters participated in the marking of Daniel
Boone's Trail in 1914 and 1915, they intended to honor the man who
marked this trace and piloted many into Kentucky. In doing so, the
Daughters also honored the men and women who made this perilous
trek during the first few decades of Kentucky's history, crossing this
rugged landscape from Cumberland Gap to the Kentucky River for
the simplest dream of the American spirit—opportunity.

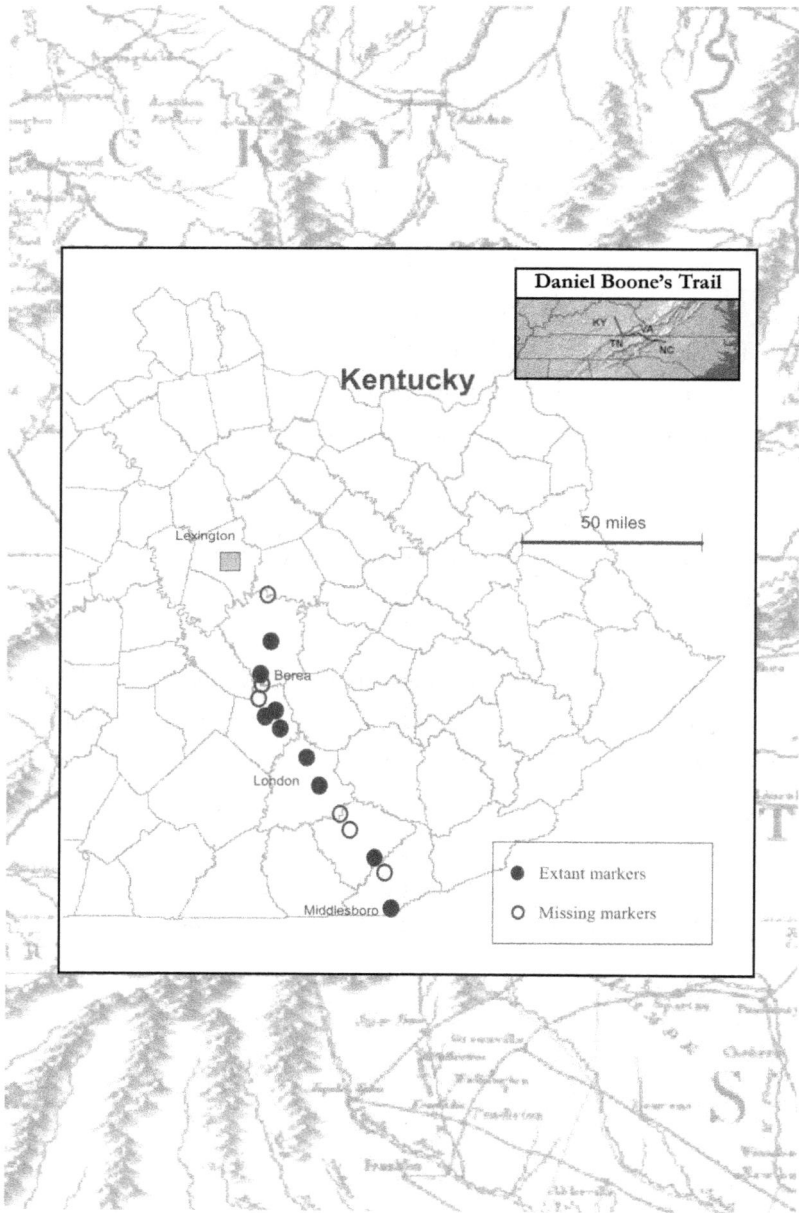

Daniel Boone's Trail

Kentucky

Lexington

50 miles

Berea

London

● Extant markers
○ Missing markers

Middlesboro

TRAILING DANIEL BOONE

Kentucky–The Real Boone Trail

From the outset of the trail-marking project, Mrs. Lindsay Patterson knew she had a capable ally in Tennessee, Miss Temple, to help in that quarter. The two challenges were finding capable Daughters to oversee the separate efforts in Virginia and in Kentucky. She had relied on Virginia's State Regent to find "a good DAR." She found another such Daughter in Kentucky.

Kentucky's Capable and Untiring Chairman

Deciding to get involved directly with the Kentucky Daughters, Mrs. Patterson attended the Kentucky state conference in October 1912. This meeting preceded her own announcement of the project in North Carolina and occurred while William Bryan was busily finishing his own commemorative monument. During the Kentucky conference, Mrs. Patterson shared both her time and her plans with Kentucky's own Boone's Trail Committee.

"The Boone Trail Committee of Kentucky met for a brief session this morning," reported committee chairman Miss Erna Berry Watson in the proceedings of the conference. "[The committee] had the pleasure of having with them Mrs. Lindsay Patterson of North Carolina, who has so successfully worked out the plan of marking the trail in her own State. The committee feels that it can do no better than to follow the lead of Mrs. Patterson and add a link to the chain so ably begun."[1]

Miss Erna Berry Watson
Courtesy of *Transylvania University Library, Special Collections*

Miss Watson was a well organized and diligent worker for the Kentucky Daughters, having been admitted as a member in 1911.[2] She was an artist and art instructor at Hamilton College, a women's school in Lexington.[3] She had studied fine art in St. Louis, Chicago, and New York, and taught in a number of schools before arriving at Hamilton College in 1909.[4] She understood organizational work, as well, having served as president of the Grand Council of Beta Sigma Omicron Sorority in 1909.[5] Miss Watson had a strong affinity for the trail-marking project and later also served on the DAR's National Old Trails Committee under whose auspices the Daniel Boone's Trail project was conducted. In fall 1912, not one marker had yet been placed anywhere on Daniel Boone's Trail, but Miss Watson could see the benefit of following the plan Mrs. Patterson proposed. She could also see the benefit of delegating the responsibility for fulfilling the project to the chapters. Accordingly the marking of the trail in Kentucky was handled more as it had been in North Carolina than in Virginia or Tennessee.

"The plan is to use natural boulders found along the road, to have iron plates bearing the name 'Boone Trail, and Erected by Kentucky D.A.R.,' and possibly the name of the Chapter," Miss Watson explained. "Each Chapter may select their own particular spot to mark and have in charge the unveiling of the marker, at which addresses can be made, or any kind of services held that the Chapter may wish."[6] Miss Watson did not intend to complete the project herself or to select every spot that would be marked on the trail. She would set the parameters and guide the process. She was relying on the two dozen or so chapters to step up and volunteer.

But Miss Watson championed the project and was very encouraging. "This [project] should be of vital interest to every Kentuckian as Kentucky was the objective point," she declared. "These [spots to mark] can be particularly interesting, as nearly every Chapter has some member who is descended from these pioneers," she added. Reminiscent of William Bryan's letter to the editor of the *Watauga Democrat* only six months before, she concluded her presentation at the conference in the imperative mood: "Urging your enthusiastic co-operation in this great work."

A year later at the state conference in October 1913, Miss Watson was able to point to the suc- cess of Mrs. Patterson's trail-marking effort in North Carolina and to put Kentucky's effort on a more definite path to success. She created a map that displayed the

The Boone Trail from North Carolina To Kentucky, 1775.

Daniel Boone's Trail in Kentucky
from flyleaf, *1913 Year Book*, Kentucky Society, NSDAR

Kentucky—The Real Boone Trail

167

general route and explained through what communities the commemorative route, defined by its 14 markers, would generally pass:

> "On the accompanying map I have marked the road, which follows the original Boone's Trail very closely as far as Pine Hill, five miles southeast of Mt. Vernon, where the trail leaves the highway and goes over the mountain and has been lost. Here we suggest that the marking go through Mt. Vernon over the Wilderness Road then out the Richmond Road where it strikes the Trail again seven miles north of Round Stone Creek, then through Boone's Gap and Richmond to Boonesboro.

> "Beginning at Cumberland Gap it will pass through Middlesboro, Pineville, Barbourville, London, Hazel Patch, Livingston, Pine Hill, Mt. Vernon, across Round Stone Creek, Boone's Gap, Berea, Richmond and end at Boonesboro, making fourteen markers in all."[7]

Miss Watson also shared information about the recent success of substantial trail-marking efforts in Missouri and continued to encourage the Kentucky Daughters to participate through their chapters in supporting the trail-marking project. She reminded them of the reputation up to which she hoped they would live. She wrote, "Kentucky is noted far and wide for the loyalty and devotion of her sons and daughters to her traditions and history and there could be no more fitting reminder of this than the marking of Boone's Trail in commemoration of its reclaiming from the wilderness by this dauntless band of pioneers led by Daniel Boone."

She closed her remarks asking the Daughters to pledge their support for the project. Whereas North Carolina Chapters had donated $20, she reasoned that if every Kentucky chapter gave $10, the Kentucky

Society, DAR would have the money it needed. "And now, Kentucky Daughters of the American Revolution," she requested, "I appeal to you as a united body, to this day pledge your Chapter to do its part in the marking of this Trail which they ["the dauntless band of pioneers"] carved through the wilderness."[8]

In the spring of 1914, at the 23rd Continental Congress in Washington, D.C., then-State Regent and former Vice–President General Mrs. W.H. (May R.) Thompson shared the status of the Kentucky Daughters' work on Daniel Boone's Trail:

> "I had the pleasure of attending the State conference of North Carolina in November. Kentucky and North Carolina are interested in the Boone Trail. Miss Erna Watson, the State chairman of the Old Trails Committee and the Boone Trail, has done great work. By the State conference in October she will have all the markers for the 150 miles placed."

Mrs. Thompson shared the wording the Kentucky Daughters had selected for their markers: "The Boone Trail from North Carolina to Kentucky, 1775."[9]

A Tangle of Tales and Trails

Miss Watson and the Kentucky Daughters had an abundance of Boone-related historic sites to commemorate and three trails to sort out in the process. All three routes overlaid one another from Cumberland Gap to Flat Lick, where Boone's Trace, the Warrior's Path, and the Wilderness Road diverged into separate routes across the landscapes of Kentucky's eastern and middle sections.

For years and certainly in the early 20th century, many people thought that the Wilderness Road in Kentucky was simply a widening of

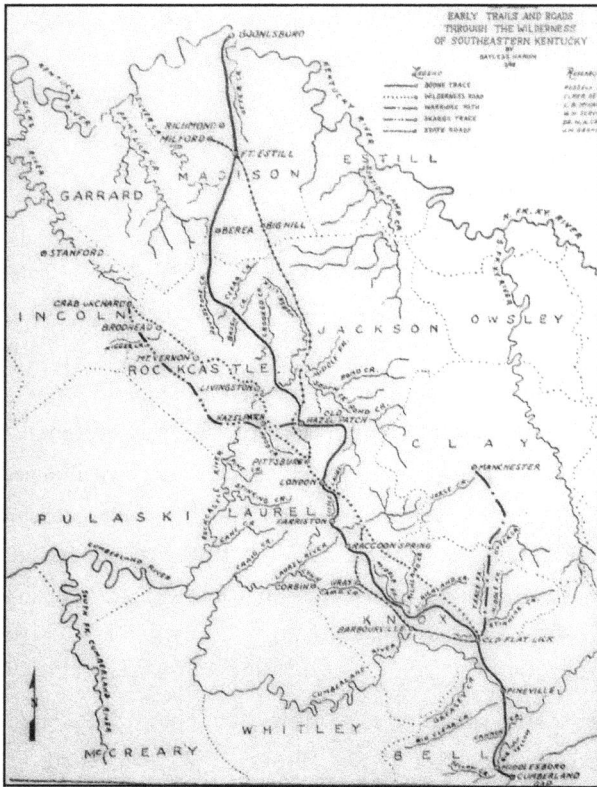

This 1948 map, "Early Trails and Roads Through the Wilderness of Southeastern Kentucky" by Bayless Hardin shows Boone's Trace and the Wilderness Road.

Boone's Trace, but scholarship over the years has reliably shown them to be much different routes, overlapping seldom at all north of Flat Lick.[10] In 1775, as he headed toward the site where he would begin settling what became Fort Boonesborough, Daniel Boone often followed the water courses along which buffalo had made passable trails through the river cane. The Wilderness Road, built by the Commonwealth beginning in 1795 often followed deer trails along the ridge lines. The former was often serpentine and suitable only for packhorses in a single file. The latter was constructed to accommodate wagons, and beyond Flat Lick headed northwesterly toward Crab Orchard, not north toward Fort Boonesborough.

The historic record of those routes was not always clear and a few of the markers perhaps intended to be placed on Boone's Trace were, in fact, placed along the Wilderness Road. Still, evidence suggests that Miss Watson, if not many other Daughters as well, distinguished between the two routes and their marking of "Daniel Boone's Trail" was to create a commemorative route which was relatively accessible to the traveling public. They were not intending to mark the literal path which Daniel Boone took in 1775, Boone's Trace.

All True Americans

Miss Watson's appeal for pledges in 1913 was not met as enthusiastically as she would have wanted. At the next annual conference in 1914, she reported her experiences. During the year, Miss Watson had written over 80 letters. The first of these had gone to the county judges along the route, "asking suggestions as to points of special interest to mark, and if we might count on any interested persons along the route to furnish the stone on which to place the marker." She continued rather disappointed, "[S]o far, none of the letters were [*sic*] answered." The bulk of the letters had been to the state's chapters asking for pledges. She reported 15 chapters pledging a total of $222.[11] In addition, she was pleased to announce the commitments made by two particular chapters: "John Marshall [Chapter] will take a Marker and place it on the farm of one of their members, which is on the route. Boonesborough [Chapter] will place one at the end of the Trail on the wall around the Boonesborough monument."[12] This commitment was particularly gratifying to the project as the John Marshall Chapter in Louisville was the fourth DAR chapter to be chartered in the country, on March 14, 1892.

Miss Watson explained in her report how the 14 markers were to be distributed among the chapters pledging $20. "I should like each Chapter to write me their first, second, and third choice of places for their marker with the exception of Cumberland Gap, as it will be marked from the smaller contributions sent by those not taking a marker." She then urged those who had made pledges to please send in the money "so we may have the actual work on the markers begun." Raising the money and getting it in hand had been more involved than Miss Watson might have imagined. A little more cooperation would certainly have been appreciated. That sense of frustration—one experienced so recently by the like-minded Boone commemorator William Bryan—might have led her to conclude her report with what may have been an intentionally nettlesome remark. "I wish to thank," she said, "all who have given me such hearty support in this great work, so dear to all true Americans."[13] If it were, she could hardly be faulted. The culmination of all of her hard work was simply awaiting the various chapters to send in the money they had pledged. As a consequence of this procrastination by the chapters, the Kentucky markers were the last to be erected along Daniel Boone's Trail, with most being completed and dedicated during the months after the celebration of the joint marker at Cumberland Gap on June 30, 1915.

In giving her report at the 24th Continental Congress in Washington, D.C., in April 1915, State Regent Hester Bryant Glore indicated the same. After praising Miss Watson's effort and sharing as much positive results as she could. She reported:

> "The past year has been marked by our bringing to a conclusion Kentucky's work on the Boone Trail through the efforts of Kentucky's capable and untiring Chairman, Miss Emma [*sic*] Watson. We have the desired amount of money for the separate

markers, as well as for the joint monument to be erected at Cumberland Gap by North Carolina, Virginia, Tennessee and Kentucky. On invitation of Mrs. Lindsay Patterson, Interstate Chairman, the State Regent of Kentucky joined her, Mrs. Wm. N. Reynolds, State Regent of North Carolina, Miss Temple, Chairman for Tennessee, at Knoxville. After a most delightful visit there, including a morning with the Bonny Kate Chapter, the party went to Cumberland Gap to select a site for this joint monument to Daniel Boone. The four States mentioned have contributed $400.00 for this cause. Kentucky hopes to have all the Boone Trail markers placed and dedicated during the summer."[14]

Daniel Boone's Trail in Kentucky

As a result of the delay in actually placing the Kentucky markers, the account published by the *New York Times* on August 1, 1915, was based on planned marker locations rather than ones actually installed and dedicated and certainly not on any firsthand knowledge by the story's writer[15]. Nevertheless, it offered a succinct accounting of Daniel Boone's Trail in Kentucky:

"The first marker in Kentucky is on Indian Rock, a few miles [*sic*] from Cumberland Gap. This rock was used by the pioneers as a place of defense against the Indians and wild beasts, and also as a signal tower.[16] Boone mentions it in some of this crude literature.

"The second marker is on the ford of the Cumberland River at Pineville. The third is at Flat Lick, in Knox County; the fourth on the farm of C.V. Wilson, hear Jarvis's store, where the old trail crosses the new road. The fifth is on the Knox and Laurel County line, on the farm of Arthur Hunfleet, near Tuttle. In Laurel County there is a marker at Fariston, near which there is an old pioneer burying ground called the "Place of Defeated Camps."

Kentucky—The Real Boone Trail

About three and half miles from East Bernstadt there are still some remains of an old fort, and there has been found a large boulder on which Boone had cut his name. This was placed in a churchyard, and the marker put on that.

"In Rockcastle County the first marker is on the farm of Philip Allen, near Livingston, the next at Boone's Hollow, near Brush Creek, then Roundstone Station, and lastly Boone's Gap. In Madison County, Berea is the first marker, then Estell [*sic*] Station, the site of Fort Estell [*sic*], and the place where Boone's party was attacked by Indians and Captain Twelty [*sic*] killed. The last marker is at Boonesboro, and is placed on the fence around the monument already erected by Boonesboro Chapter of the Daughters of the American Revolution to mark the site of the fort."[17]

Indian Rock

The first marker in Kentucky encountered by someone walking westward beyond Cumberland Gap is the marker placed at Indian Rock about a quarter-mile west of the saddle of the gap. The tablet remains today attached to the huge boulder which sits within the boundaries of the Cumberland Gap National Historical Park. This boulder is reportedly smaller today than it was in Boone's day, reduced somewhat

Indian Rock stands a quarter-mile west of the saddle of Cumberland Gap, inside the national historical park.

by the blasting and drilling that occurred in early 1900s to construct an "object-lesson road" through the Gap. The original boulder had a cleft from which Indians and, later, highwaymen pounced on unwary travelers to rob and assault them. Two men from Boone's era were said to be buried at the base of the rock, a timeless tombstone to the perils of the westward movement.

Mrs. Lindsay Patterson's grandfather, General Robert Patterson, wrote in his journal of this rock during his passage through the Gap while on his cross-country jaunt in 1835:

> "In the Gap, near the point where the road dips to descend the mountain and on the verge of the road itself is a huge isolated rock to which tradition has imparted an interest not shared by its larger and smaller brethren in the neighborhood. When this entire country was a wilderness of forests and the pioneers were guided in their movements by their knowledge of woodcraft alone with not even a sheep track to lead their footsteps this rock was selected by the [Indians] as a favorite position to waylay the unsuspecting woodsman in his journey across the mountains. Many are said to have fallen victims by that fatal rock and it was not until the country became cleared and a road opened exposing the ground around this death pass that the spot ceased to be an object of dread. Its singular formation, being cleft in the centre rendered the position peculiarly favorable for the purpose for which the natives had selected it. Tradition further says that two of the victims (white men) were buried beneath the rock but as the fragment weighs several tons and seems withal fast sealed to the mountain itself one cannot but think the placing of such a tombstone over the remains of the slain to be anything but a labor of love or hate."[18]

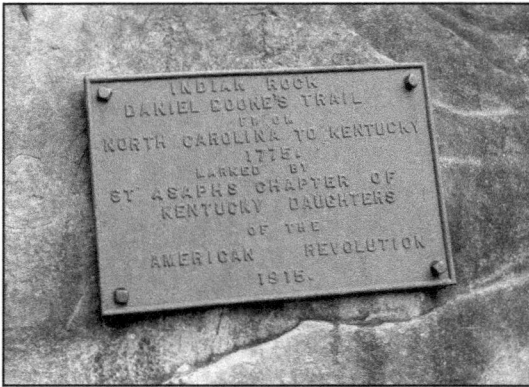

The tablet placed at Indian Rock is the only one identifying the chapter which placed it.

General Patterson may well have heard the traditional tale of the burials in the gap from his neighbor Hugh Graham, not knowing at the time of his journey in 1835 that the two families would join in a marriage (his son, William Patterson, and Graham's daughter, Cornelia) that would produce Lucy Bramlette Patterson and connect her by blood to one of the men buried there, the murdered William Bramlette.

Robert Kincaid described the passage through the Cumberland Gap as the most arduous along the Wilderness Road, noting that "every step ... had been the scene of struggle, where a fallen horse, a broken axle, a crumbled wheel, a wrecked vehicle or a scrambling team had slowed a distraught traveler." Even as late as the 1890s, lone travelers avoided the road through the gap. To assure their safe passage, they traversed instead through the tunnel. Even in groups travelers dared not go through the gap unless they were well armed.[19]

Businesses in Middlesboro used Indian Rock to advertise to travelers coming through the gap.
courtesy of *Cumberland Gap NH Park, NPS*

The tablet placed on Indian Rock was placed by the St. Asaph Chapter, Danville, the home chapter of State Regent Hester Bryant Glore. And although travelers after 1915 were not so subject to assault from robbers, during the 1920s the rock became a favorite face from which local businesses chose to spring upon unsuspecting motorists, wagoners, and pedestrians a message about their wares and services available just down the road in Middlesboro.

Cumberland Ford

The route from Cumberland Gap to Cumberland Ford followed through a low-lying area from which Yellow Creek was the only outlet. In Boone's era, the area was filled with canebrakes, but the trail was relatively good through the area as it had been trod over for centuries by migrating buffalo. By the time the DAR was marking the Trail, better roads did exist but they had only recently been so improved. The "object-lesson" road, completed in fall 1908, ran through the Cumberland Gap and put in motion efforts to improve roads throughout Kentucky. The Kentucky Good Roads Association was formed the following year and a State Department of Good Roads likewise in 1912. But the experience of travelers, including the Kentucky Daughters attempting to erect the markers, was still quite challenging. Robert Kincaid described in *The Wilderness Road*, the experience of one group of early motorists driving through southeast Kentucky along what was designated the Dixie Highway:

> "The first automobile known to travel over the major portion of the Kentucky road came from Lansing, Michigan. Four business men, with more faith than good sense, started south in January 1909 in a gaudy, brass-trimmed car with acetylene lamps and a load of spare tires. They found it fairly easy going until they reached Big Hill, south of Richmond, Kentucky. There they had

Cumberland Ford at today's Pineville was the prominent place to cross the river in Boone's day.

plenty of time to contemplate the trouble General Bragg had in getting his long wagon train over the peak where Boone first saw the glories of the Bluegrass. Slowly they churned through the bogs of the Rockcastle country until they reached London. Here they employed a guide for the rest of their journey. Making an average of three to four miles an hour, they managed to negotiate the mudholes and swollen creeks of Laurel and Knox Counties. Often they had to enlist farmers with teams of mules, horses or oxen to extricate them from particularly bad holes. At last they reached Pineville. Cumberland Mountain with its inviting stretch of "object road" was fourteen miles away, but they were told the quicksands of Yellow Creek often sucked in whole teams and wagons. Unwilling to risk such a catastrophe, they loaded their shaken and wheezing car on the train to be shipped back to Lansing."[20]

The Kentucky Daughters placed a tablet at Cumberland Ford, a water gap through the Pine Mountains. This crossing was a passage familiar to Boone and to all the Shawnees, Cherokees, and Iroquois who had followed the Warrior's Path to and from the Cumberland Gap only 13 miles farther south. The Shawnee called the river Ouasiota, meaning something akin to "valley of the deer." The name became anglicized to Wasioto, the name given since to a community in the area. "The Narrows" define the gap through Pine Mountain and can be seen from the Narrows Overlook, an observation platform at the end of a half-mile, uphill hike from a spot on Harbell Road, which departs US Hwy 25E opposite the golf course at Pine Mountain State Resort Park and immediately adjacent to the offices of the Division of Forestry, Southeastern District.

The 1914 marker no longer stands in "the Narrows" but is preserved on the lawn of the Bell County Courthouse in Pineville.

The DAR marker was placed by the Lexington Chapter[21] along the main road of the day a few hundred yards north (i.e., downstream) of where Big Clear Creek flows into the Cumberland River.[22] The marker is missing from its original spot along the river, having been moved a couple of times that are known. In the late 1970s it was reported attached to the wall of a garage building owned by D.L. Cornn at the southeast end of Park Avenue (which was US 25E at one time) until that building was demolished during construction of the flood wall. (Destructive floods hit Pineville in 1953 and 1977.) City Attorney Steve Cawood rescued the plaque during demolition; the cast iron marker was installed on the lawn on the southside of the Bell County Courthouse. Cawood's mother remembered attending the dedication ceremony in 1915 at age 7 "out in the Narrows," she said.

Standing in front of the Division of Forestry offices on US Hwy 25E is a highway historical marker recounting the naming of the Cumberland River from this spot by Dr. Thomas Walker on April 17, 1750. A mile or less farther north, in Pineville and along US Hwy 25E today, adjacent to the floodwall protecting the town at N. Pine Street, is a highway historical marker for the Cumberland Ford. The bridge for KY Hwy 66 over the Cumberland River provides a view of the river. An early settlement arose there in 1781 and took the name Cumberland Ford. The community took the name Pineville a century and more later in 1889 after the Bell County courthouse was built there in 1871.

In his 1835 journal, General Patterson recounted his June 17th experience of the passage just beyond the Cumberland Ford on what was

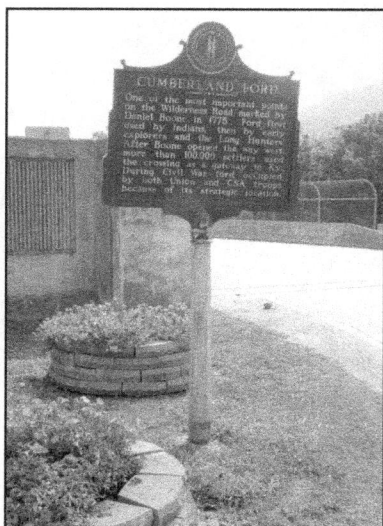

Two highway historical markers along US 25E near Pineville share the story of the Cumberland Ford.

TRAILING DANIEL BOONE

then a remnant of the Wilderness Road, but also following the route of Boone's Trace along the Cumberland River:

> "The bottom lands on the Cumberland river are very fertile but uncultivated as yet and covered with heavy timber and grape vines. There were immense canebrakes in this section in former times but these have been destroyed by the cattle of the settlers. In places inaccessible to the cattle the cane is still found. // This is the old "Wilderness road" the country between the Cumberland and the Crab Orchard still bearing that name being thinly settled and abounding in game. It is said that there are more deer in this region than in any other portion of the Union." [23]

Flat Lick

Old Flat Lick, eight miles beyond Cumberland Ford, lies in Knox County in the valley of Stinking Creek. It was a site where the Shawnee (Shawanoes) camped and made salt and where long hunters Elijah Walden and Boone also camped before continuing to the west and diverting from the Warrior's Path, which continued to the northeast to cross the Ohio River. When British Lt. Gov. Henry Hamilton was being escorted as a prisoner of the rebelling patriots from his battle post at Vincennes (today's Indiana) to Williamsburg, Virginia, in spring 1779, he observed at

The DAR marker placed at Old Flat Lick, where Boone's Trace departs from the Warrior's Path, was rededicated in 1989 (inset).
archival photo courtesy of *Knox Historical Museum*

Kentucky—The Real Boone Trail

Flat Lick some evidence of Indian activity:

"[April] 24th. forded stinking creek, and some others— at 4 p.m. passed the great War path of the Shawanese, which at this place crosses a remarkable Buffaloe salt lick— several of the trees here bear the marks of the exploits of the Savages, who have certain figures and Characters by which they can express their numbers, their route, what prisoners they have made, how many killed &ca——— they commonly raise the bark & with their Tomahawks & knives carve first and then with vermillion color their design …"24

The DAR marker placed at Old Flat Lick in 1915 was rededicated by the DAR in 1989. Today it stands mounted in a lot-sized park with garden plantings, additional tablets and a flag pole. The lot is at the intersection of Evergreen Road and Warrior's Path, north of (new) Flat Lick. The land was donated in honor of Mary Hammons Stewart, a member of the Dr. Thomas Walker Chapter, Barbourville. The site lies at the point where the Warrior's Path, Boone's Trace, and Wilderness Road diverge from each other as they served the interests and intentions of different groups. (Some cartographers unite the Boone Trace and the Wilderness Road for another four miles to the northwest before they split.)

One contemporary listing of the DAR markers placed in 1915 does not mention one at Flat Lick. It mentions, instead, placement of a marker along the Cumberland River near Elys Branch. This marker was placed by the Paducah Chapter.25 No marker can be found in that area today. It could be the Paducah Chapter placed the marker at Flat Lick instead or that it was moved there later. Or perhaps two markers were erected. Without more detailed records, any interpretation is speculative. Nevertheless, a marker does appear at Old Flat Lick today.

One of the new plaques added at the rededication in 1989 includes a map of a Daniel Boone Heritage Trail Route. It includes locations at which the DAR did not erect markers in 1913-15. It begins in the east at a spot labeled "Meakesville," North Carolina; this should be Mocksville, where Daniel Boone's parents are buried.

Boone's Trace and the Wilderness Road

In 1915, the Kentucky Daughters may have confused the routes of Boone's Trace and the Wilderness Road in some areas. Beyond Flat Lick and heading northwestwardly, the two routes diverge after several miles. Boone's Trace, the route of 1775, continued west toward Barbourville; the later Wilderness Road took a more easterly route, following closely in places today's KY Hwy 229. The two routes converged again for a short distance just south of today's London.

For 20 years after 1775, Boone's Trace, or the Kentucky Path, had been the route for immigrants entering the Caintuck "promised land" through Cumberland Gap. They came in droves. But after the American Revolution and after the statehood of Kentucky, the commonwealth had an interest in creating a better road into its settlements. In 1795, the legislature passed an act to build a new road suitable for wagons. Not surprising, Daniel Boone wrote to his friend, Governor Isaac Shelby, seeking the contract for the work. Revealing the extent of his formal education, Boone wrote:

"Feburey the 11th 1796

Sir

After my best Respets to your Excelancy and family I wish to inform you that I have sum intention of undertaking this New Rode that is to be cut through the Wilderness and I think myself intitled to the ofer of the bisiness as I first marked out that Rode in March 1775 and never re'd anthing for my trubel and sepose I

am no statesman I am a woodsman and think myself as capable of making and cutting that Rode as any other man Sir if you think with me I would thank you to wright mee a line by the post the first opportunity ... as I wish to know where and when it is to be laat [let] so that I may attend at the time
I am Deer Sir you very omble Sarvent
D. Boone"[26]

No record survives of any reply from Shelby. The contract was let to others and the Wilderness Road was constructed in 1796, following in most places a different route from Boone's Trace. In the first federal census, 1790, Kentucky had a population of 13,000. In a decade, the number of residents increased more than 15 fold to 220,000. Most of those came along the newly opened Wilderness Road. Its route and history became predominant in the minds of Kentucky's later immigrants. It is not surprising that by 1915, the Kentucky Daughters might not have distinguished between the separate routes.[27]

Indeed, in the fall of 1914, Col. James Maret, of Mt. Vernon, Kentucky, was busily organizing his Boone Way Association to promote better roads. His proposed road "mostly followed the route of the original Wilderness Wagon Road of 1796." He organized tours of automobile convoys and in 1916 the road received an inspection tour from "Bristol to Lexington" by the Southern Appalachian Good Roads Association.[28] His efforts, though greatly enthusiastic, had been preceded in December 1907 by the formation of the Society of the Wilderness. That effort by Charles Baugh was undertaken to promote local history along the route from the Cumberland Gap to the Bluegrass region while erecting markers along the way. A third stated purpose was "to work for the rebuilding of the Wilderness Road—the road that made Kentucky."[29] Conversation about the Wilderness

In 1915, Kentucky Daughters placed a tablet along the known route of the Wilderness Road near the Jarvis Store along what is now KY Hwy 229. No marker has been found there today.

Road was so prominent in the Kentucky region at the time of the Kentucky Daughters' work it is not surprising at all that they actually placed some markers on that route, intentionally or accidentally.

Jarvis Store

The Kentucky Daughters of the John Fitch Chapter, Bardstown[30], placed a marker at Jarvis Store on the route of the Wilderness Road, not Boone's Trace. Today, that route is KY Hwy 229. A country store building stands at the intersection of KY Hwy 229 and Jarvis Branch Road. This is the likely spot where the marker was placed, "where the old trail crosses the new road," as the *New York Times* article suggested. The broad valley through which KY Hwy 229 runs would have been an inviting route to build a wagon road in 1795. The area remains rural today and the store is now empty. The building may not be the same building from 1912, but that location undoubtedly served the surrounding community for decades with some store. Any marker erected in this area near the store could have succumbed to any number of calamities including vandalism, theft, or being damaged or destroyed in a vehicle accident.

No DAR marker is apparent at the Knox-Laurel county line along KY Hwy 229 where a DAR marker was placed in 1915. The marker was placed on the Wilderness Road, not Boone's Trace.

Tuttle

The Kentucky Daughters of the Henry Claggett Chapter, Shelbyville[31], placed another marker along the Wilderness Road near the county line of Knox and Laurel counties, "on the farm of Arthur Hunfleet." This also was probably erected along KY Hwy 229, known as Barbourville Road. In Laurel County, Matt Baker Road becomes Tuttle Road as it crosses KY Hwy 229 a hundred feet northwest of the county line. This intersection was the likely site where the Daniel Boone's Trail marker was placed. No marker is evident today. The area is rural and isolated. The marker could have disappeared over a century through any number of causes, or it could be tucked away on private property out of public view.

Nothing More Than a Bridle Path

Boone's Trace continued from Old Flat Lick, cutting across the headwater regions of the Cumberland River to Richland Creek north of what is now Barbourville. The route laid out for the Wilderness Road in 1796 left Boone's Trace at times lying three or four miles to the west and running through terrain more rugged than that of the Wilderness Road. In 1835, Robert Patterson was in the general area traveling from

Barbourville west to Williamsburg. He was on a poorly marked post road not actually near Boone's Trace, but was still in the headwaters of the Cumberland River. His description of the countryside and terrain in 1835, especially along the Laurel and Rockcastle rivers, suggests what Boone and others may have encountered 60 years earlier elsewhere along those rivers:

"… the country very hilly and broken while the greater portion of the road was nothing more than a bridle path. … The timber thro which we passed was very heavy and in some places so dense as to nearly exclude the rays of the sun. … [We] had again to ford the Cumberland which at this place is about 200 yards wide and deep enough to wet our saddlebags. … Our road to day lay thro a wilderness … while the last five miles of our journey was over the worst road I had ever seen. It was from the mouth of the Laurels to the mouth of Rockcastle and we were more than three hours in accomplishing the distance. In crossing Laurel we missed the main trail and had to break our way over and around stumps and fallen trees, scramble up one ravine and down another, climbing up and sliding down rocks until both our horses altho first rate animals were completely worn out. At last we reached the mouth of Rockcastle."[32]

Levi Jackson Wilderness Road State Park

A DAR marker for Boone's Trail was reported as being placed "near Fariston." That town was a railroad depot at the time and a convenient name for describing the marker's whereabouts. The actual marker was a mile and a quarter to the north-northeast at the site of one of the worst Indian massacres in Kentucky history, the McNitt Massacre, October 3, 1786. Mass graves and rude headstones comprise the McNitt Cemetery, which is surrounded by a stone wall. It marks the site of "Defeated Camp." The cemetery and the Daniel Boone's Trail

marker are in Levi Jackson Wilderness Road State Park, about two miles south of London, off US Hwy 25. Take Levi Jackson Mill Road (KY State Road 1006). The cemetery is on Mountain Life Museum Road about 100 feet northeast of its intersection with Levi Jackson Mill Road. The Millstone Museum, an old grist mill, a pond, and stream are at this intersection too.

Immediately adjacent to the intersection and south of it is a DAR boulder and tablet for Daniel Boone's Trail. It was placed by the General Evan Shelby Chapter, Owensboro.[33] The marker sits on a trail remnant of Boone's Trace, which runs through Levi Jackson Wilderness Road State Park. (Although the modern footpath may be the route, the trail does not appear to be an undisturbed road remnant. Development follows along both sides for its half-mile track through the park.) Another commemorative marker, erected in 1942 during Kentucky's Sesquicentennial, lies along this route at the southeast end of the trail segment. Also along this trail segment is a stone wall surrounding the spot where a hollow tree stood in 1786. One of the women among the McNitt settlers escaped the Chickamaugas' attack on her camp and hid inside that hollow tree through the night. Expecting a child, she went into labor and delivered the baby alone

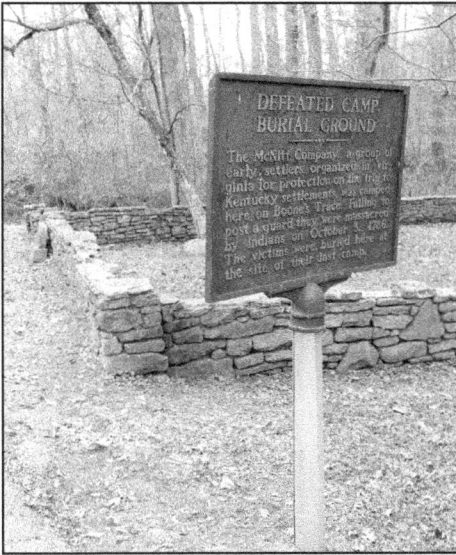

The "Defeated Camp Burial Ground" commemorates a tragic story of settlers who followed Boone's Trace more than a decade after its original marking.

and without making any sound which would have given up the hiding spot of her and her newborn to the marauders. She and the baby survived.

Beyond "Defeated Camp," the Wilderness Road and Boone's Trace again diverge. The Wilderness Road continues northwest through present London, then on to Wildcat Mountain and toward Mount Vernon. Boone's Trace runs north toward Old Hazel Patch.

Mt. Carmel Church

The Kentucky Daughters of the Jemima Johnson Chapter, Paris,[34] placed a marker north of London in Oakley along KY Hwy 490 at Mt. Carmel Church Road. The site is 3.8 miles north of East Bernstadt where KY State Road 3094 crosses KY Hwy 490. The tablet placed at Mt. Carmel Church was the first of those dedicated by the Kentucky Daughters in 1915. The occasion was a grand event prominently promoted. A letter to the editor in the May 18 *Mountain Echo* from the event chairman, J.M. Scoville, ended with a general invitation: "Everybody come, a big time expected."[35] Music and orations by learned men and women were the principal forms of entertainment for public events of the day. An article published in *The Mountain Echo*

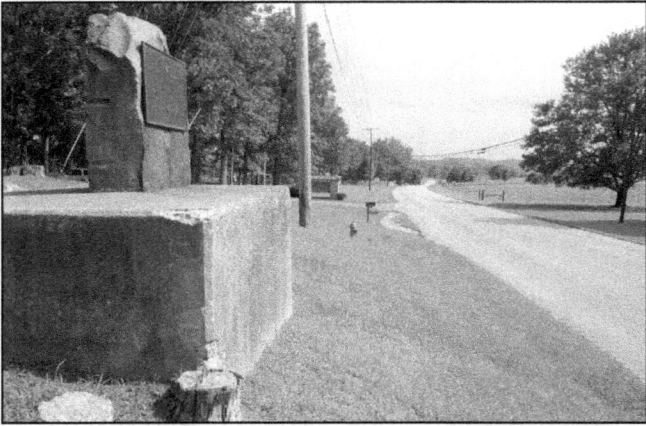

on Tuesday, June 8, 1915, described the occasion:

"The First Boone Trail Marker – Unveiled at Mt. Carmel Saturday

Last Saturday [June 5] was a day long to be remembered by the people of the Mt. Carmel neighborhood, near Oakley, this county [Laurel]. It was the occasion of the unveiling of the first of fourteen markers to be erected on the real Boone trail from Cumberland Gap to Boonesboro. Shortly before the noon hour the stalwart men, beautiful women and sweet children in that neighborhood began [illegible, *arriving*?] in wagons, on horseback and on foot until a crowd estimated at one thousand people had assembled to perform a duty uppermost in the minds of the people of Laurel County, the marking of the real Boone Trail. ...

"As the weather was rather threatening the principal portion of the exercises took place in the church building. Mr. John Scoville, than whom there is no better type of citizenship in Kentucky, presided as chairman. Music was furnished by the Mt. Carmel choir. Appropriate addresses were made … .[36] After the exercises in the church were thru the immense throng repaired to the place where the monument had been erected, the unveiling of which took place by Mrs. W. H. Whitley, [R]egent of the Jemima [*sic*, Johnson] Chapter, D.A.R. of Paris, Ky. in a few beautiful and well prepared remarks, in which she declared that the organization was interested in nothing but the truth of history. … It is an evident fact, as true as history can be, that the point indicated by this marker is as directly on the Boone Trail as is possible to get."[37]

The newspaper account also alluded to the Boone Way Association, suggesting that the DAR's project had come about after "the agitation of the Boone Way became to be [*sic*] so prominent" and as a way for the DAR to pursue the true history.[38] The Boone Way Association had, in fact, only recently announced on May 18 that unanimous agreement had been reached on the route of the road to be promoted and built. The "good roads" effort of the Boone Way Association was principally focused on economic development; Daniel Boone's Trail as marked by the D.A.R was purely commemorative and focused on historical accuracy.

A stone was erected with the DAR marker. It included the inscription "D. Boon" discovered 25 years earlier on a cliff. The DAR had a 1x3x5-ft. block of the cliff (and containing the inscription) cut out for

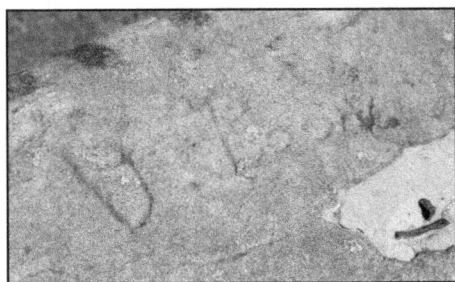

the marker. The cliff was reportedly the site of a "fort" where Boone had

The marker at Mt. Carmel Church includes the name "D. Boon" carved into the top of the stone.

Kentucky—The Real Boone Trail

191

stayed. The marker was erected along the old roadbed, Boone's Trace, which ran in front of the church toward Hazel Patch to the north. The modern church now faces west toward KY Hwy 490 and the marker was moved to stand along that highway. The old road bed, the Boone Trace, can still be seen immediately behind the church building opposite its east end.

Livingston
The Kentucky Daughters did not place a marker at Hazel Patch, but did place four markers farther north in Rockcastle County. The first of these was placed on the farm of Philip Allen (or Allin) near Livingston.

The Mountain Echo reprinted on October 26, four months after the June 15 joint ceremony at Cumberland Gap, a short article from the Louisville newspaper titled: "Boone Trail Marker unveiled on farm of Philip T. Allin on October 23." The article read:

> "Louisville, Ky. — John Marshall Chapter No. 4, Daughters of the American Revolution placed a marker on the Boone Trail on the farm of Philip T. Allin near Livingston, Rockcastle County, on October 23 which was unveiled with appropriate ceremonies on that day immediately after the arrival of a train from Louisville."[39]

The marker is attached to a stone pedestal next to the road, marking the entrance to private property. (The marker has been painted white.) This marker was placed by the John Marshall Chapter because one of its members owned land there along the route designated by Miss Watson as suitable for commemoration. According to maps prepared by Russell Dyche, a Boone's Trace authority from Laurel County during the middle of the 20th century, the marker site is most likely on the Wilderness Road which continues from Livingston northwest to Mt.

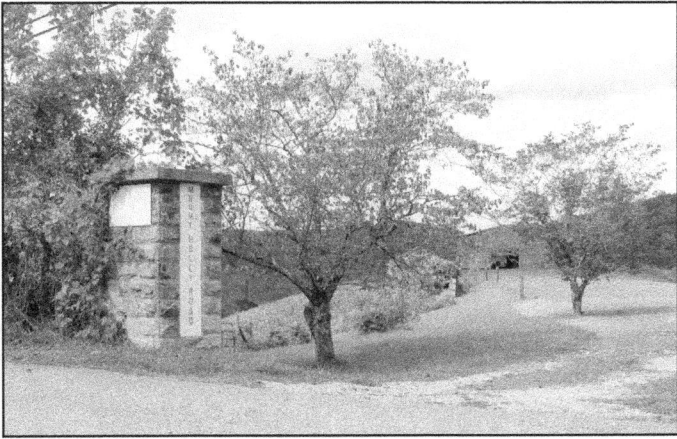

The Kentucky Daughters placed a marker for Daniel Boone's Trail in Rockcastle County north of Livingston. It sits along the Wilderness Road, but is not too far from Boone's Trace.

Vernon. Indeed, US Hwy 25 is known as South Wilderness Road.

The pedestal and marker are 0.2 miles north along Mt. Holly Road from US Hwy 25. That intersection is one-half mile north on US Hwy 25 from the center of Livingston.

Boone's Hollow at Brush Creek

The next marker along Daniel Boone's Trail was placed at a spring, which, tradition holds, was a favorite camping site of Daniel Boone. A rock overhang on the hillside above the spring would have afforded him protection. Although the site is referred to by the names Boone's Hollow and Brush Creek, the marker is along Cove Branch Road, which follows Cove Branch to its confluence with Roundstone Creek. The marker is 2.5 miles from US Hwy 25 by way of KY State Road 1004 and Cove Branch Road. The marker was placed by the Big Spring Chapter, Georgetown.[40]

The DAR marker called "Boone's Hollow at Brush Creek" is actually found on Cove Branch at a spring where he reportedly camped.

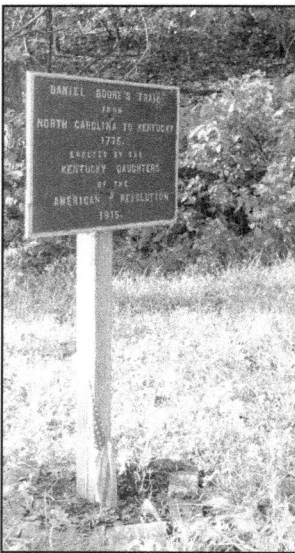

The Kentucky Daughters may have marked this site, not because it was on Boone's Trace, but because it was known as a camping site that he used. According to Dyche's maps, Boone's Trace actually crossed Brush Creek on the east side of Roundstone Creek and higher up that draw. The location of this marker and the confluence from opposite sides of both Cove Branch and Brush Creek with Roundstone Creek can be estimated on a map by locating Orlando along the CSX Railroad.

Roundstone Station

The CSX Railroad runs along Roundstone Creek. The Kentucky Daughters of the Susannah Hart Shelby Chapter, Frankfort,[41] placed a marker at a site identified as "Roundstone Station" or "Round Stone Creek." The most likely location for a station by that name would have been very close to US Hwy 25 along KY State Road 1786 (Wildie Road) at KY State Road 1617 on the site occupied today by a propane

The DAR marker along US Hwy 25 near Mt. Vernon (below) is along the Wilderness Road and may have been moved there from "Roundstone Station" along Boone's Trace (right).

gas company. No marker is evident in that area. Curiously, a Boone Trail Marker sits along US Hwy 25 just east of Mt. Vernon. No record exists that the Kentucky Daughters placed a marker there in 1915. It could be that the marker formerly at Roundstone Station was relocated to this spot perhaps because of development in the Roundstone Station area. The marker near Mt. Vernon sits on the Wilderness Road route and that location might have been favored by others during the following century. (This opinion is speculative; perhaps others have information, not yet uncovered, regarding the Roundstone Station marker or the Mt. Vernon marker.)

The DAR left no account of having placed a marker in 1915 at this location on US Hwy 25 at Mt. Vernon.

Boone's Gap

The fourth marker in Rockcastle County was placed at Boone's Gap by the Bryan Station Chapter, Lexington.[42] This pass between the watersheds of the Cumberland River and the Kentucky River is readily crossed today on US Hwy 25 about seven miles north from the supposed site of Roundstone Station and at the Rockcastle-Madison

In 1920, Dr. William A. Pusey followed the "Wilderness Road" and took this picture of Boone's Gap, which divides the Cumberland River and Kentucky River watersheds.

from *The Wilderness Road to Kentucky* by William A. Pusey, 1921

county line. US Hwy 25 cuts through a hill as it crests the rise at the county line. Old US Hwy 25 curved around the hill 100 feet to the east. Along that old highway alignment is a stone wall beyond which the ground slopes down to the railroad tracks which parallel US Hwy 25. In that stone wall stands a concrete base to which the Daughters afixed the cast iron tablet for Boone' Gap. The tablet is missing today, but the base displays an inscription. It reads:

"The Bryan Station Chapter, DAR
Erected This Base to Honored Member
Miss Erna Watson
To Commemorate Her Devotion and Perseverance
In Marking Boone's Trail in Kentucky"

US Hwy 25 continues north to Berea.

Berea

In the center of Berea, the Kentucky Daughters from the Fincastle Chapter, Louisville,[43] erected a marker which stands today in a park

The inscribed base for the missing marker at Boone's Gap remains along an abandoned stretch of Old US Hwy 25 at the county line.

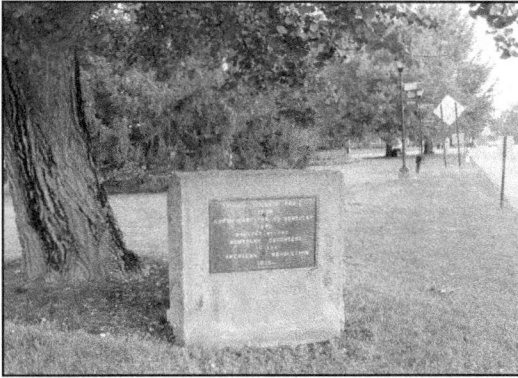

The Kentucky Daughters placed a Daniel Boone's Trail marker in Berea, in a park opposite the Historic Boone Tavern Hotel.

across the street from the Boone Tavern. The Historic Boone Tavern Hotel and Restaurant is named for Daniel Boone but has no connection to events of his life. It was built in 1909 as a guest house for visitors to Berea College. So, the Boone Tavern was six years old when the Kentucky Daughters placed the marker there.

The marker is on the southeast corner of the park bounded by Estill/Chestnut Street (US Hwy 25), Prospect Street, and Main Street South.

Estill Station

The Kentucky Daughters of the Hart Chapter, Winchester,[44] placed a marker along US Hwy 25 north of Berea and in the vicinity of the site of Fort Estill. The marker is one mile north of the intersection of KY SR 2872 and US Hwy 25. Land immediately east of US HWY 25 in this area and behind the marker is the Blue Grass Army Depot, a military installation.

In 1915, the Daughters may have confused Fort Estill with Twetty's (Twitty's) Fort. The Kentucky Daughters intended to commemorate the attack on Boone's party in April 1775 as the axmen neared their destination along the Kentucky River. Captain Twetty was killed in the

The Kentucky Daughters erected a marker on what became US Hwy 25 near the site of Fort Estill, but confused the history of that site with another.

ambush. Felix Walker was so severely wounded that the men built a makeshift fort of low cabins and remained there for a week until Walker could be carried with the party in a sling. They called the encampment Twetty's Fort. Fort Estill has a separate history of the same era. The marker was placed, nevertheless, along the likely route along which Boone' Trace fell as he and his party advanced toward Otter Creek, which would lead them to the Kentucky River.

In 1937, some of the Kentucky Daughters erected a marker at the site of Twetty's Fort, one mile southwest of the Boone Trail marker erected in 1915. The Twetty Fort marker is a stone memorial without a

In 1937, the DAR erected a stone marker at the correct site of Fort Twetty, about one mile southwest of the Fort Estill marker.

tablet attached. The marker is located within today's Acadian Senior Living Village.

Fort Boonesborough

The northernmost marker placed by the Kentucky Daughters in marking Daniel Boone's Trail was placed most appropriately at the site of Fort Boonesborough, Daniel Boone's destination in 1775. That fort was certainly one of the most celebrated sites of Kentucky's pioneer history at the time, and much of that notoriety had recently enjoyed some national attention.

In 1907, the Commonwealth of Kentucky had eagerly participated in the Jamestown Ter-centennial Exposition in Norfolk, Virginia, celebrating, of course, the founding of the first permanent English colony, Virginia, the parent of Kentucky. This exposition was a national and international affair. All of Kentucky's exhibits were presented in a replica of Fort Boonesborough, which was reported as a

This 1914 post card depicts Fort Boonesborough as it might have been. A replica of the fort housed Kentucky's exhibits at the 1907 Jamestown Exposition.
courtesy of *University of Kentucky*

Kentucky—The Real Boone Trail

great attraction to the exposition visitors after the fair's opening on April 26.

Upon the closing of the exposition on November 30, *The Courier-Journal* (Louisville) reported:

"Fort Boonesboro, the Kentucky building, was one of the first to be opened to the public and it was the very last State building at the World's Fair to close its doors on the final day. It was the only State structure open at night during the Exposition and on Saturday night, November 30, the latch string, as usual, hung out until 10 o'clock, two hours before President Tucker, of the Exposition Company, turned off the myriad of lights over the fairy city.…

"Kentucky fared reasonably well in the matter of awards at the exposition. Ten gold medals and fully as many silver ones were carried away. Great interest was always taken by visitors in the State's showing because it was the only Commonwealth represented at the exposition wholly through the patriotism and public spirit of its citizens. All other States had legislative appropriation. It is estimated that about 100,000 persons visited Fort Boonesboro during the exposition, and it is certain that no State building received more liberal praise from its guests."[45]

With such wide attention being given elsewhere to Kentucky's history, the DAR in Madison County chose to exhibit its own "patriotism and public spirit" by undertaking a special project to mark the historic site of the actual fort. "The Richmond Chapter of the Daughters of the American Revolution will erect a stone monument to mark the site of Fort Boonesboro in Madison county," reported *The Citizen* (Berea) on June 6. "The ground has been donated by the owner and the neces-

In 1907, a large crowd gathered with Boonesborough Chapter, Richmond, NSDAR, to erect a monument at the site of Fort Boonesborough. (at left)

courtesy of
Eastern Kentucky University Library

sary money has been raised to erect a handsome and fitting monument."[46] The dedication of the monument took place in the fall, on Saturday, October 5. "The monument at Fort Boonesboro was unveiled yesterday in the presence of several thousand people," reported the *Courier Journal* on October 6. "Addresses were delivered by Senator McCreary, Judge J.M. Benton, Judge George B. Kinkead and Col. J.W. Caperton."[47] It was a grand occasion locally. During the summer, however, tragedy had almost brought additional, undue attention to the cause, as a fire at the Jamestown Exposition destroyed several hotels, but spared "Fort Boonesboro," the exhibit space suffering only a "close call."[48]

In spring 1914 at the Continental Congress, Mrs. A.R. Burnam, Regent of the Boonesborough Chapter, shared: "We have arranged to place a stone wall laid in concrete around the marker on the site of Boonesborough, erected in 1907, and to adorn in other ways this beautiful historic spot."[49] One account said that the 1915 tablet was attached to that "fence," but some evidence suggests otherwise.

Kentucky—The Real Boone Trail

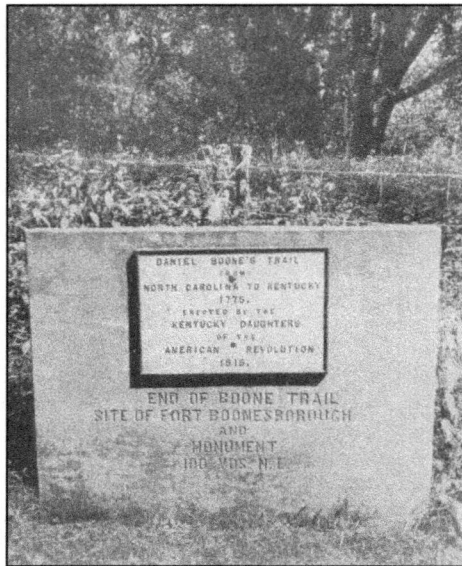

Daniel Boone's Trail ended at Fort Boonesborough, where the Kentucky Daughters placed a marker. The marker and monolith are missing today.

from *The Wilderness Road into Kentucky* by William A. Pusey, 1921

A photograph taken in 1921 by Dr. William Pusey shows the Daniel Boone's Trail tablet secured to a concrete monolith with the inscription "End of Boone Trail, Site of Fort Boonesborough and Monument 100 YDS. N.E." No marker or monolith exists at the site today and neither was there in 1996 when a member of the current park staff first arrived. The Boonesborough Chapter, Richmond, does not have any records of the Boone Trail marker dedication in 1915.

The Kentucky Daughters did place with ceremony the markers they had worked diligently to locate, fund, and erect. Kentucky's part of the trail was not completed before the joint celebration in 1915, but it was completed. The Daughters, and especially Miss Erna Watson, exhibited steadfast commitment and diligence in seeing the project through to its conclusion.

After its marking, the site of Fort Boonesborough was the scene of many educational class excursions such as the one above around 1915.

courtesy of *Eastern Kentucky University Library*

The Gateway of the Boone Trail and Dixie Highway, Cumberland Gap where Tennessee, Virginia and Kentucky state lines meet.

Cumberland Gap at the time Mrs. Lindsay Patterson and the DAR dedicated the joint monument. Post card dated 1917.

courtesy of *University of Kentucky*

The Celebration–"Four States Have Put Three in Love"

Watauga Democrat – July 1, 1915:
"Messrs. W.L. Bryan and J.P. Arthur left Monday [June 28], via Todd, to attend the unveiling of the Boone monument at Cumberland Gap. The twain almost revere the name of Boone, and it goes without saying that the ceremonies will be enjoyed by them to the fullest."[1]

Daniel Boone Marker, placed by D.A.R. in saddle of Cumberland Gap. Tenn.—Va.— Ky.

A postcard from the early 20th century for Cumberland Gap.
author's collection

In Wagons, in Hacks, in Buggies

On June 30, 1915, Daughters of the American Revolution from four states and a host of interested persons, both local and from some great distance, gathered at the historic Cumberland Gap to dedicate the one monument that would link together the paths marked across four states to create Daniel Boone's Trail. It was a grand occasion for both participants and observers. The governors of four states were expected to speak.[2] Businesses in Middlesboro were encouraged to close from 9 A.M. to 3 P.M. to allow their employees to attend the 11 o'clock ceremony.[3]

The Pinnacle News of Middlesboro further encouraged local attendance, reporting on June 24: "The citizens of this section are urged to co-operate in this work and the ladies are requested to prepare lunch that true hospitality may be dispensed to the visitors who will be present."[4] A month before, *Three States*, a Middlesboro semi-weekly newspaper, promoted the event in its "Calendar of Coming Events" emphasizing what for some had become additional reasons for celebration: "Speeches by distinguished orators. Old fashion Barbecue to be given on the mountain by people of Middlesboro and Cumberland Gap in celebration of the beginning of Boone Way and the routing of Dixie Highway through the Gap." The paper also suggested, "It is the duty of Middlesboro people to make this a memorable occasion and show their appreciation for the efforts of the D.A.R. to commemorate the name of Boone."[5]

The joint monument dedicated by DAR from four states on June 30, 1915, stood beside the crest of the road through historic Cumberland Gap.

courtesy of *Cumberland Gap National Historical Park, NPS*

After the big day, the *New York Times* recounted the event in an August 1, 1915, article:

"A few days ago at Cumberland Gap a monument was unveiled, which was erected by the Daughters of the American Revolution to commemorate the completion of the marking of the Boone Trail from Boone's home on the Yadkin River in North Carolina to Boonesboro, Ky. The monument had four faces, one for each state.

"The Regents of the State D.A.R. had charge of the unveiling exercises, which were attended not only by prominent State officials and officers and members of the Daughters of the American Revolution but by the mountain people residing in the vicinity of Cumberland Gap. They came a thousand strong. They came in wagons, in hacks, in buggies, in automobiles, on horseback and on foot. They came singly, in pairs, and in whole families. They came bringing their luncheon in baskets, and after the thrilling and patriotic exercises attending the unveiling, mountain folk and townspeople sat down together for a basket dinner.

"They sat on historic ground with portions of three States stretched out before them. They lunched off fried chicken and deviled eggs and other good things too numerous to mention and the towns folk were the guests of the people of Cumberland Gap and Middlesboro and the hospitality was truly Southern in flavor and in quantity."[6]

Closer to home, *The Pinnacle News* reported on July 1 the details of the ceremony:

"Boone Trail Monument Unveiled

Wednesday, June 30, was a gala day for Middlesboro, Cumberland Gap and the surrounding neighborhood within a radius of 200 miles when the representatives of the D.A.R. of the States of Kentucky, Virginia, Tennessee, and North Carolina dedicated the pedestal of the Boone Trail Monument, located on a slight eminence alongside the original trail at the crest of Cumberland Gap. ... The crowd began to assemble early in the morning in buggies, wagons, autos and on foot and by eleven o'clock when the dedication ceremonies began, there were at least 2,000 people present, who were grouped closely around the monument and along the hillsides. Rev. I. S. Anderson of Rose Hill, Va., delivered the invocation followed by Judge J.H.S. Morrison of Cumberland Gap in an address of welcome. ... The Bell Telephone Company installed a telephone near the monument pedestal and an operator of the Universal Film Company took motion pictures of the events and surroundings of the dedication ceremonies."[7]

A month or so later, the *Mountain Herald* reported, in part, from Lincoln Memorial University in its June/July issue on the celebration:

"Boone Pedestal Dedicated

For nearly a century and a half the history that clustered about these peaks and this ancient gateway to the West had been without a visible sign. But on the closing day of June, in the presence of such a throng as has not gathered here since the days of the Civil War, of such a peaceful throng as has not gathered since the days when Henry Clay spoke here to 5,000 people, the Daughters of the American Revolution dedicated to the memory of Daniel Boone a monument which for all time will call to mind his heroic deeds. ... The speakers were many and represented every section of America except the far West. Mrs. Lindsay Patterson acted

Cumberland Gap National Historical Park, near Middlesboro, Ky.

A post card of the Daniel Boone Monument at Cumberland Gap
courtesy of *Cumberland Gap National Historical Park, NPS*

as general chairman and introduced the speakers. … Space forbids mentioning all the speeches which were numerous, brief, and excellent in quality. At a brief preliminary meeting held in the L.M.U. Auditorium, representatives of the various East Tennessee Chapters of the D.A.R. also spoke, as well as Mrs. Reynolds, ex-state Regent of North Carolina, under whose direction the Boone trail in that state was marked."[8]

North Carolina – "something brand new"

At North Carolina's 15th State Conference, held in Waynesville at the end of September 1915, Mrs. Lindsay Patterson delivered her final report on the Daniel Boone Trail project. It was a remarkable under-taking for all the Daughters involved and she was justly proud and praising of all those who had helped. She was proud as well of the fact that the North Carolina chapters had taken the lead in bringing about the project. Appealing to a feminine nature, she reported what was, in

The Celebration–Four States Have Put Three in Love

a manner, a shared sacrifice, a small disappointment in which all the Daughters suffered for the betterment of the project.

"Ladies, it is such a pleasure to come to you with something brand new. As you know, after we marked [mapped] the trail through the States, Mrs. Reynolds and I went to Kentucky, with determination and ambition, to persuade them that Boone was a North Carolina hero. We succeeded. What we said, I do not know but whatever it was, I think it deserves to be placed along with the orations of Cicero and Demosthenes. [She no doubt paused here to enjoy a laugh with the audience.] Anyway, they trailed along with us and marked these trails. Tennessee was our daughter, so we didn't have so much trouble with her. After it was done, of course, we wanted to have a united marker. Cumberland Gap, where Tennessee, Virginia, Kentucky come together and North Carolina is not so far away, is a wonderful place.[9] I hope some day all of you can go there. Through a gap in the mountains, you look over into the blue mountains of Kentucky, over the green hills of Tennessee, and into the wonderful hills of Virginia, and a more fitting place for a marker, that four States have put three in love, I do not know. It is lovely in every way, and each of the four States contributed equal sums; each gave $100.00. The monument is right in the gap. We changed our minds a little bit; we intended to have it a D.A.R. monument, but in talking with the men, they asked us to put it in the form of a pyramid and leave a place on top of the pyramid so they might petition the Legislature, later on, to have a bronze statue of Daniel Boone. That will be the men's gift to the Daughters, and that, now, is in their hands.

"We had beautiful invitations sent out. We invited the Governors of all the States, the President, and all of the Cabinet Officers, all

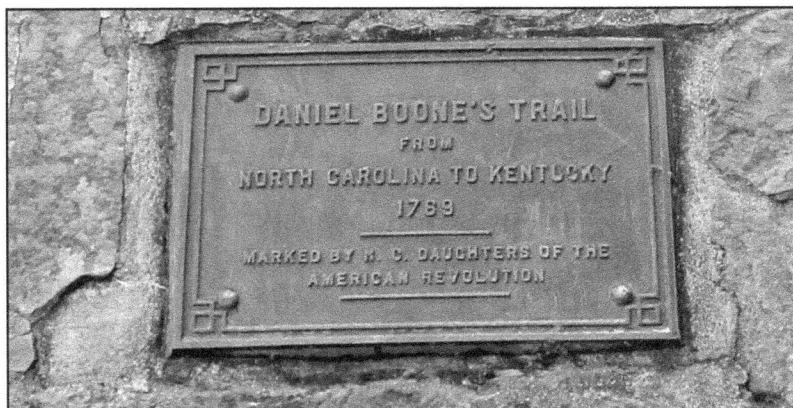

The North Carolina tablet for Daniel Boone's Trail.

of the North Carolinians scattered abroad, the Presidents of the different Historical Societies, and then, of course, our own people. We could not send invitations to each of you Daughters, because, just among ourselves, we didn't have money enough to do it. We had to send invitations to people we wanted to impress and people we didn't know. But I did wish we had another $25.00 so all of you could see the invitations."[10]

Regarding the dedication ceremony for the joint monument at Cumberland Gap, she shared anecdotes of that day, June 30, describing some of the everyday people who had come and recounting their connection to Cumberland Gap and their appreciation of the effort the Daughters had made in marking the Trail. She related with drama the story of how the most inclement weather had threatened the entire ceremony. She also shared the report with a knowing wink and a nod in places, using humor among friends to bind them closer together, as Daughters and as women, and to juxtapose the efforts, ideas, and ceremonial protocol of these "ladies" with those of "the men." She remarked:

The Celebration—Four States Have Put Three in Love

"We were disappointed that Miss Rodman couldn't come, because, many years before that, her ancestor and mine had gone through the gap, if not together, very nearly together. [Miss Lida Rodman was the State Regent in 1915-16, succeeding Mrs. Reynolds. Miss Rodman lived in Washington, North Carolina, 450 miles from Cumberland Gap.] But we had Mrs. Reynolds, who had worked so faithfully and so long and Mrs. Morrison [Regent of the Edward Buncombe Chapter], and one of the nicest people there—Allan Morrison [Asheville attorney], who had come with his mother, and little children who came from North Carolina to assist in the unveiling. Other State Regents brought little girls, and children from around there were invited. One lady came from New York with her little girl, because a century and a quarter before, her grandfather had gone through there with Boone. One man came from Philadelphia, because his grandmother was born there; he saw something about it in the papers. He stayed a couple of hours and took the next train back to Philadelphia; and he said he was more than repaid.

"The speeches were short—as women's generally are. We had a few men there, and they took up most of our time; we couldn't stop them. But they talked well.

"There were several North Carolinians there. We regretted that Governor Craig was not able to come and make the talk of the day. But they all made good talks, and we had addresses of welcome and patriotic music. And crowds and crowds of mountain people; they were everywhere. They had a wonderful time. It had been raining for five solid weeks, day and night, before the celebration. It poured in torrents, and we didn't know what to do. It rained until ten o'clock, and they said, what should we do. I said we were going to unveil the monument if there was a flood, and we decided to go right ahead and risk it. Just then there was a tiny bit of blue appeared in the sky, and soon it spread all over the heavens. It stayed clear all through the celebration, and while we ate a wonderful picnic dinner. Then the children were grabbed up and put in wagons, and just as the last of us got in the hotel, it began to rain and rained for another five weeks.

"All the newspapers sent reporters, and several magazines, and the *New York Times*. Moving picture men were there, and, altogether, it was a wonderful thing."[11]

In her closing and with intended humor that would have been obvious in her delivery to this audience of North Carolina Daughters, Mrs. Patterson harked back to her opening remarks about successfully convincing the people in Kentucky that Daniel Boone was a North Carolina hero:

"And if there is anybody in the United States now who dreams of locating Boone in Kentucky, I don't know where they are. Even Kentucky people don't claim him any longer."[12]

One can readily imagine the gregarious laughter which erupted among the Daughters at the state conference and the enthusiastic applause that followed her remarks. The North Carolina Daughters no doubt enjoyed Mrs. Patterson's humor and they also wanted to show their genuine gratitude for her leadership throughout the entire trail-marking project. It was an outstanding accomplishment and it deserved hearty recognition, generous accolades, and collective celebration. In all probability, as would befit the occasion, the Daughters gave Mrs. Patterson their rising approval, with extended applause of sincere appreciation, and heartfelt gratitude.

The Celebration—Four States Have Put Three in Love

Tennessee – "the most prominent side"

The Tennessee Daughters participated, of course, in the dedication ceremony for the joint monument at Cumberland Gap. Miss Temple was there as was one unnamed "son of Tennessee." Undoubtedly other Tennessee Daughters attended as did a good number of local residents, described as "mountain folk," from the nearby community of Cumberland Gap, Tennessee.

Miss Mary Boyce Temple reported on that dedication event only briefly, but with appropriate pride, in her remarks to the Tennessee Daughters in the fall of 1915 during the state conference in Chattanooga. She "describ[ed] the difficulties overcome and the joy felt in the finished work, with the great crowd gathered from many states to witness the ceremonies." With a particular point of pride, she noted "that Tennessee was fortunate in having the most prominent side of the base assigned to the four states, the inscription on the Tennessee side facing the highway."[13]

During the spring just preceding the dedication of the joint monument and at the 24th Continental Congress in Washington, State Regent Martha White Baxter reported the state's pride in accomplishing its marking of the Trail. She also used that opportunity to champion a related project, one that her fellow Daughter, Miss Mary Boyce Temple, would embrace and advance in coming years.

"Near this point [the Cumberland Gap]," Mrs. Baxter advised, "is a great university called the Lincoln Memorial University." With the intent of further promoting the value and significance of the Boone Trail just marked, she continued, "Recently an Advisory Board composed of women, with the State Regent of Tennessee as Chairman,

The Tennessee tablet for Daniel Boone's Trail.

has been formed to aid the University and we hope to interest the National D.A.R. in this work. The University has the most historic location of any school in America. It is situated on the Boone Trail or Wilderness Road which passes through Cumberland Gap, that wonderful stone gateway opening into four States, settled by descendants of the men who turned the tide of battle at Kings Mountain, who defeated the British veterans at the Battle of New Orleans. We ask you to add to your list of schools worthy of D.A.R. scholarships the name of Lincoln Memorial University at Cumberland Gap."[14]

In 1921, during Miss Temple's second term as Tennessee's State Regent, she delivered the presentation speech at the dedication of the D.A.R. Hall for boys at Lincoln Memorial University. She was honored that day also for having raised significant funds for the university.[15]

Kentucky – "the great triumph of completion"
At the end of October 1915, the Kentucky Daughters held their 19th State Conference in Frankfort, meeting in the chambers of the House

of Representatives. They were honored by Governor James B. McCreary, who spoke to the Daughters, saying, "There is great patriotism and great satisfaction in the memories of the American Revolution, but the American Revolution was a beginning, and not a consummation, and the duty placed upon us by that beginning is the duty of bringing the foundation then laid to the great triumph of completion."[16] It was good that Governor McCreary addressed the Kentucky Daughters then. He had not, in fact, attended the ceremonies at Cumberland Gap, citing "pressures of official duties."[17] In the spirit of reaching for such "completion," State Regent Glore announced to the Daughters that the marking of the Boone Trail was finished. (Neither did Mrs. Glore attend the ceremonies, sending in her place Mrs. W. H. Thompson, so prominent in DAR circles.[18]) The Kentucky Daughters were the last to place their markers, erecting many throughout the summer and fall even after the dedication of the joint monument. But so it was that Daniel Boone had made the last of his marks to establish the Trace on the trees that lined the streams and

The Kentucky tablet for Daniel Boone's Trail.

crossed the ridges in this same land then called Caintuck. The Kentucky Daughters, determined and committed, finished the task they had undertaken; with their help, the Trail was completed end to end.

Mrs. Glore reported as well on the ceremony that took place at Pinnacle Rock on June 30th. (Perhaps the *Lexington Leader* was mistaken in its account of her absence, or perhaps afterward she preferred to represent herself as having attended.) She recounted "that while looking out their window, she and Mrs. [*sic*] Watson found a cloud hanging over the Pinnacle Rock completely obscuring it—this, however, at 5 A.M. By eleven A.M. the sun was out in all its glory and 5000 men, women and children from the three states were waiting for the ceremonies." The minutes continued, "This tribute to the bravery of Daniel Boone and his hardy pioneers stands (entirely on Kentucky soil) high above the picturesque roadway from Cumberland Gap, Tennessee, to Middlesboro, Kentucky, and about 100 yards from the stone marking the boundary of three states of Virginia, Tennessee, and Kentucky."[19] At the 1916 Continental Congress in April, Mrs. Glore simply acknowledged in her remarks that "the monument to Daniel Boone was erected and dedicated ... last June."[20] [21]

Virginia – the chatter and laughter of a happy crowd
At the 19th Virginia State Conference in Staunton, held October 13 and 14, 1915, Mrs. Gray reported on the ceremony which completed the marking of the Daniel Boone Trail. She proudly noted that the joint monument actually sat on Virginia soil [Mrs. Glore obviously claimed otherwise] and added, "Perhaps no work has ever been done by our Society which has brought us into more public prominence." The Daughters of all four states had worked diligently to mark the Trail and to promote its importance. Local people and the press were

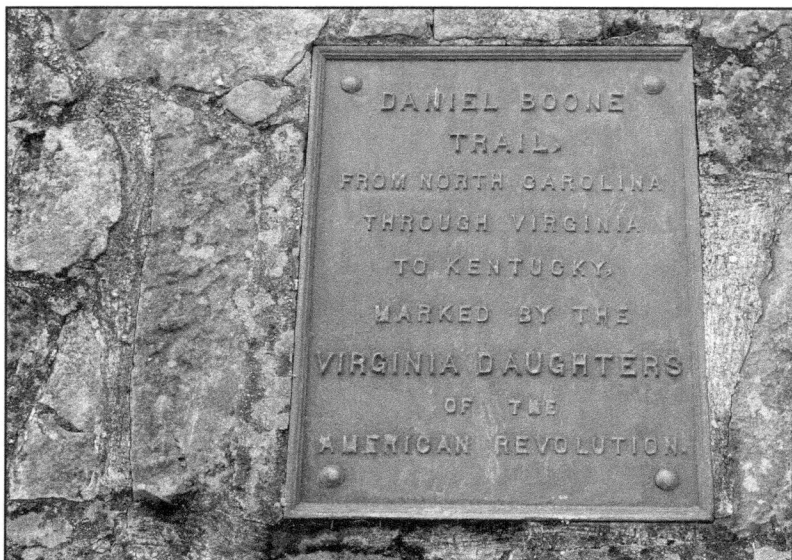

The Virginia tablet for Daniel Boone Trail.

much impressed, but elected officials were scarce that day. Mrs. Gray noted as much with a bit of humor, no doubt enjoyed by the Daughters gathered in Staunton:

"A very elaborate program was planned, and handsome invitations went out for the ceremonies on the thirtieth of June. Political perplexities, the Panama Exposition[22], and illnesses prevented President Wilson and the Governors of the four States from being with us, but North Carolina sent several of her gifted sons, and Tennessee contributed one. Virginia sent no son, but through no fault of your State Regent, who urged our Governor and four brilliant speakers to represent her; but you know it was said of men a long, long time ago, 'they all began with one consent to make excuse.' So your State was represented only by your State Regent, State Chairman, two small pages, and several very charming Daughters.

"The programme was one of deep interest from start to finish, and was witnessed by over a thousand people, but it was estimated that there would have been triple the number had not the day been showery. The sweetest part was the unveiling of the tablets by the attractive little pages, appointed by the State Regents of the four states. Those from Virginia were John M. Preston Gray, son of our State Chairman, and a descendant of Col. William Preston, Surveyor General of Virginia at the time Boone blazed his Trail through the State, and dainty little Emily Jeffrey, a descendant of Colonel Calloway, of Virginia and Kentucky."[23]

Later during the state conference, Mrs. Gray described the dedication ceremony in more poetic fashion:

"On June 30, 1915, our State Regent led our State delegation into the little village of Cumberland Gap, and we looked with awe upon the frowning battlements of the Pinnacle Rock and the mighty palisades guarding the entrance into Kentucky.

"We read in history, story and verse of the beauty and grandeur of the Palisades of the Hudson, but we Virginians need not leave our own borders to find natural beauties and wonders to which those of the Hudson 'are as moonlight unto sunlight.' The Natural Tunnel, the Pinnacle Rock, and the palisades of the Cumberland and of the Clinch River are beyond the words of a less than [Washington?] Irving to describe.

"The railroads from the three States brought into the little village that day crowds of sightseers and patriotic pilgrims; and when the hour arrived something over five thousand people (I give the estimates of reporters who were there) had congregated and were borne to the summit of the pass in every kind of vehicle, ranging from the mountain ox-cart to the sturdy little Ford and his bigger brothers.

"Mrs. Lindsay Patterson of North Carolina was hostess of the occasion, for her 'foot was on her native heath,' and also she, it was, who originated the idea of marking the Trail.

"Mrs. Wm. Reynolds, ex-Regent of North Carolina, was there to represent her State. Miss Mary Temple, Chairman of Tennessee's Committee, and Mrs. Thompson, Vice-President General from Kentucky, ably represented their States, and it is needless for me to tell a convention of Virginia women, who know their State Regent, that Mrs. Maupin was the gentle, womanly, efficient leader one instinctively looks for from the Old Dominion.

"There were addresses from each of the ladies, and one from Mrs. Guernsey of Kansas, who was the guest of North Carolina. Then there were talks, historical, reminiscent and prophetic from Judge Morrison, of Cumberland Gap, Mrs. Thomas Findlay and Mr. Arthur Bryan [no doubt a conflation in the memory of Mrs. Gray of John Preston Arthur and William Lewis Bryan who both attended] of North Carolina and others, and inspiring music by the Middlesboro, Kentucky band. At the conclusion of the exercises the State flags were drawn from the various tablets by children of the State, and a song sung by the State delegations."[24]

Six months later at the 25th Continental Congress in Washington, D.C., held April 17-22, 1916, State Regent Edmonia Maupin borrowed from Mrs. Gray's report in making her own Regent's report to the Daughters assembled in Congress, but she added a few passages fashioned from her own experience:

> "The scene on that mountain summit will linger long in memory.
> Handsome Daughters, distinguished men and mountain folks
> mingling freely together gathered in groups amid the brilliant
> blossoms of the rhododendrons, the chatter and laughter of a
> happy crowd awakening echoes in the lonely mountain."[25]

It Has Aroused the People

Mrs. Gray also reported at the Staunton meeting in October 1915 that
she had been given late notice to select a project to report to the
national society's *Memorial Magazine* as the Virginia Daughters' greatest
achievement for the year, on the occasion of the 25th anniversary of
the D.A.R. She confided that she had submitted the Daniel Boone
Trail.

Begging the Daughters' indulgence of her selecting the project of a
committee of which she was chairman, she added, "It is not our most
expensive work, not perhaps our most widely known work, but ... the
movement caused by the marking of the Boone Trail is wonderful,
and is still spreading. I have had letters from all kinds of people asking for information concerning the Trail, the families composing the
party, the Country through which they wandered. It seems to have
awakened a general interest in various subjects, historical, genealogical,
and geographical, especially. And better than all of these," Mrs. Gray
added with great enthusiasm and as a point of pride for all Daughters,
"it has aroused the people to the need for good roads. I have it from
one of the Road Commissioners that the talk of marking the Boone
Trail has done more to create interest in building good roads in this
District than any other one argument the Committee could bring
out."[26]

Indeed, the America of the second decade of the 20th century was seeing a rise in automobile travel and the need for better roads was an emerging theme across the country. On the occasion of their 25th anniversary, the Daughters of the American Revolution, founded to promote patriotism, had certainly done the country that great service and in so doing, had done another as well.

A Trail to the Past

The Daughters of the American Revolution had marked Daniel Boone's

Increased use of automobiles in the early 20th century inspired a demand for better roads.

photo taken at Cumberland Gap;
from *The Wilderness Road to Kentucky*
by William A. Pusey, 1921

Trail across a challenging landscape that had been an imposing barrier to the westward movement of European-Americans. The Daughters had completed the task in three years, but the world of 1915 was not the world of 1912. So much had happened in that time and the attention of the country had changed since the project began. U.S. Marines had been sent to Mexico, to Nicaragua, and to Haiti. The Federal Reserve Bank and the Federal Trade Commission had been established. The women of America were demonstrating for the right to vote. The 16th Amendment to the Constitution had been ratified establishing a personal income tax. Among all this and other news of the day, in August 1914 two momentous events of global importance had occurred: a great war had begun to engulf Europe after the assassination of Archduke Ferdinand, and the Panama Canal had opened, bisecting the Americas with a water passage and connecting the world's two great oceans in efficient commerce. The United States was thoroughly engaged in the world of the 20th century. Change and progress abounded. America was looking more forward and less back.

Thus it was that Mrs. Lindsay Patterson and the Daughters of the American Revolution had reached back at the last possible moment, as if snatching something from beyond a fast-closing door, and pulled an important legacy into the future. The history of Daniel Boone and America's westward movement would not be forgotten. The Daughters of the American Revolution had helped preserve the country's heritage and they had provided America a means by which to

Daniel Boone at Cumberland Gap
portrayed by Scott New; author's photo, 2005

The Celebration—Four States Have Put Three in Love

223

remember it. In good faith and dutiful fashion, they had marked a trail to the past.

In 1915, during the 25th anniversary of the founding of the Daughters of the American Revolution, Daniel Boone's Trail had been successfully marked. Cast iron and bronze tablets stood witness to that effort for another century, reminding Americans not only of the pioneers so honored, but reminding Americans today, as well, that some people do not forget. They take as their patriotic duty and as their responsibility as citizens the task of helping everyone remember, honor, and cherish America's treasured heritage. Such was then and remains today—a full century later—the purpose, mission, and service of the Daughters of the American Revolution.

TRAILING DANIEL BOONE

Epilogue

John Preston Arthur

Historian John Preston Arthur had been a great help to Mrs. Patterson in the earliest days of the Daniel Boone Trail project. He had done the yeoman's work of trekking through the region, interviewing residents, and by that process discovering as best as could be determined at the time the track of Boone's footsteps through the Blue Ridge Mountains.

John Preston Arthur
from *A History of Watauga County*
by J.P. Arthur, 1915

John Preston Arthur and William L. Bryan had made the trip to Cumberland Gap in late June 1915 to participate in the dedication ceremony of the joint monument. Arthur, in fact, was to be one of the speakers, but by his own later account and due to his own foolishness, he was not allowed to finish the speech he had begun.[1] He wrote an account of that occasion in his *A History of Watauga County* and in that passage revealed what was probably the content of his prepared remarks. He acknowledged the plans for Congress to erect a statue to Daniel Boone and then proceeded to praise the character and life of Daniel Boone in the most grandiloquent phrases, in glowing and reverential terms, declaring that no more fitting monument could honor Boone's life than one consecrated at the Cumberland Gap. He wrote:

"The whole work was crowned on the 30th of June, 1915, by unveiling at Cumberland Gap a substantial stone and concrete pedestal, bearing on its four faces tablets of the Daughters of the American Revolution of these several States. ...[2]

"Upon this pedestal in Cumberland Gap the Congress of these United States should soon erect a bronze statue of Daniel Boone, clad in hunting shirt, fringed leggings, moccasins, shot pouch, powder horn, hunting knife, tomahawk, etc., with the figure leaning slightly forward while peering from underneath the left hand toward the west, the right hand grasping the barrel of his long flint-lock Kentucky rifle, whose butt should be resting on the ground. The figure should have a coon-skin cap; for, although Thwaites says that Boone scorned the coon-skin cap of his time, it was none the less typical of the head-gear of all the pioneers of the time. Such a statue would identify this historic spot with this historic character and fix forever the costume, accoutrements and arms of the pioneers of America. It is the most significant and suggestive place in America; for, while Plymouth Rock was the landing place of the Puritans, Jamestown of the Cavaliers, Philadelphia of the Quakers and Charleston of the Huguenots, it was through Cumberland Gap that both Roundhead and Huguenot, Puritan and Cavalier passed with the sober Quaker on their way to the Golden West. Boone was their greatest and most typical leader and exemplar. He was colonel and private, physician and nurse, leader and follower, hunter and hunted, as occasion demanded, but he was never a self-seeker or a swindler. His fame is now monumental, for he had no land to sell, no private fortune to make, and his record is one of unsullied patriotism. He was simply a plain man, but a man all through. He was neither northerner nor southerner, easterner nor westerner, but all combined, and the men, women and children who followed the glowing footsteps of this backwoods lictor were the ancestors of those who people these United States today and make it the most enlightened, the most progressive and the most democratic nation in the world. That there should be no national monument to this man and on this spot seems incredible. The women and the States immediately concerned have done enough. They have marked every trail leading to this historic gateway. Let the nation act and place there a monument which shall be worthy of the place, the man, and the colossal events which they typify."[3]

Arthur may have had in mind a statue of the style completed 20-some years before by Enid Yandell (1870-1934), a noted sculptor. She creat-

Enid Yandell's 1892 sculpture of Daniel Boone; bronze placed in Louisville's Cherokee Park, 1906 (left) and at Eastern Kentucky University, Richmond, 1967 (right).

Epilogue

ed a plaster sculpture of Daniel Boone for the Filson Club. It was exhibited widely. In 1906, it was cast in bronze for the City of Louisville. (It stands today in Cherokee Park of that city. A second statue was cast in 1967 and placed on the campus of Eastern Kentucky University in Richmond.) Of course, no such statue was ever placed at Cumberland Gap despite any efforts and promises of "the men," regardless of how sincere were their intentions or the expectations of John Preston Arthur. The four-sided pedestal remained for a time an unfinished monument to America's pioneer hero, but nonetheless a fitting tribute to the effort of Mrs. Lindsay Patterson and all the Daughters of the American Revolution who did their part of the commemorative effort with style, grace, commitment, and perseverance.

Daniel Boone Statue

As it was, a statue of "Daniel Boone" had already been prominently displayed in America for 60 years. Indeed, "Daniel Boone" had attended the inauguration of President Woodrow Wilson in 1913, the year Mrs. Patterson began erecting DAR markers in North Carolina. "Boone" had been there as well for Abraham Lincoln's inaugural ceremony in 1861, the event which split the country and led her grandfather into military service as an officer in yet a third war. On the east façade of the US Capitol were two sculptures by Horatio Greenough (1805-1852). "The Rescue" depicted a frontiersman protecting his family against attack by an American Indian with an upraised tomahawk. Although the artist did not name the frontiersman, the public knew the statue as "Daniel Boone Protects His Family." The statue became a source of controversy and eventually an embarrassment, leading Congress in 1939 to consider its removal and suggesting it be "... ground into dust, and scattered to the four winds, that no more remembrance may be perpetuated of our barbaric past, and that it may

A post card reads, "President Wilson Taking the Oath of Office in Front of the Capitol, March 4, 1913, Washington, D.C." Horatio Greenough's statue, "The Rescue" is shown at left and in circle (added). *Library of Congress*

not be a constant reminder to our American Indian citizens …"[4] In 1958, it was quietly removed and placed in storage at the Smithsonian.[5] That probably served as well the legacy of Daniel Boone who was not the "Indian fighter" he was too often portrayed as being in romanticized accounts of derring-do. But in 1913, during the inauguration of President Woodrow Wilson, the statue represented for many Americans of the day at least the mythological history of the American frontier, if not the factual account, and Daniel Boone was prominent in the imagery of the public's understanding of that history. In time, Congress' suggested remedy came about by accident. In 1976, as the statue was being moved within the Smithsonian's storage areas, it was dropped from a crane and broke into numerous fragments.

John Preston Arthur died in December 1916, only a year and some months after he had published his book which included his eloquent eulogy for Daniel Boone. Another long lifetime of 80-some years would pass from the death of Arthur before another fitting statue of Daniel Boone would appear, but not at Cumberland Gap. The year 1999 was the centennial of the founding of the Watauga Academy, which became the Appalachian Training School, and eventually Appalachian State University. The founders were Blanford B. Dougherty and his brother Dauphin D. Dougherty. Dr. B.B. Dougherty served as president of the school from 1899 to 1955, and was one of the initial contributors to William Bryan's cabin monument in 1912. On the occasion of the centennial, a distinguished alumnus, the first Kentuckian to graduate from the school, presented the university with a statue of Daniel Boone. Durward W. Maynard was an admirer and a friend of President Dougherty. After leaving Boone in 1945 and after a successful career as an attorney in Kentucky, he gave the statue to honor Dr. B.B. Dougherty and his pioneering vision for the school. (That year was also the 150th anniversary of Watauga County and the creation of the town of Boone as the county seat.)

The new statue of Daniel Boone was placed along Rivers Street, at the spot, or nearly so, where William Bryan had built the Daniel Boone Cabin Monument in 1912. The bronze statue, created by Sherry Edwards, artist and faculty member of Appalachian State University, reflects the "true" Daniel Boone, the one revealed by additional years of scholarship: No coonskin cap. No fringed buckskins. This Daniel Boone is at camp, sitting on a log before a fire ring accompanied by his hunting dogs, Plott hounds. Ever ready at hand is his Pennsylvania longrifle, and on his person, clad in hunting shirt and trousers made of linsey-woolsey, wearing deerskin moccasins and donning his broad-brimmed, beaver felt hat over his clubbed and braided hair, he wears his powder horn, pouch, and patch knife. His hunting knife is tucked

Bronze casting of Daniel Boone in camp with his Plott hounds on the campus of Appalachian State University. Erected 1999.

beneath the sash at his waist. At his back, the blade of his tomahawk is secured in the log. Strong, lean, and vigilant, he is a man at peace, with and in the world.

The Boone Cabin Monument has been restored, of course, and was erected in September 2005 under the auspices of the mayor and the Town of Boone and at the direction of a committee of interested citizens. Bryan's monument had been moved in 1969 to accommodate development on the campus of Appalachian State University. When it had

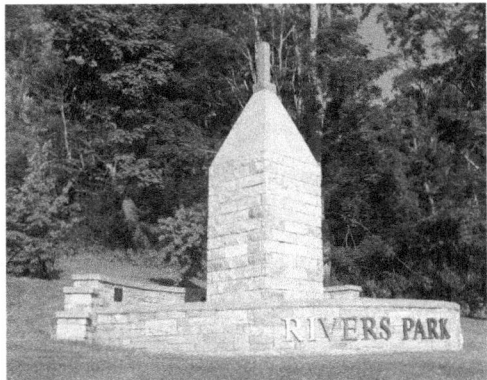

William Bryan's 1912 Boone Cabin Monument, twice moved, but restored in 2005 at Rivers Park in Boone, NC.

Epilogue

to be moved a second time in 1995, it was dismantled.[6] The stones were numbered and placed in storage. When a suitable site could be found, Rivers Park,[7] the near-century-old monument was brought out again and reconstructed as a tribute to Daniel Boone, to William Bryan, and to the citizens of Watauga County who treasure their pioneer heritage.

The Joint DAR Monument

Whatever were the intentions of "the men" who suggested that the "the ladies" build their joint monument in the shape of a pedestal to hold a statue of Daniel Boone and whatever were the efforts these men undertook in that regard, no statue was ever erected. But that does not mean no effort was made by someone. As soon as the fall of 1915, the Kentucky Daughters, at least a few, realized that the responsibility for erecting that statue would fall to "the ladies." Miss Erna Watson, Kentucky's chairman for Daniel Boone's Trail, proposed a means of raising funds for the statue. "The plan was for each chapter to show the motion pictures of the Unveiling of the Joint Marker which I had secured, and give the proceeds to the Boone Statue Fund," she reported in 1916. "A vote was taken and my plan accepted." The movie was purchased at a cost of $25. She continued explaining, however, that after writing to all the Kentucky chapters, most letters went unanswered. Only one chapter participated in the project. "Jemima Johnson [Chapter, Paris] gave an entertainment and used them [the motion pictures] and forwarded to me $16.39 to start the fund. I am hoping that others will take hold of the work this year and help me."[8]

One year later in the fall of 1917, Miss Watson made her report "fully realizing that it is a very poor one," she said, "as there has been practically nothing done during the year." She continued her report suggesting a resolution of the matter aware that since April, America had entered the Great War and the nation's soldiers were then sailing over dangerous waters to fight on foreign soil:

"If it seems best to use the returns from the display of the film for some other more pressing need at this time I make no objection. ... If the sturdy pioneers who made these trails were with us at this time I feel that they would wish our efforts centered on the things that will make the world safe for Liberty, so if it is the desire that the work for the inanimate figure of Boone be dropped while we turn our attention to suffering humanity, you have only to give utterance to the desire."[9]

The National Society, Daughters of the American Revolution, was already deeply involved with supporting relief aid for the citizens of Belgium.

The distractions of a changing world during the 1920s left the pedestal

America's hero of the Great War, Sgt. Alvin C. York, laid a wreath at the DAR's joint monument in Cumberland Gap on June 9, 1925.
from *Mountain Herald*, July 1925
courtesy of *Carnegie-Vincent Library, Lincoln Memorial University*

monument bare. It remained, nevertheless, representative of the pride the nation placed in its pioneer heroes and in the history of its unrelenting progression toward Liberty. Indeed, 10 years after its dedication, another special ceremony took place there in the spring of 1925. During the time of commencement ceremonies for Lincoln Memorial University, the Daniel Boone Post of the American Legion invited celebrated Tennessee war hero Sergeant Alvin C. York[10] to participate in the Pioneer's Day Convocation and to lay a wreath at the DAR monument in Cumberland Gap.[11] The site remained in the minds of many as a symbol of American spirit and patriotism and Alvin York was a living reminder of what these Tennessee mountain folk, the descendants of these early frontiersmen, could do when called upon. But in only a few more years that pride began to fade in the minds of others. To them, the pedestal was just an unfinished monument—conveniently forgetting, as they had, of course, exactly how that came to be its status.

In the closing years of the 1920s, as automobile travel had become more popular and as improved roads had become more prevalent, tourism became a viable and appealing industry for economic growth. Enticing people to visit an area and enabling them to spend their money locally looked to have a promising future. The Cumberland Mountains were attractive and majestic and they were within the railroading and driving reach of a large percentage of the American population. The views from the pinnacle of Cumberland Gap would afford visitors broad, panoramic vistas of three states—of six some claimed. This experience was something community leaders thought they could sell. So it was that plans began in earnest for building a road to the top of the mountain. It went nowhere else. It was a road for tourists—the first of its kind in the country.

Engineers were engaged and plans developed for building the Skyland Highway. The road to the Pinnacle would ascend from the saddle of Cumberland Gap. The gap was crossed and connected to the rest of the country by the Dixie Highway, an improved driving route that ran from Cincinnati to Florida. This Skyland Highway was a project for the region's future, reasoned the powers-that-be, and nothing would interrupt it, certainly not an old, unfinished monument that was

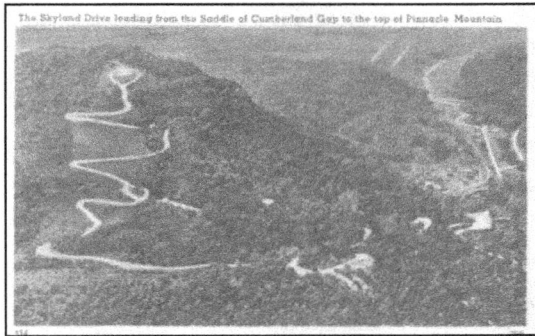

Postcard promoting the Skyland Drive to Pinnacle
Kentucky Historical Society

squarely in the way of the new, grand plans of these men.

The Sky Land Company, Middlesboro, Kentucky, used private capital to build the Pinnacle Loop (Skyland Highway), a toll road, which ascended two miles to what was called a "Garden of Gazes" at Pinnacle Mountain. From there, they declared, visitors could see six states. "If the Empire [State] Building in New York City were situated in Cumberland Gap," they promoted, "it would be 400 feet below the Pinnacle." The advertising included incidental mention in a history of the Gap that Daniel Boone had come through it in 1769 and 1775, but when the sights to be seen on a visit were listed, the writers referred to "the historic marker in Cumberland Gap."[12] Without the Daniel Boone statue on the pedestal, in only a decade and a half some understanding had been lost in the meaning of the DAR's joint marker of 1915.

It is not surprising then that to build the Skyland Highway to the Pinnacle in 1929, the joint monument was relocated to the southwest about 100 feet. (This was 30 years before this area became a national park.) It would be more accurate, however, to say the monument was

Epilogue

The reconstructed and relocated Daniel Boone's Trail joint monument. A new dedication marker for the Skyland Highway stands across the road.

courtesy of *Kentucky Historical Society*

dismantled and reconstructed than just moved. The replacement monument was smaller and not as well made. The 1915 monument was taken down from its site adjacent to the road on the south side of the gap and moved to a spot where it would be out of the way. The original monument was a four-sided pedestal with each trapezoidal side maybe 14 feet at the base and four feet at the top. That original pedestal was well more than six feet high. Each face was constructed of successive courses of rough stone.

The replacement pedestal was built by embedding each plaque into a monument face constructed of flagstone and mortar. Each side was about 12 feet at the base and the pedestal was about the same height. (Some say the original was one-and-half feet taller than the replacement.) In reconstructing the monument, its orientation was changed as well, rotating it about an eighth of a full rotation (i.e., 45 degrees) and changing the order of the plaques. Tennessee had been especially pleased that its plaque faced the road through the gap. In clockwise order from there the plaques were Tennessee, Virginia, Kentucky, and

The reconstructed Daniel Boone's Trail joint monument just before opening day of the Skyland Highway, June 4, 1929.
from *The Cincinnati Enquirer* (Kentucky Edition), May 24, 1929, courtesy of *Cumberland Gap National Historical Park, NPS*

then North Carolina. Afterwards the clockwise order was Tennessee, Kentucky, North Carolina, and then Virginia, whose face then most prominently faced the new improved road.[13]

The Skyland Highway was dedicated on June 4, 1929, with a host of governors, US Senators, and dignitaries invited and many attending. In his address at the opening ceremonies, Gov. Myers Cooper of Ohio offered in his remarks, "Not only do we have here one of America's beauty spots fully adorned by nature, but here is the spirit of the Pioneer, and the spirit of the Patriot to grip and challenge all who love their country while standing on this sacred soil."[14] He and others painted the history of the Cumberland Gap

Men and their cars gathered at Cumberland Gap on June 4, 1929, for the opening of Skyland Highway.
courtesy of *Kentucky Historical Society*

Epilogue
237

Proponents and supporters of the Skyland Highway were joined by governors, senators, and other dignataries at the grand opening. Gov. Flemon Sampson of Kentucky and Gov. Myers Cooper of Ohio are in front row, center.

from *The Story of the Pinnacle*, 1929

with broad brush strokes of general reference, offering no details which would have lent meaning.

For the few hundred years of America's brief history, the mountains had been a barrier to western movement. Passage across by man and beast was restricted to the lowest gaps that could be found. It was ironic perhaps that early in the 20th century, the history of the place thus made famous was then superseded by the spectacle from the height of the mountains themselves. The men cut the ribbon; the crowds dashed to the top of the mountain. In their haste to gratify their senses, they had overlooked the opportunity to consider and to revere the significant.

In time the highway through Cumberland Gap was widened more. With it came more traffic. The monument became a familiar fixture along the roadside. With that familiarity—as human nature too often

A widened road through the Cumberland Gap, c1930s. Inset detail shows DAR monument on hillside behind gasoline station.
courtesy of *Cumberland Gap National Historical Park, NPS*

unfortunately dictates—came disregard and eventually contempt. In time, vandals attacked the monument; stones were dislodged from the mortar. The tablet placed by the North Carolina Society, NSDAR, was broken and shards of it disappeared. A few more decades of inattention and neglect combined with the effects of time and weather on the mortar left a crumbling and nearly forgotten monument at the side of a busy highway. "Daniel who?" the passing motorists might well have asked.

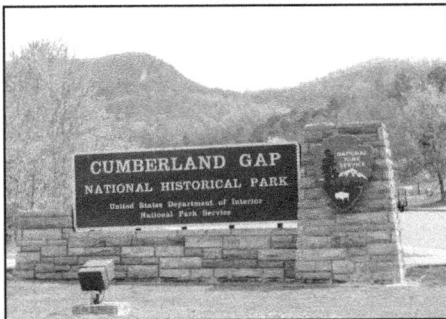

Cumberland Gap National Historical Park was established in 1959.

The Cumberland Gap National Historical Park was formed in 1959. There was much to do in creating and forming the park, so the crumbling monument received little attention for another 40 years. By then, it had been forgotten even by

Epilogue

some in various chapters of the Daughters of the American Revolution. But, these same, sisters to those who had made the trail in 1915, would rally again when called upon to do so.

In 2001, a Tennessee man with Kentucky roots and an interest in local history, included the DAR's joint monument in a research project he was completing for a class at Southeast Kentucky Community and Technical College. James Schenkenfelder of Harrogate, Tennessee, called himself "The Roaming Historian" and was concerned about a handful of local commemorations which he called "forgotten monuments." He used his unpublished paper and his unrelenting commitment to preserve the DAR monument—the one he called, "old friend"—to help rally the interest of others in repairing the marker. Prominent among these were Carol Burkhart of the National Park Service at Cumberland Gap National Historical Park and the State Regents, Daughters of the American Revolution, from Kentucky, Tennessee, North Carolina, and Virginia. Kentucky State Regent Lynda Closson took the lead. Money was raised on the order of $27,000 and repairs were made to the deteriorating 1929 monument.

1929 relocated DAR monument was in need of repairs long before 2004.
courtesy of *Cumberland Gap NH Park, NPS*

The shattered North Carolina tablet was replaced by one which vandals in that state had apparently stolen and then tossed aside. Around 1988, the replacement tablet was found in the town of Boone in a ditch on the campus of Appalachian State

University. It was cracked but repairable. So many of those tablets erected in the area had been taken over time, no one knew which tablet had been found. The Daughters of the Daniel Boone Chapter, Boone, offered it to the restoration project, and it was sent to Cumberland Gap to grace the joint monument.[15] In June 2004, the restored joint DAR monument was rededicated by the Daughters of the American Revolution in a ceremony and program at Cumberland Gap National Historical Park. The program was completed with appropriate pride and celebration 75 years after the joint monument's relocation.[16]

Today, the natural passage Cumberland Gap has been restored as well. The National Park Service removed the highway and rebuilt the landscape to match, it believed, its form at the time of Daniel Boone. Today, the repaired 1929 monument greets those visitors to Cumberland Gap National Historical Park who hike on foot to the saddle of the gap in a manner akin to that of the hundreds of thousands of men, women and children who were venturing west well

Epilogue

more than two centuries ago. A visit to that monument should remind them of the effort made in 1915 to place the original monument in completion of Daniel Boone's Trail and in honor and commemoration of America's pioneer hero and all those who moved westward by this route to build a new America.

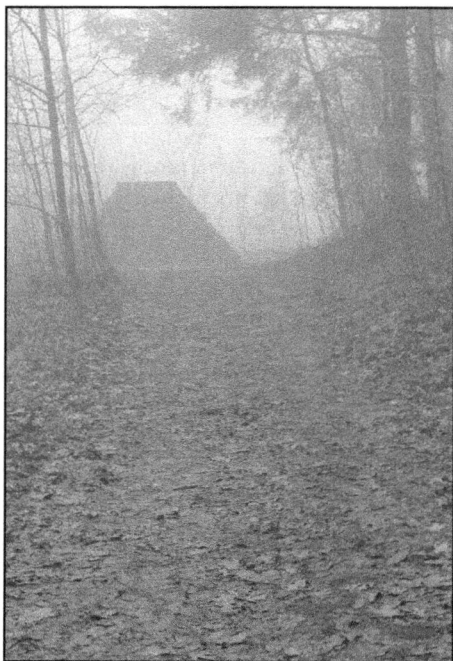

The restored DAR monument stands proudly today at Cumberland Gap, a symbol of America's frontier history and a continuing reminder of the vigilance and effort required to keep heritage and legacy ever-present in the consciousness of the citizenry.

Equal Suffrage

During the time of the marking of Daniel Boone's Trail, women of the United States were striving for equal suffrage—the right to vote and to hold public office. The effort had begun in earnest during the childhood of Mrs. Patterson, when Susan B. Anthony drafted a Constitutional Amendment in 1878. That victory would take another 40 years to be achieved.

Some western states had passed such laws, but for the nation as a whole in the early 20th century, the matter was hotly contested. A march, the "Woman Suffrage Procession," was held in Washington, D.C., in March 1913 and preceded by five weeks the 22nd Continental Congress of the Daughters of the American Revolution. President Wilson was against the women's cause at first, a stance which may have made his speaking before the DAR in 1916 to the 25th Continental Congress a little awkward. But following demonstrations in front of the White House in 1917 (the first cause to do so), and through what influence one might assume First Lady Edith Wilson may have brought to bear, he became a champion of women's right to vote. In fall 1918, he personally spoke before Congress urging the passage of the matter as a war measure. After two successive, failed votes, success came in the spring of 1919 and after the armistice with Germany.

President and First Lady Wilson leave Continental Hall after he addressed the DAR in 1916.

courtesy of *Woodrow Wilson Presidential Library and Museum*

Epilogue

On June 4, 1919, Congress passed the joint resolution to amend the Constitution and the matter was put to the states for ratification. Tennessee enjoyed the honor of being the 36th of the 48 states to ratify the Nineteenth Amendment (although by the narrowest of margins, 50 ayes out of 99 representatives[17]), thus making suffrage for women the law of the land on August 18, 1920, just in time for the elections of 1920.

The Daniel Boone Highway Memorial Association

J. Hampton Rich, of Winston-Salem, had capitalized on the efforts of Mrs. Lindsay Patterson and Mrs. William Neal Reynolds to mark Daniel Boone's Trail by championing the building of a highway along the route they had marked. Mrs. Reynolds had, in fact, been the one to suggest "building a graded highway called the Boone Trail Highway along the heritage trail."[18] Rich helped form the Daniel Boone Highway and Memorial Association in October 1913, intending to promote the investment of state and local money into building better roads into the western mountains of North Carolina. In time, he must have broadened his vision, and he seems to have enjoyed the minor celebrity status he achieved. Soon enough he was crossing the state and then the country drumming up support for the erection of markers in local communities to the legacy of Daniel Boone. He was a showman and a promoter and placed more than a few markers in places that had no historical connection to Daniel Boone at all, including Virginia Beach, Virginia, and at the Golden Gate Bridge in San Francisco. He erected, by some counts, 384 markers. As part of his appeal to patriotism, each tablet contained some metal he had acquired that was salvaged from the *USS Maine*, the ship sunk in Havana Harbor in 1898, at the outset of the Spanish American War.

Everett G. (Gary) Marshall is the authority on the work of Hampton Rich. He wrote *Rich Man: Daniel Boone* and has tracked down over 100 of the markers that remain intact and in place. The Daniel Boone marker near Hanes Park in Winston-Salem, attached to an elegant stone arrowhead, is regarded as the "Mother Marker," although it was not erected until October 29, 1927. The dedication followed a day-long competition in Hanes Park of Boy Scout patrols exhibiting frontiersman skills. The evening ceremony was illuminated by a procession of students from the nearby school, carrying torches.

J. Hampton Rich erected tablets honoring Daniel Boone from 1913 to 1938. Not all are as elaborate as the "Mother Marker" at Hanes Park, Winston-Salem, NC.

Boy Scouts of America

Mrs. Lindsay Patterson, the Daughters of the American Revolution, William L. Bryan, and J. Hampton Rich were not the only persons and groups championing Daniel Boone in the early 20th century. One notable group was the Boy Scouts of America. Scouting began in Great Britain in 1907, founded by Robert Baden-Powell. The organization came to the United States in 1910. When it arrived, the largest boys' organization in the country was the Society of the Sons of Daniel Boone. That group was folded into the Boy Scouts of America and the society's founder, Daniel

Epilogue

Carter Beard, became the first national commissioner of the Boy Scouts of America. In 1914, the BSA published *Scouting with Daniel Boone*, a book which embraced the legacy of Daniel Boone to promote the character traits and skills the BSA supported. In the book's preface, author Everett Tomlinson wrote:

> "There has never been a time when the development of a true patriotism was more needed that it is to-day. Our perils and problems are ... no less dangerous than those which confronted our forefathers. How to meet them, what qualities ought to be strengthened in the life of an American boy, how best to inspire the younger generation with love and devotion for our country, are vital questions for the present. The author believes there is no better way of doing this than by interesting our boys in such heroic men as Daniel Boone."

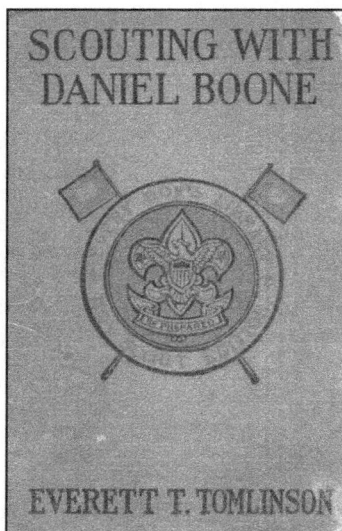

Scouting with Daniel Boone was published in 1914 by the Boy Scouts of America. It was illustrated by a young Norman Rockwell.

The artwork for that 1914 book was drawn by a 20-year-old illustrator just getting started in his career, Norman Rockwell.

"The scout, with his family, returned to Boonesborough"

Mrs. Lindsay Patterson

Mrs. Lindsay Patterson had a history of taking on monumental projects at significant milestones in the history of America. She was equally engaged in social causes of equality, in the advancement of education, and in promoting good literature. So it was that in 1915, and probably even before the ceremony at Cumberland Gap, Mrs. Patterson immersed herself immediately in preparing for the North Carolina observance of the 300th anniversary of the death of William Shakespeare. This national event as observed in North Carolina colleges led to the construction and dedication of an amphitheatre at the University of North Carolina at Chapel Hill. It is known today as Forest Theatre. Her colleague in this endeavor was Archibald Henderson, a professor of mathematics at the University of North Carolina and a noted drama critic. He had helped Mrs. Patterson, of course, in her early work to discover the route of Daniel Boone's Trail. He had provided family papers of Judge Richard Henderson, the man who hired Daniel Boone to mark Boone's Trace in 1775.

After the Great War, the Daughters of the American Revolution took on relief work for a battered Europe. Mrs. Patterson undertook humanitarian work abroad in Belgium, Romania, and Serbia, receiving the Cross of Mercy from King Alexander, the first king of Yugoslavia, and becoming personal friends with Queen Marie of Romania. She travelled extensively, reportedly having been very likely to every country in the world. She was an international figure and one of national note as well, serving in her last years on the Republican National Committee.

Her husband, J. Lindsay Patterson, died in 1922. She retained her home in Winston-Salem, *Bramlette*, but built in Russellville, Tennessee, a summer home that she called *Long Hope Hill*. According to some, the

The deteriorating remanants of "Cavanalee" (also known as "Long Hope Hill"), Mrs. Lindsay Patterson's summer home built in Russellville, Tennessee, in the 1920s. Razed c2010.

courtesy of *Bill Henderson*

house was known also as *Cavanalee,* the name of the birthplace in Tyrone County, Ireland, from which her grandfather Hugh Graham was exiled at age 14.[19] After her death, the house remained in the family but with no inhabitants. During the latter part of the 20th century, "the old Patterson house" became well known as the local "haunted house," the object of dares and other foolishness among the young people in Hamblen County. The house was razed around 2010.

Mrs. Patterson's showcase home, *Bramlette,* burned in the 1930s. At the time, it contained "priceless books, silver, furniture, paintings, china, autographed pictures, rare documents and letters."[20]   That home was on Patterson Avenue at 15th Street. During the time of their great influence on the community, the road name had been changed from Depot Street to Patterson Avenue to honor Mr. and Mrs. J. Lindsay Patterson.

Mrs. Patterson died in 1942, on June 20 at 8 o'clock in the morning in the hospital at Winston-Salem, North Carolina, after a few years of declining health and an illness of five weeks. She was 76. After a local funeral service, the newspaper reported, "... the body [was] placed on the 12:45 p.m. train Sunday for Morristown, Tennessee."[21] She was interred at Bethesda Cemetery in Russellville, her summer home in the Holston River valley amidst the haunts of her Graham and Nenny ancestors, not 40 miles from her birthplace in the Clinch River valley of East Tennessee. It is fitting for the Daughter who marked Daniel Boone's Trail, "the beloved road of her heart's desire," that the road to Bethesda Cemetery runs off Old Kentucky Road.

An obituary which ran in the *Winston-Salem Journal* on June 21, 1942, gave a concise synopsis of this most accomplished woman's engagement with life.

"Mrs. Lindsay Patterson

Few women were more friendly than Mrs. Patterson; few were more versatile in talent, more catholic in interests, tastes, and sympathies. Mrs. Patterson could do many things well, and there were few matters pertaining to social, political, cultural, or economic life in which she did not take a keen and active interest.

"In 'Who's Who' may be found a comprehensive list of the various organizations and movements with which this gifted alumna of Salem College [*sic*, Salem Female Academy] and long-time resident of Winston-Salem was connected.

"But mere listing of her memberships and offices in different civic and cultural organizations does not give an adequate picture of Mrs. Patterson's long life of leadership and service to the people of Winston-Salem, the state and nation. For many years she had been a leader of the Republican party in this state and was a member of the Republican National Committee.

"As a writer whose articles were published in newspapers and magazines over a period of many years, she was equally adept in discussing rural sociology and economy, historical events or fine points of fiction, biography or poetry. For several years one of the best features of *The Progressive Farmer* was the weekly column for women which Mrs. Patterson wrote for the periodical.

"A wide traveler, Mrs. Patterson had a broad background of personal observation and experience. Her interest in social welfare carried her into Serbia after the World War, and she received a decoration at the hands of King Alexander for her notable work there. A few years ago she toured Soviet Russia and wrote a series of intriguing articles on life in that country. Many of these articles were published by *The Journal*.

"As a speaker Mrs. Patterson was much in demand and her lectures were redolent of the spicy flavor which seasoned her writings. Always she was an initiator of progressive movements; a humanitarian who had the common touch; the encourager of all young writers and others who aspired to higher things. Truly here was a woman of rare genius and heroic mold, whose radiant spirit will long remain as a gentle, persuasive influence in the lives it touched, both directly and indirectly."[22]

"… and on the pinnacle
we will carve the name of Mrs. Lindsay Patterson."[23]

**Engraving of Cumberland Gap above, Samuel Valentine Hunt;
artist, Harry Fenn; c1872**

Library of Congress

Epilogue

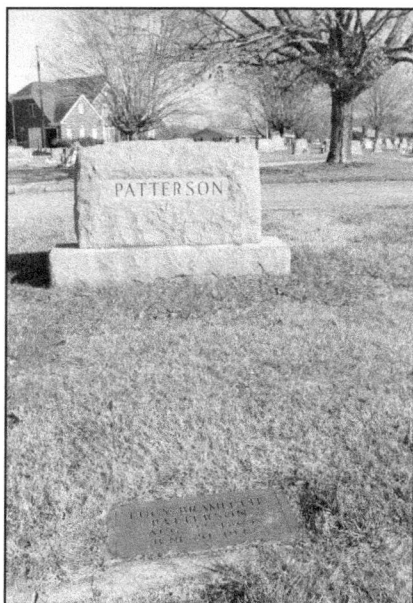

Lucy Bramlette Patterson
August 22, 1865
June 20, 1942
Bethesda Cemetery
Russellville, Tennessee

As Mrs. Lindsay Patterson was laid to rest in Tennessee, that same summer two Kentuckians oversaw the placement of a series of stone markers for Boone Trace in Laurel County on the occasion of Kentucky's Sesquicentennial (1792-1942). In the spirit of what the DAR had accomplished, Russell Dyche and L.B McHargue honored the legacy of Daniel Boone with another marking of his trail.

The legacy endures; the story continues.

Acknowledgements

No book of this detail and scope could possibly be compiled by one person. I was gratified by the willingness of so many people to assist me in finding markers, finding photographs, and finding historical accounts and records. I am grateful to them all. Each has helped to enrich the story by his or her efforts and I thank all for their kindness and assistance to me and for enabling this story to be told much better than it could have been otherwise. Any failings or shortcomings, however, and all errors are mine and mine alone.

I wish to thank (in alphabetical order):

Sue Anderson, State Regent, North Carolina Society, NSDAR, (2010-2012) for her interest in resurrecting the century-old story of the trails marking which began in her state and for inviting me to speak at the North Carolina state conference in advance of the book's publication;

Rebecca Baird, Archivist, Office of the Historian General, NSDAR, for providing during my visit to Memorial Continental Hall guidance and access to the public records of the Daughters of the American Revolution;

Fam Brownlee, Forsyth County Public Library, North Carolina Room, for help in locating *Bramlette*, the home of Mrs. Lindsay Patterson;

Steve Caudill for his continuing service in first-person portrayal of "Daniel Boone of Kentucky" and for the use of his image;

Betsy Burch, Regent, Boonesborough Chapter, Richmond, KY, for her help in accessing the chapter's excellent scrapbook of articles;

Sam Compton, President, Boone Society Inc., for his support in the pursuit of this project to enhance a renewed telling of the broader story of Daniel Boone and the Westward Movement;

Ross Cooper, Reference Librarian, Watauga County Public Library, for help in finding archival photos of the Town of Boone and for their use;

Loretta Cozart, Colonel Frederick Hambright Chapter, Kings Mountain, for her early and continuing support of the effort to recover this story and to engage the broader community of North Carolina Daughters in celebrating their role during the centennial occasion;

Kim Cumber, archivist, North Carolina State Archives, for assistance with the 1905 photograph of President Theodore Roosevelt in Raleigh;

Dana Dorman, Researcher, The Historical Society of Pennsylvania, for locating and supplying the relevant portions of Robert Patterson's 1835 diary;

Margaret Foote, archivist at Eastern Kentucky University, Special Collections, for enumerable kindnesses and assistance in my research both on my behalf beforehand and during my visit to the collection;

Brian Fannon, accomplished scholar and dedicated reenactor, for sharing his master's thesis and knowledge about the original trails through Watauga County, North Carolina;

Tommy Fields, third-generation and childhood resident and local historian, for his personal tour of the ford at Powell River and environs and for sharing his evidence and arguments regarding the site of

James Boone's murder;

Dr. Lawrence Fleenor, historian and author, for his personal tour of Wallens Creek and the Duffield area of southwest Virginia, for his exploration of Scott's Fort, and for his dedication to pursuing the historic details which tell the factual story, and for his tour of Fannon Springs and sharing his evidence and arguments regarding the site of James Boone's murder;

Dr. John Fox, for hospitality and a personal guided tour to specific markers along Boone's Trace through Kentucky and for his enthusiastic dedication to resurrecting public interest in "that little road," and for his leading me to Kentucky's Sesquicentennial markers placed in 1942;

Michelle Ganz, librarian, Carnegie-Vincent Library, Lincoln Memorial University, for sharing her knowledge of the campus's history and for providing archival photographs for use;

Gordon Garrett (as William Calk) and all the reenactors whose period interpretations add volumes to the public's appreciation of history, and for the use of their images;

Ms. B.J. Gooch, librarian, Transylvania University Library, Special Collections, for her pursuit of an image from Hamilton College archives, and image that has made Miss Erna Watson more than a name;

Neal Hammon, Esquire, consummate Kentucky author and celebrated authority, for the kind use of his transcription of the William Caulk Journal.

Terry Harmon, researcher, writer, and Boone descendant, for his 2008 account of the DAR markers in Watauga County, North Carolina;

Bill Henderson, career teacher, local historian and author of Morristown, Tennessee, and the surrounding region, for this encyclopedic knowledge of the Patterson, Graham, and Nenny families, and

Acknowledgements

for his undaunted pursuit of a photo of *Cavanalee*;

Camille Hunt, Museum Registrar, North Carolina Museum of History, for access to the William Houston Patterson Memorial Cup for photographing;

Betsy Kuster for her kindness is escorting me to the Kentucky Society, NSDAR, archives at Duncan Tavern and for her guided tour of the road from Lexington to Paris which by serendipity brought to this book one photograph which would otherwise never have appeared;

Laurel County Public Library research staff for kind assistance during several visits;

Kate Lukach, reference librarian and her volunteer staff at Kingsport Public Library for help in uncovering DAR marker history;

Rev. Gary Marshall, author of *Rich Man:Daniel Boone*, for his help and friendship in several efforts to celebrate Daniel Boone and the Boy Scouts of America.

Kay McKnight, archivist for Salem Academy and College Library, for her interest in the project, for her perusal of historic accounts, and for providing access to the school's public records of the early 20th century;

Sherry Myers, librarian at the Lonesome Pine Regional Library in Lee County, Virginia, for her research help in locating the town of Boone's Path and for providing archival photographs for use;

Scott New for his continuing commitment to educating the public about Kentucky's pioneer era through his first-person portrayal of Daniel Boone and for the use of his image;

Billie Page, resident of Clinchport, Virginia, for sharing her recollections of the Daniel Boone Trail marker attached to the school building;

Molly Grogan Rawls, Forsyth County Public Library Photography Collection and author, for her interest in this project, for introducing me to the legacy of Mrs. Lindsay Patterson, for providing archival images for use, and for contributing images from her personal collection of post cards;

Jay Richiuso, Tennessee State Library and Archives, for securing special remote access to published records on the history of the Tennessee DAR;

Tony Scales, geologist and author of *Natural Tunnel: Nature's Marvel in Stone*, for sharing his intimate knowledge of Natural Tunnel.

James Schenkenfelder, "the Roaming Historian," for sharing his personal research and for his unrelenting pursuit after 2001 to see the DAR joint monument at Cumberland Gap restored and thus removed from his personal list of "Forgotten Monuments";

Tom Shattuck, author of *The Cumberland Gap Area Guidebook*, for providing his book and knowledge of the geology and history of the area;

Sherrod Library research staff, East Tennessee State University, for providing access to their collection of Tennessee newspapers;

Mike Silliman, Chief Forester, Southeastern District, Pineville, Kentucky Division of Forestry, for pointing out and sharing the history of Cumberland Ford at Wasioto;

Herman Tester, volunteer and curator, Butler Museum, for providing archival photos and the story of their DAR marker;

Peggy Troxell, State Regent, North Carolina Society, NSDAR, (2012-2014)for her support of celebrating the centennial anniversary of this historic trail-marking effort, which began in North Carolina;

Harold Wade, resident of Clinchport, Virginia, for sharing information about the location of the "old school";

Acknowledgements

Jessieanne Wells, State Regent, Kentucky Society, NSDAR , for championing the story of Boone's Trace and current efforts to recover that story for the general public, and for inviting me to speak at the Kentucky Society's state conference in advance of the book's publication;

Martha Wiley, historian for Cumberland Gap National Historical Park, for her general support of this project, for research assistance, and for providing archival photographs for publication;

Janet Wooten, eagle-eyed proof reader, champion of proper usage;

All the scholars, writers, and researchers who have compiled histories and accounts, from which I was able to draw to understand the times and the actions of the people in this story, with special appreciation for the work of Dr. William A. Pusey in 1920 to follow the Wilderness Road and note in description and photographs the condition and status of the route within a decade of the Daughters marking Daniel Boone's Trail;

And last and most special, all the Daughters of the early 20th century whose efforts made possible Daniel Boone's Trail and all those who wrote and published detailed accounts of the project, as well as those who later made the effort to document additional information before it slipped away into oblivion.

For those whose assistance and kindnesses are not specifically noted above, I offer you my thanks as well as my apologies. I kept a list because the memory fails me sometimes; and, when the list fails me, I can only rely upon your gracious understanding and forgiveness.

Thank you all.

Notes

Notes from: **Chapter 1 - This Rugged Way**

1 Mary S. Mercer, "Report on Committee on Patriotic Education," *14th Annual State Conference of the NSDAR in North Carolina* (Durham), (Raleigh: NCDAR, 1914), 88-92
2 Mary Speed Mercer was a poet and songwriter of note. Mrs. William. N. Reynolds, State Regent, in her address in Charlotte on Nov. 4, 1913, called her "a gifted writer of our country's songs ... whose 'United' has been around the world with Sousa and whose latest poem, 'Carolina,' you will have the pleasure of hearing at this conference."
3 Mrs. Lindsay Patterson, "Report of Mrs. Lindsay Patterson, chairman Boone Trail Committee," *13th Annual State Conference of the National Society, Daughter of the American Revolution* (Charlotte), (Raleigh: NCDAR, 1913), 40-43

Notes from: **Chapter 2 - This Great and Good Work**

1 Michael C. Hardy, *Short History of Old Watauga County*, (Boone, NC: Parkway Publishers, 2005)
2 Daniel J. Whitener, *History of Watauga County*, 1849-1949, (Boone, NC: unk., 1949)
3 Donna Akers Warmuth, *Boone: Images of America Series*, (Charleston, SC: Arcadia Publ., 2003)
4 Whitener, p. 36
5 W.L. Bryan, "The Daniel Boone Monument," *Watauga Democrat*, Boone, NC, (April 25, 1912)
6 Ad placed by J. Lindsay Patterson, *Watauga Democrat*, Boone, NC, (June 13, 1912)
7 $5: W.L. Bryan, F.A. Linney, B.B. Dougherty; $1: Rev. E.F. Jones, J.J.T. Reece, E.J. Norris, Thos. A. Love, L.L. Critcher, D.J. Cottrell, Wyatt Hayes; $0.50:John Sherrill, W.N. Thomas, Tom Watson, D.N. Coffey, L.W. Gross, A.J. Campbell, T.L. Critcher, R.C. Rivers; $0.25: J.R. Reece, J.W. Smith, Dr. M.F. Greer, Miss Royster Critcher.
8 W.L. Bryan, "The Daniel Boone Monument," *Watauga Democrat*, Boone, NC, (May 30, 1912)
9 W.L. Bryan, "General Notice," *Watauga Democrat*, Boone, NC, (June 20, 1912)
10 W.L. Bryan, "Please Read This," *Watauga Democrat*, Boone, NC, (July 25, 1912)
11 R.C. Rivers, *Watauga Democrat*, Boone, NC, (July 25, 1912): p 3
12 "North Carolina Good Roads Association," *Watauga Democrat*, Boone, NC, (Aug. 22, 1912)
13 W.L. Bryan, "Read This", *Watauga Democrat*, Boone, NC, (Sept 12, 1912)
14 R.C. Rivers, "Watauga County Fair, an editorial," *Watauga Democrat*, Boone, NC, (Oct. 3, 1912)
15 ___ , *Watauga Democrat*, Boone, NC, (Sept 26, 1912)
16 "Col. Roosevelt Shot," *Watauga Democrat*, Boone, NC, (Oct. 17, 1912)
17 "Local News," *Watauga Democrat*, Boone, NC, (Oct. 31, 1912)
18 Email exchange with Bryan family genealogist Randy Bryan, January 28, 2012.
19 Hardy, p. 128

Notes from: **Chapter 3 - Mrs. Lindsay Patterson--Lady Bountiful**

1 John Kivett, "The Grahams of Early Tazewell." *Claiborne Progress*, July 30, 1997, 12A.
2 John Kivett, "The Grahams of Early Tazewell." *Claiborne Progress*, Aug 6, 1997.
3 Patterson was too old to be an effective general at the outset of the War Between the States.

Notes

He was roundly criticized for his inaction at the Battle of Bull Run (a.k.a. First Manassas), but through the intervention on his behalf by President Lincoln, he avoided court martial and retired. – as per Bill Henderson interview.

4 Robert Patterson, *Robert Patterson Diary*, Historical Society of Pennsylvania, Philadelphia, (Am .11150)

5 The tri-state marker is actually about a quarter-mile south from Indian Rock.

6 Mrs. Lindsay Patterson, "Marking Daniel Boone's Trail Through North Carolina," *Daughters of the American Revolution Magazine*, NSDAR, 44, no. 4 (April 1914): 221-4.

7 Bramlette was destroyed by fire. "It contained priceless books, silver, autographed pictures, rare documents and letters." (J.A. Yarbrough, Mrs., "Interesting Carolina People - Mrs. Lindsay Patterson," *Charlotte Observer*, May 4, 1941).

8 "Mrs. Lindsay Patterson," *Winston-Salem Journal*, (June 21, 1942).

9 The first such club, Sorosis, was founded in New York City. The botanical name "Sorosis" means "a collective fruit formed by the union of many flowers." "Federated Women's Club Is Vital Force in North Carolina History," (*Winston-Salem Journal*, May 4, 1941).

10 Adelaide L. Fries, ed., *Records of the Moravians in North Carolina*, (Raleigh: NC Historical Commission, 1943), Vol.VI, p. 2688.

11 "Women's Clubs - National Secretary to Form a State Federation in This City," *Winston-Salem Journal*, (May 21, 1902), p.1.

12 Sallie Southall Cotton, *History of the North Carolina Federation of Women's Clubs*, 1902-1925. (Raleigh: Edwards and Broughton Printing Company, 1925.

13 J.A. Yarbrough, Mrs., "Interesting Carolina People - Mrs. Linday Patterson." *Charlotte Observer*, (May 4, 1941).

14 Algine Neely, "Mrs. Patterson," *State Magazine*, May 1941, p. 10 +.

15 "The S.F.A. Centennial," *Union Republican*. Winston-Salem, NC, May 22, 1902.

16 *The Academy*, Salem Academy and College, Winston-Salem, NC, November 1901

17 *The Academy*, Salem Academy and College, Winston-Salem, NC, (February 1902), p. 2129-30

18 "Something of the Program - Splendid Reception to Mr. Aycock," *Winston-Salem Journal*, (May 21, 1902)

19 Copper King Mansion. http://www.thecopperkingmansion.com/waclark.htm. (accessed Dec. 13, 2011).

20 "Colonel Joseph Winston Chapter History - The First Hundred Years, 1904-2004," Colonel Joseph Winston Chapter, NSDAR, http://www.ncdar.org/ColonelJosephWinstonChapter_files/about_our_chapter.htm, (accessed Dec. 10, 2011)

21 The cup if various described as gold, gold plate, and silver plate. The author personally photographed the cup. If it is gold, it is white gold rather than yellow gold.

22 "Our Lady of Letters." *Sky-Land Magazine*, September 1914: 626-8.

23 E.E. Moffitt, Mrs., "Mrs. Lindsay Patterson." *The North Carolina Booklet*, XII, no. 1 (1912): 162-6.

24 "Patterson Memorial Cup," *Winston-Salem Journal*, October 19, 1905.

25 "Glenn Funeral," *Winston Salem Journal*, October 19, 1905: 1.

26 "President is Greeted by Cheering Thousands," *Winston-Salem Journal*, October 20, 1905: 1. A misreading of this incident has given rise to the incorrect account that President Roosevelt presented the Patterson Cup in its first awarding. He did not.

27 "North Carolina Literary and Historical Awards," http://www.history.ncdcr.gov/affiliates/lit-hist/awards/patterson.htm. (accessed Dec. 10, 2011).

28 E.E. Moffitt, Mrs., "Mrs. Lindsay Patterson." *The North Carolina Booklet*, XII, no. 1 (1912): 162-6.

29 Mrs. Lindsay Patterson, "The Old Patterson Mansion, the Master and His Guests," *Pennsylvania Magazine of History and Biography* (Historical Society of Pennsylvania) 39, no. 1 (1915): p. 81.

30 Ibid., p.86
31 "Union Generals – General Robert Patterson, USA,"
http://www.historycentral.com/bio/UGENS/USAPatterson.html, (accessed Dec. 12, 2011)
32 Mary Hilliard Hinton, "North Carolina Historical Exhibit at the Jamestown Ter-Centennial Exposition," (Raleigh: North Carolina Historical Commission, 1908).
33 "North Carolina Historical Exhibit. Jamestown Ter-centennial Exposition," North Carolina Historical Commission, 1907, (NC Archives: Outer Banks History Center)
34 Mary Hilliard Hinton, "North Carolina Historical Exhibit at the Jamestown Ter-Centennial Exposition," (Raleigh: North Carolina Historical Commission, 1908).
35 Virginia Foundation for the Humanities, "Encyclopedia Virginia: Jamestown Ter-Centennial Exposition of 1907," http://www.encyclopediavirginia.org/Jamestown_Ter-Centennial_Exposition_of_1907, Sept, 23, 2009, (accessed Dec. 10, 2011)
36 Mary Hilliard Hinton, "North Carolina Historical Exhibit at the Jamestown Ter-Centennial Exposition," (Raleigh: North Carolina Historical Commission, 1908).

Notes from: **Chapter 4 - North Carolina--A Long and Weary Hunt**

1 The words to The Old North State were written by N.C. Supreme Court Justice William Gaston in 1835 while living in Raleigh. In 1927, the N.C. Legislature adopted the song as the official state song. [http://digital.ncdcr.gov/u?/p249901coll37,4603]
2 "Proceedings of 12th Annual Sate Conference of the National Society of the DAR in North Carolina," (Asheville: NC Society, DAR, 1912), p. 8-9.
3 Postscript to "Daniel Boone Monument," *Watauga Democrat*, April 25, 1912
4 Local News, *Watauga Democrat*, May 9, 1912
5 See Our Lady of Letters in Chapter 3.
6 Mrs. William Neal Reynolds, "North Carolina State Regent's Report," Proceedings of the 22nd Continental Congress NSDAR. Washington, DC: NSDAR, 1913. 465-6.
7 Kate Bitting Reynolds's husband, always called "Mister Will," served as president of R.J. Reynolds Tobacco Company for six years following the death of founder R.J. Reynolds in 1918.
8 "Marking Daniel Boone's Trail Through North Carolina," *Proceeding of the 13th State Conference of the NSDAR in North Carolina* (Charlotte Nov 4 & 5, 1913) (Raleigh: NC Society, NSDAR, 1913), 40-43.
9 "Address of Mrs. Cummings Story," *Proceedings of 13th State Conference of NSDAR in North Carolina* (Charlotte, Nov 4 & 5, 1913), (Raleigh: NC Society, NSDAR, 1913), 35.
10 "Daniel Boone Memorial," *New York Times*, May 1, 1910
11 "Celebration in Boone [township]," *Lexington Dispatch*, Nov. 3, 1913
12 "Marker Is Unveiled at the Boone Cabin," *Salisbury Evening Post*, November 3, 1913.
13 "Celebration in Boone [township]," *Lexington Dispatch*, Nov. 3, 1913
14 "Marker Is Unveiled at the Boone Cabin," *Salisbury Evening Post*, November 3, 1913.
15 "Marking Daniel Boone's Trail Through North Carolina," *Proceeding of the 13th State Conference of the NSDAR in North Carolina* (Charlotte Nov 4 & 5, 1913) (Raleigh: NC Society, NSDAR, 1913), 40-43.
16 "DAR Meets," *Winston-Salem Journal*, Oct. 5, 1913
17 "Boone Tablet Unveiled in Yadkin County," *Statesville Landmark* repeated in *Lexington Dispatch*, October 22, 1913.
18 "Third Boone Tablet Unveiled Tuesday," *Winston-Salem Journal*, October 30, 1913.
19 "Unveiling of Daniel Boone Trail Marker in Wilkesboro," *Wilkes Patriot*, Nov. 27, 1913, p. 2
20 John Preston Arthur, Western North Carolina, a history. (Raleigh, NC: Edward Buncombe Chapter, DAR, 1914), p 82
21 "Wilkes County Witnesses Largest Flood in its History," *Wilkes Patriot*, July 20, 1916: 1, col. 5 & 6.
22 "Complete Destruction in Wilkesboro Region," *Winston-Salem Journal*, July 21, 1916: 1.

Notes

23 *Wilkes Patriot,* July 27, 1916

24 "Last Boone Marker," *Watauga Democrat,* May 7, 1914: 1.

25 "Boone's Popularity," *Watauga Democrat,* April 30, 1914.

26 "New Marker Marks Original Trail of Boone thru Watauga," *Watauga Democrat,* June 25, 1964.

27 John Preston Arthur, *History of Watauga County,* (Richmond: Everett Waddey Co., 1915): 32

28 Ibid.

29 "Unveiling the Boone Marker," *Watauga Democrat,* October 16, 1913.

30 "Marking the Trail of Boone," *Watauga Democrat* repeated jn *Lexington Dispatch,* Nov. 5, 1913

31 John Preston Arthur, *History of Watauga County,* (Richmond: Everett Waddey Co., 1915): 34

32 Ibid.

33 Ibid., p. 35

34 John Preston Arthur, *History of Watauga County,* (Richmond: Everett Waddey Co., 1915): 32

35 "DAR Historical Marker is Rededicated," *Watauga Democrat,* June 7, 1982.

36 Terry Harmon, "Daniel Boone Days: Marking Boone's Local Trails," *High Country Press,* August 2008.

From John Preston Arthur's *Western North Carolina, a history,* page 80: "If they did this by the easiest and shortest route, they passed up the Shawnee trail on the ridge between Elk and Stony forks through Cooks gap, down by Three Forks of New river, through what is now Boone village and Hodges gap, across the Grave Yard gap down to Dog Skin creek, following the base of Rich mountain to State Line gap between Zionville and Trade to the head of Roan creek to the crossing of the two Indian trails at what is now Shoun's Cross Roads, and thence over the Iron mountains. Any other route would have been deliberately to go wrong for the sake of doing so. From any eminence that route seemed to have been marked out by nature."

37 Terry Harmon, "Daniel Boone Days: Marking Boone's Local Trails," *High Country Press,* August 2008.

38 John Preston Arthur, *Western North Carolina, a history,* (Asheville: Edward Buncombe Chapter, NSDAR, 1914), page 40

39 Brian R. Fannon, "Buffalo Trail: Searching for Lost Landscapes through Historical Geography: a thesis," (Boone: Appalachian State University, 2006).

40 W.L. Bryan, "My Trip to Zionville," *Watauga Democrat,* November 13, 1913.

41 "Boone Trail's History Cited," *Winston-Salem Journal,* February 18, 1932.

42 J. Hampton Rich, "The Boone Trail Highway," *Winston-Salem Journal,* Dec. 14, 1913

43 "November 5th and 6th 'Good Roads Days,'" *Davie Record,* October 22, 1913

44 The errors in writing and spelling may be his or the typesetter's.

45 H.W. Horton, "Boone Trail Highway Association," *Davie Record,* November 12, 1913.

46 "Helen Keller Is Heard By Large Audience Here," *Winston-Salem Journal,* October 7, 1913.

47 Mrs. Lindsay Patterson, "Marking the Daniel Boone Trail in North Carolina," (Washington, D.C.: Daughters of the American Revolution Magazine, April 1914), 221-4.

48 Mrs. W.N. Reynolds, "State Regents Reports - North Carolina." *Proceedings of the 23rd Continental Congress,* NSDAR. Washington, D.C.: NSDAR, 1914. 861-2.

49 John Filson, *The Adventures of Colonel Daniel Boon,* 1784

50 Proceedings of the *14th Annual State Conference of the North Carolina Society,* DAR (Durham), (Raleigh: NC Society, DAR, 1914), p 10

Notes from: **Chapter 5 - Magic City**

1 Robert L. Kincaid, *The Wilderness Road,* (Indianapolis: Bobbs-Merrill Company, 1947), p 318.

2 Charles Dudley Warner, "excerpt from Harper's 1888," in *The Wilderness Road,* by Robert L. Kincaid, (Indianapolis: Bobbs-Merrill Company, 1947), 320.

3 Kincaid, p. 321

4 Kincaid, p. 324

5 Kincaid, p. 338-9

Notes from: **Chapter 6 - Tennessee--Something Worthwhile**

1 Mary Rothrock. *French Broad-Holston Country: A History of Knox County*, Tennessee, (Knoxville: East Tennessee Historical Society, 1972), p. 495

2 Jack Neely, "The Temple House Downtown's Last Single-family House," *Metropulse*, October 19 2006, http://m.metropulse.com/news/2006/oct/19/secret_history-2006-42/, (accessed Dec. 24, 2011).

3 Ossoli Circle is a literary and book club for women organized in Knoxville in 1885 by noted feminist and suffragist Lizzie Crozier French (1851-1926). It was inspired by the Sorosis Woman's Club she visited while studying in New York and named to honor Margaret Fuller (Ossoli) (1810-1850), regarded as "the best read person in New England." [http://www.discoveret.org/ossoli/HISTORY(A).html]

4 "Biography of Mary Boyce Temple," Bonny Kate Chapter, TNDAR, http://www.tndar.org/~bonnykate/templebio.htm (accessed Dec 23, 2011)

5 Jack Neely, "The Temple House Downtown's Last Single-family House," *Metropulse*, October 19 2006, http://m.metropulse.com/news/2006/oct/19/secret_history-2006-42/, (accessed Dec. 24, 2011).

6 Actually the weapons were manufactured by Remington in America and were being shipped by way of Germany for political cover.

7 "Patriotic Daughters," *Knoxville Journal & Tribune*, (April 21, 1914).

8 "First Americans Are Killed at Vera Cruz, Mexico." *Knoxville Journal & Tribune*, (April 22, 1914).

9 "D.A.R. Chapter Holds Election," *Knoxville Journal & Tribune*, (May 15, 1914).

10 "Boone's Trail Now Well Marked," *New York Times*, (August 1, 1915).

11 Kate K. White, *Tennessee State History of the Daughters of the American Revolution*, (Knoxville: S.B. Newman & Co., c.1930), p. 66-8

12 Herman Tester of Butler Museum provided photos and information by email about the DAR marker. Dec. 28, 2011.

13 "Tribute to Daniel Boone Paid at Elizabethton," *Bristol Herald Courier*, (August 16, 1914).

14 Kate K. White, *Tennessee State History of the Daughters of the American Revolution*, (Knoxville: S.B. Newman & Co., c.1930), facing p.73

15 "Watauga," *Bristol Herald Courier*, (August 20, 1914), p.7.

16 "Boone Trail Marker Is Formally Dedicated," *The Comet* (Johnson City, TN), (Aug 13, 1914).

17 Ibid.

18 John Preston Arthur, *History of Watauga County*, (Richmond: Everett Waddey Co., 1915): 40

19 Lawrence J. Fleenor, Jr. and Dale Carter, *Forts of the Holston Militia* (Big Stone Gap. VA: Fleenor, 2004): 9

20 Wm. Allen Pusey, *Wilderness Road to Kentucky: Its Location and Features*, (New York: George H. Doran Co., 1921): 19

21 "Tennessee To Be the Scene of Woman's Suffrage Activities During Next Two Months," *Knoxville Journal & Tribune*, (September 26, 1914).

22 "Good Roads Association," *Knoxville Journal & Tribune*, (October 7, 1914).

23 "Anniversary of Kings Mountain," *Knoxville Journal & Tribune*, (October 8, 1914).

24 "Anniversary of Battle," *Knoxville Journal and Tribune*, (October 9, 1914).

25 Ibid.

26 "Mrs. and Miss Baxter Return" *Knoxville Journal & Tribune*, (September 17, 1914).

27 "State Regent's Address Made Before D.A.R. Conference," *Knoxville Journal and Tribune*, (November 11, 1914): 9.

28 Ibid.

29 Ibid., p.10

30 Mrs. Thomas William Willis, ed., "Excerpts of the Minutes of 9th State Conference of the

Notes

DAR, Knoxville, 1914." *History of the Tennessee Society Daughters of the American Revolution 1892-1990*, Knoxville: Tennessee Society, DAR, n.d.), p. 19.

Notes from: **Chapter 7 - Virginia--Such Rapid and Thorough Work**

1 Mrs. James S. Maupin, "State Reports – Virginia," *Proceedings of the 23rd Continental Congress*, (Washington, DC: National Society, DAR, 1914): 947-8.

2 *Proceedings from 16th Virginia State Conference* (1912, Onancock), (Charlottesville: Michie Company, 1913): 63

3 *Proceedings from 17th Virginia State Conference* (1913, Richmond), (Charlottesville: Michie Company, 1914): 108

4 "Minutes from April 22, 1914 meeting in Washington, DC," *Proceedings from 18th Virginia State Conference* (Alexandria, 1914), (Charlottesville: Michie Company, 1915): 102

5 *Proceedings from 18th Virginia State Conference* (Alexandria, 1914), (Charlottesville: Michie Company, 1915): 16

6"Report of the Daniel Boone Trail Committee," *Proceedings from 18th Virginia State Conference* (Alexandria, 1914), (Charlottesville: Michie Company, 1915):p. 91

7 "Report of Committee on Daniel Boone Trail," *Proceedings from 19th Virginia State Conference* (Staunton, 1915), (Charlottesville: Michie Company, 1916): 72-78

8 Ibid., p. 77

9 Ibid., p. 74

10 Interview Dec. 30, 2011 with Otis Rhotan, former principal of the school at Clinchport.

11 Interview Dec. 28, 2011 with Harold Wade and his sister Billie Page, local residents of Clinchport, VA

12 "Report of Committee on Daniel Boone Trail," *Proceedings from 19th Virginia State Conference* (Staunton, 1915), (Charlottesville: Michie Company, 1916): 76-7

13 On August 1, 1915, the *New York Times* reported, "From Clinchport the trail leads along the water course now known as Stock Creek, around the Natural Tunnel, where the third tablet is placed, and down Purchase Ridge to the little town of Duffield."

14 Local geologist and author Tony Scales shared in a 2012 interview regarding a DAR marker at the tunnel, "I never came across such a reference in my research and having been through the tunnel hundreds of times, have not seen a marker or the remains of where it might have been mounted."

15 Wm. Allen Pusey, *Wilderness Road to Kentucky: Its Location and Features*, (New York: George H. Doran Co., 1921): 101

16 Field trip with local, life-long resident, Dr. Larry Fleenor, March 21, 2012. Dallie (sp?) Tate was the driver of car that hit the DAR marker in the 1950s.

17 "Report of Committee on Daniel Boone Trail," *Proceedings from 19th Virginia State Conference* (Staunton, 1915), (Charlottesville: Michie Company, 1916): 75

18 With the store was a cabin which was built, reportedly, from the logs that comprised Scott's Fort. In the 1990s, that cabin was purchased and moved to Kingsport, TN, where it stands today as part of the exhibits at the Netherland Inn, serving as the Children's Museum. Some claim that Daniel and Rebecca Boone lived in that cabin for a time after the murder of their son, James, along Wallen Creek in October 1773. Dr. Larry Fleenor has looked at the cabin and observed that the logs are from second growth trees; moreover, he notes that the construction techniques used on that cabin are typical of post-1820 practices. March 27, 2012 email.

19 20"Report of the Daniel Boone Trail Committee," *Proceedings from 18th Virginia State Conference* (Alexandria, 1914), (Charlottesville: Michie Company, 1915):p. 91

21 "Report of Committee on Daniel Boone Trail," *Proceedings from 19th Virginia State Conference* (Staunton, 1915), (Charlottesville: Michie Company, 1916): 75

22 Ibid,

TRAILING DANIEL BOONE

23 It is beyond the scope of this book to explore the issue of where James Boone was killed. However, the author enjoyed exploring the issue with local historians and gained such grateful appreciation for the depth of analysis applied to the matter by those engaged in it arguing their positions. Dr. Larry Fleenor favors Fannon Springs along Wallen Creek a few miles southwest of Stickleyville. A third-generation resident of the 30 miles farther southwest, Tommy Fields, argues convincingly for the ford over Powell River where Wallen Creek flows in. Dr. William Allen Pusey, in The Wilderness Road to Kentucky (1921), also offered accounts and arguments in support of a location closer to Stickleyville. (Wm. Allen Pusey, Wilderness Road to Kentucky: Its Location and Features, (New York: George H. Doran Co., 1921): 108n) Most parties agree that no commemorative marker currently sits at either of the two most credible sites. Accordingly, no marker is exactly correct, thus any marker that commemorates James Boone and Henry Russell's death is an appropriate place to reflect on their lives and experiences.

24 "Mrs. Patterson's Letter," Proceedings from 18th Virginia State Conference (Alexandria, 1914), (Charlottesville: Michie Company, 1915): 98

25 "Minutes of the State Meeting of the Virginia D.A.R. in Washington, Tuesday, April 20, 1905 [sic]", Proceedings from 19th Virginia State Conference (Staunton, 1915), (Charlottesville: Michie Company, 1916): 20

26 Ibid.

27 Ibid., p. 21

28 Erroll Morris, "Anosognosic's Dilemma: Something's Wrong but You'll Never Know What It Is (Part 3)," Opinionator, June 22, 2010, http://opinionator.blogs.nytimes.com/2010/06/22/the-anosognosics-dilemma-somethings-wrong-but-youll-never-know-what-it-is-part-3/, (Accessed March 4, 2012).

29 "Edith Boling Galt Wilson," Wikipedia, http://en.wikipedia.org/wiki/Edith_Bolling_Galt_Wilson, (accessed Dec. 27, 2011).

Notes from: **Chapter 8- One Man's Journey--Everyman's Dream**

1 Excerpts from the journal of William Calk also appear in The Wilderness Road to Kentucky by William Pusey, 1921, page 41-49.

Notes from: **Chapter 9 - Kentucky--The Real Boone Trail**

1 Report of Boone Trail Committee, 1912 Year Book, (Lexington: Kentucky Society, NSDAR, 1912): 21-22

2 Member 88598, "Supplement Directory, NSDAR," (Washington, D.C., NSDAR, 1911)

3 "Monument Unveiled Where Boone Entered Kentucky," Lexington Leader, (June 30, 1915).

4 Erna Berry Watson curriculum vitae, Crimson Year Book, (Lexington: Hamilton College, 1916): 179

5 Ida Shaw Martin, Sorority Handbook, (unk,: Rorburgh Press, 1909): 67

6 Ibid.

7 Report of Boone's Trail Committee, 1913 Year Book, (Lexington: Kentucky Society, NSDAR, 1913): 60-61

8 Ibid.

9 "State Regents' Reports – Kentucky," Proceedings from the 23rd Continental Congress, (Washington, D.C., NSDAR, 1914): 699

10 Karl Raitz, "Kentucky's Frontier Trails: Warrior's Path, Boone's Trace, and Wilderness Road," (a map), (Lexington: University of Kentucky, 2008)

11 "I have written 80 letters which resulted in the following pledges: St. Asaph, $10.00; Bryan Station, $20.00; Fort Jefferson, $10.00; General Samuel Hopkins, $5.00; Lexington, $20.00; Big Spring, $20.00; Jemima Johnson, $20.00; General Evan Shelby, $20.00; Susannah Hart Shelby, $10.00; Hart, $20.00; Fincastle, $20.00; John Fitch, $20.00; Henry Claggett, $20.00; Israel

Notes

Putnam, $2.00; Frankfort, $5.00. Total $222.00."

12 Report of Boone's Trail Committee, *1915 Year Book*, (Lexington: Kentucky Society, NSDAR, 1915) 59-60; Miss Watson's report for 1914 apparently appears in the 1915 Year Book. No copy of the 1914 Year Book has been found.

13 Ibid.

14 "State Regent's Reports – Kentucky," *Proceedings of the 24th Continental Congress*, NSDAR, (Washington, D.C., NSDAR, 1915): 611

15 "Boone's Trail Now Well Marked," *New York Times*, (August 1, 1915).

16 The writer may be referring to a rock atop Pine Mountain 13 miles away, which would have been more useful as a "signal tower."

17 "Boone's Trail Now Well Marked," *New York Times*, (August 1, 1915).

18 Robert Patterson, *Robert Patterson Diary*, Historical Society of Pennsylvania, Philadelphia, (Am .11150)

19 Robert L. Kincaid, *The Wilderness Road*. (Indianapolis: Bobbs-Merrill Company, 1947), p 351.

20 Ibid., p. 353-4

21 "Monument Unveiled Where Boone Entered Kentucky," *Lexington Leader*, (June 30, 1915).

22 Wm. Allen Pusey, *Wilderness Road to Kentucky*: Its Location and Features, (New York: George H. Doran Co., 1921): 121

23 Robert Patterson, *Robert Patterson Diary*, Historical Society of Pennsylvania, Philadelphia, (Am .11150), p. 22-3

24 John D. Barnhart, ed., "Henry Hamilton and George Rogers Clark in the American Revolution with The Unpublished Journal of Lieut. Gov. Henry Hamilton," (Crawfordsville, IN: R.E. Banta, 1951)

25 "Monument Unveiled Where Boone Entered Kentucky," *Lexington Leader*, (June 30, 1915).

26 Robert M. Addington, *History of Scott County, Virginia*, (1932) (Johnson City, TN: Overmountain Press, reprint 1992): 27-8

27 Ibid.

28 Russell Dyche, "Boone Way" Was First Highway Effort," *History of Laurel County*, (London, KY: Laurel County Public Library, n.d.): 196

29 "Society of the Wilderness," *London Sentinel*, December 12, 1907.

30 "Monument Unveiled Where Boone Entered Kentucky," *Lexington Leader*, (June 30, 1915).

31 "Monument Unveiled Where Boone Entered Kentucky," *Lexington Leader*, (June 30, 1915).

32 Robert Patterson, *Robert Patterson Diary*, Historical Society of Pennsylvania, Philadelphia, (Am .11150), p. 23

33 "Monument Unveiled Where Boone Entered Kentucky," *Lexington Leader*, (June 30, 1915).

34 "Monument Unveiled Where Boone Entered Kentucky," *Lexington Leader*, (June 30, 1915).

35 J.M. Scoville, "Program," *Mountain Echo*, (May 18, 1915).

36 "by Judge W.L. Brown, Col. R.R. Perry, of Winchester, Judge Sam Hardin, Judge Wm. Lewis, and Messrs. A.R. Dyche [publisher, *Mountain Echo*], Allan Pennington, and C.L. Luker."

37 "The First Boone Trail Marker – Unveiled at Mt. Carmel Saturday," *Mountain Echo*, (June 15, 1915)

38 "First Boone Trail Marker," *Mountain Echo*, (June 8, 1915)

39 "Boone Trail Marker unveiled on farm of Philip T. Alin on October 23," *Louisville Courier-Journal* (?) repeated in *Mountain Echo*, Oct. 26, 1915.

40 "Monument Unveiled Where Boone Entered Kentucky," *Lexington Leader*, (June 30, 1915).

41 "Monument Unveiled Where Boone Entered Kentucky," *Lexington Leader*, (June 30, 1915).

42 "Monument Unveiled Where Boone Entered Kentucky," *Lexington Leader*, (June 30, 1915).

43 "Monument Unveiled Where Boone Entered Kentucky," *Lexington Leader*, (June 30, 1915).

44 "Monument Unveiled Where Boone Entered Kentucky," *Lexington Leader*, (June 30, 1915).

45 "Home Again, All Kentucky's Exhibits Back from Jamestown," *Courier-Journal* (Louisville), December 9, 1907, p. 2

46 *Citizen* (Berea), June 6, 1907

47 *Courier-Journal* (Louisville), October 6, 1907

48 *Interior Journal*, (Stanford, KY), June 28, 1907

49 "State Regents' Reports – Kentucky," *Proceedings from the 23rd Continental Congress*, (Washington, D.C., NSDAR, 1914): 700

Notes from: **Chapter 10 - The Celebration--Four States Have Put Three in Love**

1 "Local News," *Watauga Democrat*, (July 1, 1915).

2 "Boone Monument," *Three States*, Middlesboro, KY, (June 8,1915).

3 "Everybody Going to the Boone Pedestal Dedication," *Three States*, Middlesboro, KY, (June 29, 1915).

4 "Boone Trail Celebration June 30," *The Pinnacle News*, (June 24, 1915).

5 "Calendar of Coming Events," *Three States*, Middlesboro, KY, (May 28, 1915).

6 "Boone's Trail Now Well Marked," *New York Times*, (Aug. 1, 1915).

7 "Boone Trail Monument Unveiled," *The Pinnacle News*, (July 1, 1915).

8 T.B. Ford, ed., "Boone Pedestal Dedicated," *Mountain Herald*, Harrogate, TN, xviii, 6, (June/July, 1915)

9 The text transcribed into the record, perhaps jumbled from her intent, reads: "Cumberland Gap, where Tennessee, Virginia, Kentucky and North Carolina come together, is not so far away. And it is a wonderful place."

10 Mrs. Lindsay Patterson, *15th State Conference of the North Carolina Society*, NSDAR, (Waynesville, 1915), (Raleigh: NCDAR, 1915): 58-60.

11 Ibid.

12 Ibid.

13 Mrs. Thomas William Willis, ed., "Excerpts of the Minutes of 10th State Conference D.A.R, - November 3,4,5, 1915, Chattanooga," *History of the Tennessee Society Daughters of the American Revolution 1892-1990*, Knoxville: Tennessee Society, DAR, n.d.): 20.

14 Mrs. Margaret White Baxter, "State Regents' Reports – Tennessee," *Proceedings of the 24th Continental Congress of DAR*, (Washington, D.C.: NSDAR, 1915): 877

15 "History of Bonny Kate Chapter, DAR," (2007), <http://www.tndar.org/~bonnykate/chapterhistory.htm>, (accessed Dec. 24, 2011)

16 Mrs. Bacon Moore, Burchett, and Wooten, *History of the Kentucky Society Daughters of the American Revolution*, (Frankfort: Hulette Printing Co., 1966): 21-2

17 "Monument Unveiled Where Boone Entered Kentucky," *Lexington Leader*, (June 30, 1915).

18 Ibid.

19 Ibid.

20 Hester Bryant Glore, "State Regents' Reports, Kentucky," *Proceedings of the 25th Continental Congress*, NSDAR, (Washington, D.C.: NSDAR, 1916):523.

21 Mrs. Glore was state regent for 1914-1915. *History of DAR in Kentucky, 1890-1929* by Anna Dickson Roe-Keith, ed., 1929 says on page 32, "No report could be secured of her administration."

22 The Panama-California Exposition ran from March 1915 through December 1916 to celebrate the opening of the Panama Canal in August 1914 and to promote San Diego as the first port of call for ships passing through the canal east to west.

23 Elizabeth Preston Gray, "Report of Committee on Daniel Boone Trail." *19th Virginia State Conference*, DAR. (Staunton, VA, 1915), (Charlottesville: Michie Company, 1916): 72-78

24 Ibid.

25 Mrs. Edmonia Maupin, "Viriginia State Regent's Report," *Proceedings of the 25th Continental Congress of the DAR, April 17-22, (Washington, D.C.: NSDAR, 1916): 791.*

26 *Eliza*beth Preston Gray, "Report of Committee on Daniel Boone Trail." *19th Virginia State Conference*, DAR. (Staunton, VA, 1915), (Charlottesville: Michie Company, 1916): 72-78

Notes

pages 225 - 251

Notes from: **Chapter 11 – Epilogue**

1 John P. Arthur, "Address of John P. Arthur at the Masonic Picnic Held in Boone Saturday, August 14," *Watauga Democrat*, (Aug. 26, 1915).
2 John Preston Arthur, *History of Watauga County*, (Richmond: Everett Waddey Co., 1915): 35
3 John Preston Arthur, *History of Watauga County*, (Richmond: Everett Waddey Co., 1915):36-37
4 United States Congress, House, 76th Congress, 1st session, April 26, 1939, House Joint Resolution 276.
5 Vivien Green Fryd, "Two Sculptures for the Capitol: Horatio Greenough's 'Rescue' and Luigi Persico's 'Discovery of America'" *American Art Journal*, Vol. 19, No. 2 (Spring, 1987); http://en.wikipedia.org/wiki/The_Rescue (statue)
6 "University plans moving monument of Daniel Boone; erecting sculpture," *Herald-Journal*, Spartanburg, SC, (Dec. 5, 1994), p. B5
7 Rivers Park was the home site of Rachel Rivers Coffey (1943-1999), donated in 2000 to the town for historical purposes.
8 "Report of Boone's Trail Committee," *1916 Year Book*, (Lexington: KSDAR, 1916): 91
9 "Boone's Trail," *1917 Year Book*, (Lexington, KSDAR, 1917): 80-81
10 Distinguished Service Cross and Medal of Honor
11 "The Visit of a True Patriot," *Mountain Herald*, Lincoln Memorial University, (July, 1925): 9, 11,15
12 *The Story of the Pinnacle*, (Middlesboro: Sky Land Company, 1929)
13 James W. Schenkenfelder, "Forgotten Monuments," Appalachian Seminar, Southeast Kentucky Community College, 2001
14 *The Story of the Pinnacle*, (Middlesboro: Sky Land Company, 1929)
15 Terry Harmon, "Daniel Boone Days: Marking Boone's Local Trails," *High Country Press*, August 2008.
16 "DAR to dedicate park monument," *Daily News*, Middleboro, KY, (June 12, 2004).
17 Carroll Van West, (ed.) "Woman Suffrage Movement," *Tennessee Encyclopedia of History and Culture*. Thomas Nelson, 1998.
18 H.W. Horton, "Boone Trail Highway Association," *Davie Record*, (November 12, 1913)
19 "A Brief History of Speedwell Manor (Formerly Castle Rock of Tazewell, TN." Claiborne County Public Library, Tazewell, TN ,n.d.).
20 J.A. Yarbrough, Mrs., "Interesting Carolina People - Mrs. Lindsay Patterson," *Charlotte Observer*, (May 4, 1941).
21 "Mrs. Lindsay Patterson," *Winston-Salem Journal*, (June 21, 1942).
22 Ibid.
23 Mary S. Mercer, "Report on Committee on Patriotic Education," *14th Annual State Conference of the NSDAR in North Carolina* (Durham), (Raleigh: NCDAR, 1914), 88-92

Bibliography

Books

_____. Supplement Directory, NSDAR. Washington, D.C., NSDAR, 1911.

_____. *The Story of the Pinnacle*. Middlesboro, Sky Land Company, 1929.

Addington, Robert M. *History of Scott County, Virginia*. Johnson City, TN: reprint 1992, Overmountain Press, 1932.

Arthur, John Preston. *History of Watauga County*. Richmond: Everett Waddey Co., 1915.

Arthur, John Preston. *Western North Carolina, a history*. Raleigh, NC: Edward Buncombe Chapter, DAR, 1914.

Cotten, Sallie Southall. *History of the North Carolina Federationof Women's Clubs, 1902-1925*. Raleigh: Edwards and Broughton Printing Company, 1925.

Dyche, Russell. *History of Laurel County*, (London, KY: Laurel County Public Library, various dates)

Fannon, Brian R. "Buffalo Trail: Searching for Lost Landscapes through Historical Geography: a thesis." Boone, NC, Appalachian State University, 2006.

Filson, John. *The Adventures of Colonel Daniel Boon*, 1784

Fleenor, Jr., Lawrence J., and Dale Carter. *Forts of the Holston Militia*. Big Stone Gap Publishing, Big Stone Gap, VA, 2004.

Fries, Adelaide L., ed., *Records of the Moravians in North Carolina*, (Raleigh: NC Historical Commission, 1943)

Hamilton, Henry. *Henry Hamilton and George Rogers Clark in the American Revolution with The Unpublished Journal of Lieut. Gov. Henry Hamilton*. Edited by John D. Barnhart. Crawfordsville, Indiana: R. E. Banta, 1951.

Hardy, Michael C. *A Short History of Old Watauga County*, Boone, NC: Parkway Publishers, 2005.

Hinton, Mary Hilliard. *North Carolina Historical Exhibit at the Jamestown Ter-Centennial Exposition*. Raleigh: North Carolina Historical Commission, 1908.

Kincaid, Robert L. *The Wilderness Road*. Indianapolis: Bobbs-Merrill Company, 1947.

Marshall, Everett G. *Rich Man: Daniel Boone*, Dugspur, VA: Sugartree Enterprises, 2003.

Martin, Ida Shaw. *Sorority Handbook*, unk,: Rorburgh Press, 1909.

Moffitt, Mrs. E.E. "Mrs. Lindsay Patterson." *The North Carolina Booklet* XII, no. 1 (1912): 162-6.

Moore, Mrs. Bacon, Mrs. Thomas Burchett, and Mrs. Bailey Wooten. *History o f the Kentucky Society Daughters of the American Revolution*. (Frankfort: Hulette Printing Co., 1966).

North Carolina Commission, "North Carolina Historical Exhibit, Jamestown Ter-centennial Exposition, 1907," Raleigh, 1907.

Pusey, William Allen. *The Wilderness Road to Kentucky: Its Location and Features*. New York: George H. Doran Co., 1921.

Roe-Keith , Anna Dickson, ed. *History of DAR in Kentucky, 1890-1929*. KSDAR, 1929

Rothrock, Mary. French Broad-Holston Country: A History of Knox County, Tennessee. Knoxville: East Tennessee Historical Society, 1972.

Schenkenfelder, James W. *Forgotten Monuments.* Appalachian Seminar, Southeast Kentucky
    Community College, 2001
Whitener, Daniel J. *History of Watauga County, 1849-1949.* Boone: unk, 1949.
Warmuth, Donna Akers. *Boone: Images of America Series.* Charleston, SC: Arcadia Publishing,
    2003.

Periodicals

*The Academy.*Salem Academy and College. Salem, NC.
Bristol Herald Courier, Bristol, TN
Charlotte Observer, Charlottte, NC
The Citizen, Berea, KY
Claiborne Progress, Tazewell, TN
The Comet, Johnson City, TN
Courier-Journal, Louisville, KY
Crimson Year Book, Hamilton College, Lexington, KY,
Daughters of the American Revolution Magazine, NSDAR, Washington, DC, 1914
Davie Record, Mocksville, NC
High Country Press, Boone, NC
Interior Journal, Stanford, KY
Knoxville Journal & Tribune, Knoxville, TN
Lexington Dispatch, Lexington, NC
Lexington Leader, Lexington, KY
London Sentinel, London, KY
New York Times, New York City, NY
Mountain Echo, London, KY
Mountain Herald, Lincoln Memorial University, Harrogate, TN
Pennsylvania Magazine of History and Biography. Historical Society of Pennsylvania, Philadelphia,
    1915
The Pinnacle News, Middlesboro, KY
Salisbury Evening Post, Salisbury, NC
Sky-Land Magazine, unk. 1914
State Magazine, Charlotte, NC
Three States, Middlesboro, KY
Union Republican, Winston-Salem, NC
Wilkes Patriot, Wilkesboro, NC
Winston Salem Journal, Winston-Salem, NC
Watauga Democrat, Boone, NC

DAR Proceedings
National Society, DAR
Proceedings of the 22nd Continental Congress NSDAR. Washington, DC: NSDAR, 1913.
Proceedings of the 23rd Continental Congress, NSDAR. Washington, DC: NSDAR, 1914.
Proceedings of the 24th Continental Congress, NSDAR. Washington, DC: NSDAR, 1915.
Proceedings of the 25th Continental Congress, NSDAR. Washington, DC: NSDAR, 1916.

North Carolina Society
*12th Annual Sate Conference of the National Society, Daughters of the American Revolution in North
Carolina,* Asheville: (Raleigh: NCDAR, 1912)
13th Annual State Conference of the National Society, Daughters of the American Revolution in North

Carolina, Charlotte, (Raleigh: NCDAR, 1913)

14th Annual State Conference of the National Society, Daughters of the American Revolution in North Carolina, Durham, (Raleigh: NCDAR, 1914)

15th Annual State Conference of the National Society, Daughters of the American Revolution in North Carolina, Waynesville (Raleigh: NCDAR, 1915)

Tennessee Society

Mrs. Thomas William Willis, ed., *History of the Tennessee Society Daughters of the American Revolution 1892-1990*, TN DAR.

White, Kate K. *Tennessee State History of the Daughters of the American Revolution*. (Knoxville: S.B. Newman & Co., c.1930).

Virginia Society

Proceedings of 16th Virginia State Conference (1912, Onancock). Charlottesville: Michie Company, 1913.

Proceedings from 17th Virginia State Conference (1913, Richmond). (Charlottesville: Michie Company, 1914.

Proceedings of 18th Virginia State Conference (1914, Alexandria). Charlottesville: Michie Company, 1915.

Proceedings of 19th Virginia State Conference (1915, Staunton). Charlottesville: Michie Company, 1916.

Kentucky Society

1912 Year Book. Lexington: Kentucky Society, NSDAR, 1912

1913 Year Book. *Lexington:* Kentucky Society, NSDAR. 1913

(No *1914 Year Book* could be located and probably was not published.)

1915 Year Book. *Lexington:* Kentucky Society, NSDAR. 1915

1916 Year Book. *Lexington:* Kentucky Society, NSDAR. 1916

1917 Year Book. Lexington: Kentucky Society, NSDAR. 1917

Online

Copper King Mansion. http://www.thecopperkingmansion.com/waclark.htm (accessed 12 13, 2011).

Humanities, Virginia Foundation for the. *Encyclopedia Virginia: Jamestown Ter-Centennial Exposition of 1907*. September 23, 2009. http://www.encyclopediavirginia.org/Jamestown_Ter-Centennial_Exposition_of_1907 (accessed December 10, 2011).

NC Literary and Historical Awards. http://www.history.ncdcr.gov/affiliates/lit-hist/awards/patterson.htm (accessed 12 10, 2011).

Union Generals - General Robert Patterson, USA. http://www.historycentral.com/bio/UGENS/USAPatterson.html (accessed 12 12, 2011).

Bonny Kate Chapter, TN DAR. Biography of Mary Boyce Temple. http://www.tndar.org/~bonnykate/templebio.htm (accessed 12 23, 2011).

Bonny Kate Chapter, TN DAR. History of Bonny Kate Chapter DAR. 2007. http://www.tndar.org/~bonnykate/chapterhistory.htm (accessed 12 24, 2011).

Neely, Jack. The Temple House - Downtown's Last Single-family Home. October 19, 2006. http://m.metropulse.com/news/2006/oct/19/secret_history-2006-42/ (accessed 12 24, 2011).

Bibliography

Trent, Kim. Mary Boyce Temple House. 07 12, 2009.
http://blogs.metropulse.com/saving_places/2009/07/mary-boyce-temple-house.html
(accessed 12 24, 2011).

Dedman, Bill. *At 104, the mysterious heiress Huguette Clark is alone now* . 9 8, 2010.
http://www.msnbc.msn.com/id/38719231/ns/business-small_business/#.TujhvXrfVxo
(accessed 12 14, 2011).

O.L. Brown, Rev. "John Preston Arthur Early Day Scholar, Boone Resident Historian: Plagued
By Loneliness." http://toto.lib.unca.edu/findingaids/mss/moore/john_preston_arthur.htm
(accessed Feb. 12, 2012).

"Colonel Joseph Winston Chapter History - The First Hundred Years, 1904-2004," Colonel
Joseph Winston Chapter, NSDAR,
http://www.ncdar.org/ColonelJosephWinstonChapter_files/about_our_chapter.htm, (accessed
Dec. 10, 2011)

Erroll Morris, "Anosognosic's Dilemma: Something's Wrong but You'll Never Know What It
Is (Part 3)," Opinionator, June 22, 2010,
http://opinionator.blogs.nytimes.com/2010/06/22/the-anosognosics-dilemma-somethings-
wrong-but-youll-never-know-what-it-is-part-3/, (Accessed March 4, 2012).

"Edith Boling Galt Wilson," Wikipedia,
http://en.wikipedia.org/wiki/Edith_Bolling_Galt_Wilson, (accessed Dec. 27, 2011).

Vivien Green Fryd, "Two Sculptures for the Capitol: Horatio Greenough's 'Rescue' and Luigi
Persico's 'Discovery of America'" *American Art Journal*, Vol. 19, No. 2 (Spring, 1987);
http://en.wikipedia.org/wiki/The_Rescue (statue)

Other

Patterson, Robert. *Robert Patterson Diary*, Historical Society of Pennsylvania, Philadelphia, (Am
.11150), 1835

Raitz, Karl. Kentucky's Frontier Trails: Warrior's Path, Boone's Trace, and Wilderness Road.
map, Lexington: University of Kentucky, 2008.

Interviews

Page, Billie interviewed by phone by author. Local resident. December 28, 2011.

Rhotan, Otis, interviewed by phone by author. Former principal of Clinchport school.
December 30, 2011.

Wade, Harold interviewed in-person by author. Local resident and brother to Billie Page.
December 28, 2011.

Index

Index

General Fed. of Women's Clubs, 31-2, 38
General Fed. of Woman's Clubs of TN, 104
Gen. Joseph Winston Chapter, (see Col. Joseph Winston Chapter)
General William Davidson Chapter, Lexington, 59
Gist, Christopher, 69
Gist, Nathaniel, 20, 69
Glenn, General James Dodge, 41
Glenn, Gov. Robert B., 40, 42
Glore, Kentucky State Regent Mrs. Scott (Hester Bryant), 124-5, 151, 172, 177, 216-7
Graham, (General) Hugh, 24-7, 44, 176, 248
Graham, Catherine (Nenny), 25, 26
Grant, Ulysses S., 26
Graveyard Gap, (*see* Straddle Gap)
Gray, John M. Preston, 219
Gray, Mrs. Robert (Elizabeth Preston), 130-147, 151, 217-221
Great Bridge Chapter (VA), 131
Great War (World War I), 125, 182, 233, 247
Great White Fleet, 17, 48,
Green, Richard, 72
Greene, General Nathanael, 62
Greenhough, Horatio, 228
Greer, Cicero, 82
Guernsey, Mrs., (of Kansas), 220

Hamilton, (Brit.) Colonel Henry, 181
Hamilton College, 166
Hammon, Neal, 158
Hanes, P.H., 83
Harrogate (TN), 99, 240
Hart Chapter, Winchester, 197
Hazel Patch (KY), 162, 168, 189, 192
Henderson, Archibald, 42, 56, 65, 247
Henderson, Judge Richard, 56, 91, 113, 133, 156, 158, 247
Hendren, F.B., 67
Henry Claggett Chapter, Shelbyville, 186
Hinton, Miss Mary Hilliard, 48-9
Historic Boone Tavern Hotel, 197
Hodge's Gap, 76, 79-83
Holman's Ford, 58, 69, 71, 80
Holston River, 91, 120, 122, 133, 249
Home Moravian Church, 34
Horton, H.W., 85
Hunfleet, Arthur, 173, 186
Huntsville (NC), 64-5, 85

Indian Creek (VA), 148, 159
Indian Rock, 173, 174-7

Irving, Washington, 219

Jamestown Historical Commission, 45
Jamestown Ter-Centennial Exposition, 45, 48, 199
Jarvis's Store, 173, 185
Jeffrey, Emily, 219
Jemima Johnson Chapter, Paris (KY), 189, 232
John Carter Chapter, Elizabethton, 112-3
John Fitch Chapter, Bardstown, 185
John Marshall Chapter, Louisville, 171, 192
John Sevier Chapter, Johnson City, 114, 117
Johnson City (TN), 115, 117
Jonesville (VA), 143-4

Kane's Gap, 139-142
Keller, Helen, 87
Kelly Tavern, 64-5
Kentucky Good Roads Association, 177
Kentucky River, 157, 158, 163, 195, 198
Kentucky state conference, NSDAR, 1912, 165-6
Kentucky state conference, NSDAR, 1913, 167-9
Kentucky state conference, NSDAR, 1914, 171-2
Kentucky state conferences, NSDAR, 1915-1917, 232-3
Kentucky's Sesquicentennial (1942), 188
Kesterson, M. Wheeler, 148
Kincaid, Robert, 95-6, 176-7
Kinkead, Judge George B., 201
Kings Mountain, Battle of, 29, 47, 65, 116, 124, 215
Kingsport (TN), 91, 107, 120-3,
Kitchin, Congressman (NC), 35
Knox County (KY), 173, 181
Knoxville (TN), 25, 94, 103, 104-6, 115, 122, 124, 126, 127, 173
Knoxville Journal & Tribune, 105, 123, 124, 127
Kramsch, Rev. Samuel, 31

Lake Watauga (TN), 110
Laurel County (KY), 173, 186, 190, 192
Laurel River, 161
Lee County (VA), 143, 147
Lenoir (NC), 72
Lenoir, William, 29
Levi Jackson Wilderness Road State Park (KY), 161, 187, 188
Lexington, NC, 58, 60, 62

Index

Index

* 9 7 8 0 9 7 6 9 1 4 9 6 9 *